Emancipation of Dalits and Educational Reservation

Emancipation of Dalits and Educational Reservation

Sadanand Paswan

ADHYAYAN

ADHYAYAN PUBLISHERS & DISTRIBUTORS

NEW DELHI (INDIA)

Published by
ADHYAYAN PUBLISHERS & DISTRIBUTORS
4378/4B, 105, J.M.D. House, Murari Lal Street
Ansari Road Darya Ganj, New Delhi - 110002
Ph.: 011-23263018, 011-23277156, Fax: 011-23280028
Email: adhyayanpublishers@yahoo.com

Emancipation of Dalits and Educational Reservation

Edition 2011
ISBN 978-81-8435-240-5

Printed in India

Published by Harish Chandra Yadav for Adhyayan Publishers & Distributors, Laser Typeseting at A.V. Rao and Printed at Tarun Offset Printers, Delhi

Preface

Dalit is a broad concept, which includes most deprived persons of the society, such as scheduled castes, scheduled tribes and other backward classes. The Government of India has introduced several development programs with special budgetary allocation to help the underprivileged sections of the society including an extensive scheme of affirmative action, encompassing reservations in education, public sectors employment as well as legislative bodies.

Even after five decades of state intervention, conditions of Dalits and tribes have not improved. Most of the Dalit and tribals remain at the bottom of human development indicators. The Dalits still suffer from not only poverty, unemployment, Illiteracy and malnutrition, but from caste discrimination, and also systematic violence. Most of the Dalits are homeless and landless, besides they earn less than Rs. 50 a day. It is necessary to empower the socially disadvantaged groups of the society. The government should chalk out long term programs and policies for Dalits and implements effectively for their sustainable development in future.

In this book, an attempt has been made to discuss about empowerment of Dalits in India. It analyses the role of government in the emancipation of Dalits, and suggests measures for empowerment of theses socially disadvantaged groups. It explores the nature and role of education and its relationship to empowerment of Dalits. This book will be of interest to practitioners in the fields of development, sociology, cultural studies and education; caste, gender, post-modern and subaltern academics and students, the general public and policy makers.

Sadanand Paswan

Contents

1

Status of Dalit in India

The issue of Caste, when raised at international platform is averted by Indian authorities as an "internal social matter of Indian society". Often people and groups outside India and other Asian counties try to compare 'caste' with 'race'. It is natural that people who are directly and adversely affected by caste, find it almost impossible to understand Caste and it is influence on the psyche of those who are at the receiving end.

Caste system as an institution has division of various social groups as ' Caste'. Each Caste has it's own customs and rituals which are visible. The system also has a religion-sanctioned ideology which ranks Castes as 'higher' or 'lower', which is invisible. The net product to this hierarchy is untouchability. The Higher Caste Persons would be defiled if they physically touched 'Dalits' the lowest class of untouchable Caste. It is this invisible ideology that forms the dominant part of one's socialisation. A child as old as three years, under the socialisation process is convinced above any doubt one's Caste-based social status as 'just' and 'natural'

To that extent Caste system is a *double edged sword*. It convinces without any doubt to the so called 'upper Caste' that his/her social status in society and behaviour which may affect others adversely is 'just' and 'rightful'. It convinces people who are the sufferers that their exploitation and hardships are 'God given', a punishment for the sins of their previous births. The remedy for the same is beyond the human reach.

The Caste system has sustained itself for more than three thousand years because it has been validated by religion. The structural poverty and Caste inferiority of Dalits instills in them a permanent sense of insecurity and helplessness. For a Dalits, to oppose Caste and Caste-based oppression is tantamount to opposing religion and rebellion especially the poor ones, as generally poverty goes with orthodoxy, i.e. fear of social disapproval. That is why Dr. Ambedkar, the Dalits leader said, " Untouchability will vanish only when Caste Hindus will unlearn their way of life...which is sanctified by their religion. To change their way of life is almost to change their religion".

It is not worthy that all attempts to change or question the exiting social, economical and political system having its roots in the Caste system, have been defected on religious grounds. Even the religious movements such as Buddhism and been countered in the like manner.

Caste system is justified by Dalits themselves because it's ideology gives a person the 'meaning' or 'convincing explanation' about one's position and it's value in society, and a hope to look forward to better prospects in the next birth, according to the theory of rebirth.

The *Internalisation* of caste ideology has resulted in affecting Dalits adversely by creation of the *sub-Casteism*. Dalits, within themselves have not only hierarchy, but even untouchability. Therefore, one does not complain about being 'low' since he/she can find oneself 'higher' to some other person and group. The only exception to this is the scavenger community, which has no one lower to them.

Those who are not part of the Caste society shall perhaps understand how deep rooted the caste system is by looking dispassionately at the *Christianity* that had and continues to have interaction with the Caste system. Let us remember that Christianity as a system is 2000 years old. Moreover of the world's population. It has it's roots into a previous couple of centuries old culture. Southern part of India is believed to have embraced Christianity in as early as 1st century AD, much before the British invasion, had a different dimension. The first converts were Iyengar Brahmins, considered as the highest Caste in the social order. (The present Hindu fundamentalist who are targeting Christians as the product of forceful conversion from Hinduism do not answer why Iyengar Brahmins embraced Christianity.) But the later converts were from fisherman, Dalits and Tribals. In the state of Gujarat, The conversion to Christianity that started a hundred years back, has been only from Dalits and tribals.

Not surprising for Indian population, the *church* has maintained *segregation* between those who originated from the so called 'high' and 'low' Caste. Not only the churches that are separate for Dalits and Non Dalits but even the burial spaces for those who are already dead in search of heavenly abode are maintained and protected separately. There have been incidents where the corpse of a Dalit has been removed from the grave by Brahmin Christians on grounds of untouchability. The influence of Caste ideology on clergy is more than visible. To that extent, Christianity which proclaims equality has failed to influence the Caste system, indirectly certifying the pervasiveness of Caste system.

The Tribals are considered outside the Caste system since they were never influenced by the culture of the plains. Their subsistence on the forest was endangered by the encroachment of the plains over the hills who subsequently over exploited of the natural resources. The Tribals had no option but to come to the plains as 'migrant workers' wandering here and there in search of labour, homeless almost through out the year.The tribals who were never part of the Hindu society on having to interact with the Hindu culture of the plains have started observing untouchability towards Dalits, who were socially, educationally and economically much ahead than them.

In a Caste based society the status of a women irrespective of her Caste and class background is as low as the one that a Dalit has. The status of Dalits women in this context can be imagined.One often does not make a distinction between the fact that while the feminist movement in the west has a focus on the development of women, in India the primary concern for women is the very existence, which is in danger. One does not also visualise the role that the Caste system play behind the women's present conditions.

The Dalits and the women movement for liberation from their Caste based status is crippled by the internalisation of Caste ideology. This internalisation does not allow the growth of class consciousness.

The inequalities between the rich and poor are glaring. About 60 % of Indian population, fall under the so called poverty line'. Even though over 25 % of workers are landless farm workers, the nation does not have a uniform legislation to govern the wages and working conditions. A bill has been pending for approval in parliament for the past twenty years.

Farm workers wages in Gujarat are as low as Rs. 12/- per day, which is one third of the official minimum wage. As if the government supports these facts of underpayment, they announce schemes such as widow pension for those whose monthly earnings do not exceed Rs. 200 a month.

The constant insecurity of employment therefore forces people to migrate for more than six months in a year. This is the story of Gujarat which is considered the most developed state in the nation. Now, under the WTO pacts, it is expected that the present lobar laws would be further relaxed in favour of the MNCs.

But in spite of exploitation that Dalits and the non-dalits poor face alike, one requires great patience and herculean efforts to unite them as a class, because according to the invisible rule of Caste system, to relate with Dalit means defilement, which can only earn social boycott from the fellow-Caste men.

1.1. Influence of Caste Ideology on Dalits

Marx said religion is the opium of the masses. This belief can be extended in the context of poor within Caste system, that religion can convince people to justify those very actions that bear a direct threat to their own life and liberty. This may happen even though deep down some of them may also doubt, about the rightfulness of their own belief. This mixture of belief and disbelief creates a schizophrenic state of mind for the awakened and enlightened Dalits with modern consciousness.

But for many Dalits, just as for most non-dalit Hindus, life without Caste as unthinkable, because Caste ideology is product of the unique Hindu-Brahmanic rural, agricultural, feudal, unchanging, closed universe of socio-economic-religious-cultural order which cannot be described as "society" in the modern western sense.

1.1.1. Insecurity

The question naturally arises : Why Dalits continuously allow themselves to be fooled ? The answer lies in their situation. Insecurity takes control over their action, and pushes the person towards security on matter where it comes from and at what price.

In the case of an enterprising, bright or educated Dalits, in spite of being equipped with required qualifications, natural talents and intellect, he / she would not have the same opportunities as the non Dalit would have. One can therefore imagine the systemic insecurity that the Dalits experience in all areas of public life. The competition that Dalits face in society is not only in the areas of finance, knowledge, education and technology, but largely from the Caste mind.

1.1.2. Divide and Rule

The ruling Caste, i.e. the dominant Caste-class making up what is known as "authorities" know that in cases of any trouble - complaint or dissent against any injustice poor ordinary Dalits can be managed (silenced, suppressed, frightened or bought over) by local district level or state level Dalit sub caste, of course for a price. That is how a handful of British ruled over India for 200 years. In most such cases the poor, frightened Dalit-in-trouble has no use for the critical awareness and the sanehonest practical advice or help by the modern, secular-minded and honest social activist (even of the same sub Caste) because that advice can benefit only in the long run for which the insecure Dalit has no patience or confidence. And it will be difficult to blame him for that perception. For Dalits, the intense struggle for survival leaves attention remains focused only on self and the community.

1.1.3. Impact on Children

Children are considered to be playful and innocent. But in the case of children from Dalit communities, there is something more awaiting them.

The following true life story shall prove the point.

In 1996, a public school in the small town of Dhandhuka, in Ahmedabad district of Gujarat caught attention of the state. A boy from

Scavenger community aged around 10 years, was accused by the teacher of kicking his scooter to engine immediately. Various please and apologies by the father went to deaf ears of the teacher who insisted on dismissal of the boy with a bad character certificate.

It was only after long persuasions and having tendered the written apology, the father thought that the matter was settled, until late evening when his son did not return home. The family was dumbfounded on suddenly hearing that the dead body of their son cut into three pieces was lying on the railway tracks near their house. It was taken as an accidental death until a piece of paper that was proved in the forensic lab to be the child's own handwriting was discovered during the autopsy from the boy's clothes. The last paragraph of a long letter that gave the account of the happenings since the morning of that day read thus :

> "I would not have felt bad if the teacher had slapped me. I would not have felt bad if the teacher had abused me. But the way my father was humiliated, i felt very bad. And lastly, after my father left and as i was entering the class room, the teacher stopped me and told me that he would see how i will manage to study further and go ahead in life, I felt extremely hurt and if i am going to be allowed to study further and go ahead in life, what is the meaning of living the life. I am therefore committing suicide"

One hears many such stories from the mouth of these tender kids.

Their complaints include: other children not playing with them in school, the teacher being rude only with them, they being served meals separately from other kids during the Government sponsored midday meal, the teacher asking them to sit at the end of the classroom, not allowed to drink water from where others drink and on and so forth.

1.1.4. Caste System and the Freedom of Religion

How does one bring about equality among the poor, when many of them believe that it is better to be poor or die of hunger than to dine with a Dalit ?

There is a Constitutional catch which discourages such attempts though not directly. The Constitution of India guarantees fundamental right to all its citizens, "the right to practice, profess and propagate the religion according to their conscience."

There were some isolated instances of conversion of Dalit groups to Christianity in some religions of Gujarat during the first half of this century. The largest conversion movement of Dalits to Buddhism on Maharashtra was led by Dr. Ambedkar, the father of India Constitution. In a historic statement he said, " To be born as a Hindu was not in my hand, but i shall not die as a Hindu."

Change of Religion and Loss of Special Constitutional Status : Constitutionally, person who ceases to be a Hindu, also ceases to be a member of 'scheduled Castes', (The schedule, a part of the Indian Constitution, is drawn up of Caste communities suffering untouchability) and therefore he / she can not avail of various special benefits. These benefits include various welfare schemes and benefits of 'reservations' in jobs and educational institutions, because it is assumed that Caste is an integral part of Hindu only and no other religion.

Although it has been proved again and again by various studies that the change of religion has neither brought any change in the social or economic status of Dalits nor in the treatment meted out to them by Caste Hindus. The demand to treat such converts as 'scheduled Caste', do not find many takers, including the Supreme Court of India.

1.1.5. Politics of Conversion

Lately in 1997 just before it's fall the previous national government expressed its intentions to extend the 'scheduled Caste' status to Christian converts, Which met with stiff resistance from Hindu groups, only to reinforce the point that the so called benefits can be extended only to those who are in the *Hindu fold*.

Surprisingly, almost at the same time the same status was extended to Neo Buddhists, who followed Ambedkar to *Buddhism*, without the slightest opposition. In the present times, Ambedkar has been portrayed as great man by all the political parties, including the Hindu fundamentalists, to woo Dalits, definitely a large (14.5 %) vote bank.

1.1.6. Freedom of Religion and Politics of Reconversion

This, Constitutional catch, is not only taking away a citizens right to freedom of religion, but it also indirectly promotes the Caste system by offering special incentives and schemes under the banner of provisions for scheduled Caste. To be a Hindu means to belong to a hierarchical Caste structure with untouchability as its integral part, a fact that the highest authority of the nation acknowledges.

Interestingly, as part of the Hindu fundamentalists program to bring back the converts in the fold of Hinduism, there are many who choose to return to Hinduism for number of reasons. The procedure of reconversion is simple and the religious ceremony for the purpose is called "*SUDDHI*" means "*Becoming clean*"

This is only to Sanction that Dalit's impure status in Caste society was the result of his/her fate but his/her conversion to other religion has made him impure, which is earned to voluntarily. Naturally, you have to purify yourself of your voluntarily impurity to return to your God-given impure status.

The logical conclusion is that apart from becoming eligible for special benefit as member of scheduled Caste you also save your children from suffering due to your voluntary impurity.

1.1.7. Caste System and Right to Knowledge

Historically, it was Mahatma Jyotirao Phule and his wife Savitridevi who started the first school for Dalits and women in 1848. Jyotirao, a non-Dalit activist from Maharashtra addressed the issue of untouchability in a major way. According to the Hindu scriptures, both Dalits and women did not have a right to knowledge. The attempt of Phule met the toughest hostility including physical attacks from Brahmins, who accused phule of defiling religion. In response to British Government more to open public schools to Dalits, the Brahmin teacher preferred to resign from their jobs rather them educating Dalits finally it was some Muslim teachers who took up the job to educate Dalits.

1.1.8. Bureaucracy's Contempt for the Poor

One our activist colleague had a public protest program to the district education officer, complaining that apart from the teacher not attending the school in a particular village, there were no elementary schools in many villages. The children affected were the Dalits and the poor. The education officer replied, "Why do you bother about these children who are not going to be doctors or engineers anyway ?"

1.1.9. Attempts to Divide Dalits, Muslims and Tribals

Serious attempts are how at work by the fundamentalist parties to pose Dalits against the Muslims during the communal riots only to divide them and break whatever linkages (of poverty, food, residential locality etc.) they share, to make sure that in future they do not pose a united threat to their dominance. The same plans are at work where Dalits and Tribals are pitted against the Christians, the converts from Dalits and Tribals.

1.2. Dalits and Political Power

1.2.1. Pre-Independence

Dr. Ambedkar, the dalit leader demanded "*Separate Electorate*" for Dalits in 1932. Under the envisaged system Dalit candidates were required to be elected primarily by Dalit voters only. This according to him would ensure effective political representation where the candidates would remain loyal and committed to their primary electorates. The demand reflected long term political empowerment for Dalits.

He apprehended that once Independence was achieved, Dalits would continue to be treated as 'second class citizens' as they had been for centuries. In fact the provision for separate electorate had already been exiting for Muslims and Anglo-Indians.

Dr. Ambedkar's apprehension was rooted in recent history, showing the weakness of pro-reform Hindus in the national independence movement, which, though started on two fronts of social reforms and political independence, later on dropped the agenda of social reforms, saying that once independence was achieved, social reforms would follow. The reforms were aimed at abolition of untouchability and discrimination based on Caste; stopping cruelty on women by banning child marriages, promoting window remarriages, banning 'sati' system, (Inducing widows to immolate themselves after the death of their husbands) etc.

The sole reason for denial to Ambedkar's demand came under the leadership of Gandhiji who went on fast unto death until Ambedkar dropped his demand saying, "*It would divide the Hindu society*". According to Gandhiji the present inequalities based on Caste, which promoted ambedkar to raise his demand, was an internal matter of Hindus society. Therefore the British had no business to concede the demand and went to the extent of saying that his fast was "a gift of God".

1.2.2. Opening of Temples for Dalits

Gandhiji's appeal to Hindus to do away the Caste discrimination resulted into opening some temples for Dalits. Ambedkar argued that his demands were part of the long term political strategy to ensure that the legitimate demands of Dalits were guaranteed. For him, the temple entry was temporary emotional spur of Caste Hindus, on which he would not base his decisions. After all, temples which otherwise open to dogs were now open to Dalits.

1.2.3. Formula for Political Reservations

Dr. Ambedkar had no option but to drop his desmand and accept unwillingly the system of present political reservations. The provincial election that followed after three years witness Ambedkar's defeat at the hand of an unknown Dalit candidate, sponsored by the Congress party. This was so because under the system of reservation the Dalit candidate had to depend on the votes of non-Dalits, the majority. It became very clear therefore, that a Dalit candidate who would not pose a challenge to the non-Dalit interests, would be elected.

Dr. Ambedkar's apprehensions have proved right after independence.The nation which evolved and accepted the concept of political 'reservation' or 'affirmative action' as termed in USA., for Dalits, Tribals and lately for other poor communities on the *basis of Caste* was originally envisaged only for 10 years. No such time-limit was set for reservations in government jobs, since the 'Equality' as guaranteed in the Constitution was supposed to be achieved by then. Today, after 50 years, it has become a '*trap*' for the Dalits masses. The system seems so attractive to politicians who enjoys people's goodwill without delivering anything substantial to messes. All Political Parties are trying to perpetuate it. Poor, Dalits people are a powerful vote bank open to cheating.

1.2.4. Impact of Political Reservations

One dose not have to go very far to understand this as the living example of what has been the result of political reservations for the Dalits is right in front of our eyes. We have reached a point where the loyalty or commitment of Dalit candidates, is more and absolute to the political party than to their own communities, contrary to the very objectives of the Constitutional provision for reservation.

It was painful to witness total silence from all the 13 Dalit assembly members, elected on reserved seats, on the issue of manual scavenging. The issue had already caught the national attention. This was in spite of lobbying, where all relevant details about this crude from of human right violation was supplied to all these members at their door step.It has become a precondition that a dalit politician should cease to be a Dalit in sense of representing his interests or sharing their pains after elections.

Thus political representation of Dalits has proved to be a mere eyewash wherein political parties have learned to keep them divided by promoting sub- Casteism. During the last fifty years, all natural resources and benefits of development have been cornered by the small minority of upper Caste classes.

Gandhiji's description of the living condition of scavengers in a colony of Bombay in 1992, would also apply to their condition in Gujarat and other states in 1998.

Political power is helpful only if it can bring about effective political representation, i.e. by addressing the agenda of social change, Which has not yet happened. And so political reservation have to be understood only as *tokenism*.

1.2.5. The Brahmins

Traditionally, they are supposed to be the supreme Caste (in Caste or Varna hierarchy) because of living a pious life and engaged in learning, teaching and preservation of religion and knowledge, and some of then in priestly duties. But during the last 200 years they have increasingly taken to secular jobs and dominated politics, professions, civil services, all white collar jobs, arts, journalism and literature.

According to one estimate based on the 1931 census (which included caste category for the last time) Brahmin were 3.5 percent of the population in parts of the present-day Maharashtra state formed only in 1960. According to one estimate, their all India average could be less than seven percent. But at one time their representation in the national parliament was more than 30 percent. The top *leadership* in all major political parties are in the hands of upper Castes, and particularly the Brahmins.

Lately, in the last decade one finds a visible change in the political parties, where one finds representatives coming from Dalit or Tribal communities as party office bearers. But it is all part of the survival game. By the total failure of poverty alleviation programs and increasing suffering of the poor there is a rise in political awareness amongst the poor. This is because the struggles of the poor, including Dalits to survive has intensified so as to cause the 'law and order' problems, and tilt electoral results.

1.2.6. New Labels for the Old Disease

In this context Politicians have begun to worry about the votes of 'Dalits' 'Tribals' and 'women'. Earlier the votes that could be secured on 'Poverty Alleviation' card has become defunct. Hence the same has now been replaced with the card of 'Social justice'. Lately, some of the state government are renaming the 'Social Welfare Department' which carry out social welfare programs for the poor as Department of social justice and Empowerment'.

1.2.7. Acceptance of the Issues is not Sufficient

Learning to Distrust Politicians. The moment the state recognises the issue one begins to feel hopeful. The next step is to join hands with the state agency. The communities affected already full of desperation are waiting for the results with open mouth. The aspirations of the communities loads an additional psychological stress on the social workers, who mediate with the state on behalf of the people.

Once an activist has joined hands with the state, naturally the weapon of criticism ceases to operate, thereby reducing pressure and embarrassment for the state. The media which has a limited interest-based role are no more your allies now. It is only much later you realise that what you received as progress or a hopeful signal has turned out to be a mirage. The only role that you are subsequently left with is it try to explain to your desperate communities as to why things have failed, a task which otherwise the state is bound to perform.

1.2.8. Ambedkar and Dalit Leadership

Ambedkar is described by Louis Fischer as, "a distinguished lawyer with international experience who had played a big part at the Round Table Conferences in London, owned a powerfully built body and strong stubborn, superior intellect. The accumulated bitterness against Hindus that rankled for centuries in millions of Harijan breasts found expression in Ambedkar's Himalayan hatred." He was humiliated in his life time since he questioned the core of the Caste system under the pretext of Hinduism not mincing words.

Ambedkar who laid a corner stone of the Dalit movement for self-assertion is now hijacked by the very political parties who destroyed him. Almost all the Government have taken up some populist measures such as naming roads after him that lead only to Dalit location and setting up his status in Dalit location, while the pathetic conditions of Dalits are safely ignored. Lately, one finds incidents of desecration of Ambedkar's statues, causing riots and enabling opposition parties to turn the episode against the ruling party as its failure to protect his statues. The state of Maharashthra alone has witnessed 508 such incidents of desecration of statues in the last decade.

1.3. Issues for Dalits Today

When does one ever cease to be a 'Dalit' is moot fundamental question in the context of dalit identify at this stage of our history. Even assuming that the rising at critical mass awareness, questioning the unjust system is a giant leap towards liberation, it is definitely not sufficient. The fight against the Caste system has to continue on several fronts. Though Caste is a social stigma it's influence on economic and Political structure of the nation is dominating. The major issues of Dalits can be summarised as the following.

1.3.1. Existence

The primary concern is to ensure protection to the person and property of dalits.

During our experiences of past 18 years, working with Dalits, we have witnessed the following.

a. According to Police reports, in Gujarat the general crime rate has decreased by 1.35% during 1990-1993, but the crime against Dalits have gone up by 90%.

b. The Police reports are based only on registered crimes. It is learnt that 13.50% victims of atrocities are criminally pressurised not to lodge complaints with Police, while complaints of another 15.75% victims though recorded by Police, the same is not shown on records.

c. 20% of crimes against Dalits are of serious nature, which includes rape, murder and grievous bodily injuries.

1.3.2. Survival

Structural poverty adds to the already degrading living conditions of majority Dalits, both in urban as well as rural areas.

a. *Scavengers*: The attached paper on living conditions of scavenger portrays their pathetic conditions.

b. *Landless agriculture workers* : Though the combined numerical strength of the Dalits and Tribals in Gujarat is 23% of state's Population, 54% of State's landless agriculture workers belong to this class. This is the same for the nation. The specially enacted lobar courts to protect their rights have failed to do so. The under Payment of wages to this class of farm workers in the state is estimated to 5,000 million rupees a year. They are not governed by any central legislation as the wages for then differ one state to another.

c. *Child labour*: Normal thinking of the rural community is that it is better it be illiterate of less educated and be employed locally, than to be better educated and find oneself unemployed always in search for a job. The children of the rich and upper Castes are in better position to complete for jobs in organised sector.

d. *The unorganised urban labour force*: Most Dalits self employed as cotton weavers in rural areas had no option but to migrate to cities to join the British introduced high Productivity oriented weaving technology based textile industries. Now with the shift from cotton to Poly Yarn and high technological innovations, the old mills have shut down rendering thousands unemployed. It is a common sight to see their children polishing shoes or employed in tea shops, their women working as domestic servants and the unemployed Workers as casual construction workers.

1.3.3. Development

Existence and survival are the preconditions for development Scores of promises were made to Dalits pre and post independence, including the constitutional guarantees aimed at providing them opportunities for their development. These promises and guarantees have Proved to be tigers.

a. *Land reforms* : Was a major programme of Agricultural land redistribution. It aimed at Protecting the rights of tenants over land and fix a ceiling of Land holding. In Gujarat, Only 7,00,000 tenants could become landowners as against 13,00,000 registered talents. 3,71,000 tenants lost their over land, for fear of retaliation and assault from landlords, if they claimed their rights. It is estimated that under the land reforms while majority of beneficiaries were the Dalits and Tribals, more than 1 Million acres of agricultural and has slipped away is the hands of rich landlords. The state and Judiciary have remained mute spectators to the ugly implementation of land Reform programme. However, it has to be noted that the land under the reforms has gone more in the hands of middle Castes than to the Dalits and Tribals. Successive Government, barring the Marxist, speak about social justice, but not about land reform.

b. *Government welfare measures*: It is learnt that the implementation of Government sponsored welfare measures have not been above 40% Needless to say, that even this Scantly implementation has not remained untouched from the corruption.

1.3.4. Struggle

There are some psychological blocks, which impede the growth of the organisation

a. *Organisation the poor on a non-party basis*: The poor who believe their Caste to be their fate, later become victims of the system by co-option, as political agents, who try to defeat the non-party movement for personal and ultimately party's political gains. The influence of upper Caste and money in political parties is not always visible.

b. *Ideological deceptions*: But the major fight is with the State which continuously creates a web of ideological deceptions about Law, Justice, Neutrality, Equality, Equal Opportunity and the worst of all "Democracy" Whereas in practice they will do just the contrary : Bureaucrats, judged, and the police carry their Caste prejudices wherever they work.

In July 1998, in the state of Uttar Pradesh a district judge, (empowered to award any sentence including capital punishment) on being transferred and taking charge of his new office, washed the entire office space with 'Gangajal' (water from the holy river Ganga) to purify it since the previous occupant to that office was a judge from dalit community.

1.4. Positive Discrimination

India was a country with a very rigid caste based hierarchal structure where the higher casts enjoyed most of the benefits while the lower casts were looked down upon by the higher casts. The majority of the population was backward socially, economically, educationally, and politically. The backward classes were classified as the Scheduled castes (SC), Scheduled tribes (ST), and other backward classes. Reservation, in India, is a type of affirmative action that tries to allocate fixed number of seats in educational and social institutions for various under-represented communities.

It is stated as a response to the thousands of years of discrimination done by upper caste persons in India. Thus, when India attained independence, the constitution gave special provision for certain communities to have a minimum representation in various fields. The initial provision was to have ended in a few years, but the practice continues till now, and the government of India kept on increasing the quotas in the matter of employment and education.

Article 46 stated that the state shall promote with special care the educational and economic interest of the weaker section of the people, also protecting them from social injustice and all forms of exploitation. Article 46 was complimented by the inclusion of many other articles for the empowerment of the backward classes. Since they were the oppressed classes this was thought to be the best mechanism to correct the mistake that was being practiced for many hundreds of years. Under Article 340 of the Indian Constitution, it is obligatory for the government to promote the welfare of the Other Backward Classes (OBC).

Article 340(2) states, "A commission so appointed shall investigate the matters referred to them and present to the president a report setting out the facts as found by them and making such recommendations as they think proper Consequent to the notification of the Constitution (Ninety-Third Amendment) Act, 2005, effecting the 104th Amendment to the Constitution in January this year, the Government of India indicated its intention to provide reservation for students coming from the socially and educationally backward classes of citizens, popularly known as Other Backward Classes (OBCs) in higher educational institutions.

Therefore, Article 15 of the Constitution, after clause (4), the following clause is inserted; (5) Nothing in this article or in sub-clause (g) of clause (1) of article 19 shall prevent the State from making any special provision, by law for the advancement of any socially and educationally backward classes of citizens or for the Scheduled Castes or the Scheduled Tribes in so far as such special provisions relate to their admission to educational institutions including private educational institutions, whether aided or unaided by the State, other than the minority educational referred to in clause (1) of article 30 of the Constitution.

The 93rd Amendment Act, 2005 inserting Article 15(5) is without doubt introduced to overcome the law laid down by the Hon'ble Supreme Court in an unanimous judgment by 7 judges in P.A. Inamdar & Ors. v. State of Maharashtra & Ors declaring that the State can't impose its reservation policy on minority and non-minority unaided private colleges, including professional colleges. This judgment was an attempt to bring clarity to two previous judgments by the Hon'ble Supreme Court in T.M.A. Pai Foundation & Ors. v. State of Karnataka & Ors and Islamic Academy of Edn. & Anr. v. State of

Karnataka & Ors by a constitution bench that interpreted the Pai Foundation judgment.

In the landmark Judgement in the case of Ashok Kumar Thakur Vs. Union of India, 2008 the supreme court states that the the constitution 93rd Amendment Act,2005 is valid and does not violate the "basic Structure" of the constitution so far as it relates to the state maintained institutions and aided educational institution. The creamy layer be excluded from the benefit of this provison. Although the reservation policy is an exception to the equality rule it is still considered an essential element of equality.

As equality has many dimensions and one such dimension is the reservation policy for the backward classes. From a simple reservation of about 15% for the SC's & ST's in educational institutions now the percentage has gone up and also the other backward classes (OBC's) have been brought within the fold of reservation by the suggestion of the Mandal Commission. But even after 59 years of independence the people still fall back on reservation. It is not that the backward have not progressed but the percentage is less because those who have already availed reservation and progressed keep getting it again.

This results in the formation of the creamy layer. Instead of having a reservation policy we feel the emphasis of the government should be to build good schools in the rural as well as urban areas so that the poor have an opportunity to study. All kinds of encouragement from the government should be there in the implementation of such policies. The mid day meal program was a successful one and we should see more of such schemes which encourage the poor to study. The existing system has not been able to fulfill the equality clause of the constitution under Article 14 of the Constitution due to the lack of infrastructure in the rural areas where a proportionate amount of the backward classes reside.

Neither has it been successful in abolishing the caste system. A disturbing sign has been the demanding of reservation by the other backward class whereby the majority would not be left with seats proportional to their numbers. The policy of reservation has never been subject to a widespread social or political audit. Before extending reservation to more groups, the entire policy needs to be properly examined, and its benefits over a span of nearly 60 years have to be gauged.

REFERENCES

Das, Gurcharan. *India Unbound.* New York: Alfred A. Knopf, 2001.

Department of Social Welfare, Government of India. *Report of the Committee on Untouchability, Economic and Educationl Development of the Scheduled Castes and Connected Documents* (Delhi,1969).

Fuller, C.J., ed. *Caste Today.* New Delhi: Oxford University Press, 1996.

Galanter, Marc. *Competing Equalities: Law and the Backward Classes in India.* New Delhi: Oxford Univeristy Press, 1984.

Gautam, D.N., ed. *Fifty Years of Indian Constitution.* New Delhi: Manak Publications, 2001.

Gupta, S.K. *The Scheduled Castes in Modern Indian Politics: Their Emergence as a Political Power.* New Delhi: Munshiram Manoharlal Publishers Pvt. Ltd., 1985.

2

Historical Background of Reservations Policy

Jati, or caste, is a second factor specifying rank in the Hindu social hierarchy. Jatis are roughly determined by occupation. Often region-specific, they are more precise than the sweeping varna system which is common across India and can be divided further into subcastes and sub-subcastes. This is also the case among untouchables. Andre Beteille defines caste as "a small and named group of persons characterised by endogamy, hereditary membership, and a specific style of life which sometimes includes the pursuit by tradition of a particular occupation and is usually associated with a more or less distinct ritual status in a hierarchical system."

Jatis in the three highest varnas in the hierarchy—Brahmins, Kshatriyas, and Vaisyas—are considered "twice-born" according to Hindu scripture, meaning they are allowed to participate in Hindu ceremonies and are considered more "pure" than the Sudras and "polluting" untouchables. This concept of pollution versus purity governs the interaction between members of different castes. The touch of an untouchable is considered defiling to an upper-caste Hindu. In southern India, where caste prejudice has been historically most severe, even the sight of an untouchable was considered polluting. Untouchables usually handled "impure" tasks such as work involving human waste and dead animals. As a result, until reforms began in the 19th century, untouchables were barred from entering temples, drawing water from upper-caste wells, and all social interaction with upper-caste Hindus (including dining in the same room). These social rules were strictly imposed and violators were severely punished; some were even killed.

Despite constitutional prohibitions and laws, most recently the Scheduled Castes and Scheduled Tribes (Prevention of Atrocities) Act of 1989, violence and injustices against untouchables continue today, particularly in rural areas of India. Accounts of caste-driven abuses continually appear in Western media and surely affect foreigners' perceptions of India. American economist Thomas Sowell drew on a 1978 case in which an untouchable girl had her ears cut off for drawing water from an upper-caste well in one of his books. More recent examples include Dalit students at a government school in Rajasthan who were punished for asking to drink water from a pitcher used by higher caste students and a Dalit in Punjab who was murdered by "affluent Rajput Hindu youths" after his dog ran into a Hindu temple.

In its latest published report, the Government of India's National Commission for Scheduled Castes and Scheduled Tribes states that "...even after 50 years of Independence Untouchability has not been abolished as provided in Article 17 of the Constitution & incidents continued to be reported." For 1997, the Commission lists 1,157 "registered" cases of abuse of untouchables and tribals. An independent overview is provided annually by the U.S. Department of State in its annual report to Congress on worldwide human rights practices. For India in 2001, the Department commented, inter alia, that

— Dalits are among the poorest of citizens, generally do not own land, and often are illiterate. They face significant discrimination despite the laws that exist to protect them, and often are prohibited from using the same wells and from attending the same temples as higher caste Hindus, and from marrying persons from higher castes. In addition they face segregation in housing, in land ownership, on roads, and on buses. Dalits tend to be malnourished, lack access to health care, work in poor conditions, and face continuing and severe social ostracism.

— The Scheduled Castes and Scheduled Tribes (Prevention of Atrocities) Act lists offences against disadvantaged persons and provides for stiff penalties for offenders. However, this act has had only a modest effect in curbing abuse. Under the Act, 996 cases were filed in Tamil Nadu and 1,254 cases in Karnataka in

2000. Human rights NGO's allege that caste violence is on the increase.

— Intercaste violence claims hundreds of lives annually; it was especially pronounced in Uttar Pradesh, Bihar, Rajasthan, Madhya Pradesh, Tamil Nadu, and Andhra Pradesh.

In addition to specifying an economic and social role, caste is also accompanied by certain popularly held generalisations. Brahmins, for instance, are often believed to be fair-skinned, sharp-nosed, and having more "refined" features, consistent with their Aryan roots.

Untouchables, on the other hand, are commonly held to be dark-skinned and possessing coarse features. Beteille has pointed out that lighter skin colour has a higher social value, making Brahmins highly conscious of their appearance. A dark-skinned Brahmin girl, for example, is a source of anxiety for her parents since the task of finding a husband is made harder. Matrimonial advertisements, a staple in Indian newspapers, are full of families seeking "wheatish" brides for their sons.

Nevertheless, there is increasing social mobility, especially in India's urban areas. Some untouchables and sudras have tried to move up in the hierarchy by adopting customs of upper castes, a process labelled *sanskritisation*. Others have attempted to escape the system entirely by converting to Buddhism or Christianity. The prominent Dalit politician and lawyer, Bhimrao Ramji Ambedkar (1891-1956), who saw the demolition of the caste system as necessary for the emancipation of India's Dalits, converted to Buddhism at the end of his life. Over time, significant numbers, although only a tiny portion of India's Dalits, have followed his example; in November 2001, thousands of untouchables participated in a mass conversion to Buddhism in Delhi.

2.1. Pre-Independence Initiatives against Untoucability

Christian missionaries took the lead in adopting the cause of the Depressed Classes seeking to provide welfare for them. By the 1850s, either inspired or shamed into action by the missionaries' example, Hindu reformers emerged. Jyotiba Phule was one such activist, and in 1860 he called attention to the plight of victims of caste discrimination in Maharashtra.

British and other Indian leaders soon followed suit, spurred on in part by reports of discrimination against Indians in South Africa. Thus, in the 1880s, British officials set up scholarships, special schools, and other programs to benefit the Depressed Classes. Forward-thinking maharajas (princes) in "native" states like Baroda, Kolhapur, and Travancore, which were not under direct British administration, established similar initiatives. Ambedkar, from the Mahar caste of Maharashtra, was one beneficiary. The Mahars had a long association with the British-organised Indian Army, in which Ambedkar's father and grandfather had served. One result was that Ambedkar was able to attend government primary and secondary schools. The Maharaja of Baroda, recognising Ambedkar's gifts for scholarship, sponsored his study abroad, first at Columbia University in New York, where Ambedkar obtained a Ph.D. in Economics, and later at London University, where he earned a DSc. and entrance to the Bar from Grey's Inn.

As early as 1858, the government of Bombay Presidency, which included today's Maharashtra, declared that "all schools maintained at the sole cost of Government shall be open to all classes of its subjects without discrimination." Although a 1915 press note revealed that this policy was not being enforced—in one case, a Mahar boy was not allowed to enter the school room, but was relegated to the veranda—the Bombay government maintained its position on the issue, and, in 1923, announced a resolution cutting off aid to educational institutions that refused admission to members of the Depressed Classes. Other initiatives followed including the 1943 Bombay Harijan Temple Entry Act and the 1947 Bombay Harijan (Removal of Civil Disabilities) Act. In the United Provinces, now Uttar Pradesh, the 1947 United Provinces Removal of Social Disabilities Act was put in force.

In what is now Kerala, the Maharaja of Travancore announced the "Temple Entry Proclamation" in 1936, in what has been called a "pioneer [effort] in the field of reforms relating to the eradication of untouchability before independence." Stating that "none of our Hindu subjects should, by reason of birth or caste or community, be denied the consolations and solace of the Hindu faith," the Maharaja declared the removal of all bars on those denied entry to temples controlled by the Travancore government. Other measures affecting what would become the present state of Kerala included the 1938 Madras Removal of Civil Disabilities Act and the 1950 Travancore-Cochin Temple Entry (Removal of Disabilities) Act.

2.1.1. The Government of India Act of 1919

Caught in the turmoil of World War I, Britain focused its attention on Europe, not on India. Nevertheless, the British passed important legislation during this turbulent period that would have a significant impact on the development of Indian governmental institutions: The Government of India Act of 1919.

The Act had its immediate origins on August 20, 1917. With Britain in a war for survival in Europe, in need of continued support from India and the Empire, and desiring to avoid confrontation with the Indian independence movement, Secretary of State for India Edwin Montagu, in an announcement in Parliament, defined Britain's India policy as:

> increasing [the] association of Indians in every branch of the administration and the gradual development of self-governing institutions with a view to the progressive realisation of responsible government in India as an integral part of the British Empire.

Montagu and Lord Chelmsford, then Viceroy, embarked on an analysis of the Indian situation, eventually laying out proposals forming the basis for the 1919 Government of India Act. Despite mention of greater Indian participation in politics, the 1919 Act still contained provisions guaranteeing a continued active British presence and dominance:

> While we do everything that we can to encourage Indians to settle their own problems for themselves we must retain power to restrain them from seeking to do so in a way that threatens the stability of the country.

The reforms included devolution of more authority to provincial governments and dyarchy, a system in which elected Indian ministers, responsible to the legislatures, were to share power with appointed British governors and ministers. The Act also addressed minority safeguards, including the particularly vexing issue of communal electorates.

Montagu and Chelmsford firmly rejected communal electorates, characterising the system as a "perpetuat[or] of class division" and a "very serious hindrance to the development of the self-governing principle." The authors also pointed out another related problem that:

> A minority which is given special representation owing to its weak and backward state, is positively encouraged to settle down into a feeling of satisfied security; it is under no inducement to educate and qualify itself to make good the ground it has lost compared with the stronger majority. On the other hand, the latter will be tempted to feel that they have done all they need do for their weaker fellow countrymen and that they are free to use their power for their own purposes. The give-and-take which is the essence of political life is lacking. There is no inducement to the one side to forbear, or to the other to exert itself. The communal system stereotypes existing relations.

Despite their repudiation of communal electorates, Montagu and Chelmsford realised it would be unfeasible to take away communal representation already granted to Muslims by the 1909 Morley-Minto reforms. At Lucknow in 1916 the Indian National Congress and the All India Muslim League had agreed to separate electorates for Muslims. Britain for political reasons was not willing to risk the combined ire of these Indian groups. Other, including Sikhs, Anglo-Indians, Europeans, Indian Christians, and non-Brahmins, also clamored for special representation, but Montagu and Chelmsford largely resisted their demands—they did grant the Sikhs (described as a "gallant and valuable element to the Indian Army") communal representation—proposing instead a system of nomination. If nomination proved ineffective, they proposed reserving seats for communities in plural constituencies, but with a general electoral roll.

In Britain, the decision against communal electorates was controversial. Indian moderates and some British members of Parliament (MPs) supported the Montagu-Chelmsford position. (One MP effusively praised the Montagu Report, but lamented that such an excellent product came from a Jew and not a "real" Englishman.) However, most feared an "oligarchy of Brahmins" if communal electorates were not set up for non-Brahmin Hindus. Several factors contributed to such "Brahminophobia," a fear that had been developing even before the Montagu-Chelmsford Report.

Some Britons perceived Brahmins as "untrustworthy," oppressive towards the lower castes, and subversive regarding British governmental and social reforms. Valentine Chirol, a prominent *Times* correspondent, published *Indian Unrest*, in which he asserted that Brahminism was the biggest threat to the British. The Rowlatt Report of 1918, the product of a study on the causes of political violence in India, described Brahmins as "revolutionaries." Annie Besant, English-born leader of the "Home Rule" movement for Indian independence, accused Brahmins of repressing the lower castes.

Another important feature of the 1919 Act was the provision for the appointment of a statutory commission after ten years

> for the purpose of enquiring into the working of the system of government, the growth of education and the development of representative institutions in British India...and ...report...to what extent it is desirable to establish the principle of responsible government, or to extend, modify or restrict the degree of responsible government then existing therein.

2.1.2. The Simon Commission

In keeping with the 1919 Government of India Act, the British government in 1927 appointed a commission to assess the Montagu-Chelmsford reforms and "whether, and to what extent it [was] desirable to establish the principle of responsible government, or to extend, modify, or restrict the degree of responsible government existing therein." The seven-member commission was headed by John Simon, MP, and included MP Clement Attlee.

This "all-white" panel proved controversial. The competence of the nominees was not at issue, but rather the lack of any Indian representatives. In protest, Gandhi and the Congress Party, the dominant Indian political party, boycotted the Commission and protest demonstrations in India were widespread.

The Simon Commission toured every Indian province. Its findings were based largely on memoranda from the Government of India, from committees appointed by the provincial legislative councils, and from non-official sources. The final report contained recommendations for reform.

One area the Commission identified was the need to safeguard minorities and other disadvantaged members of Indian society. Noting that "the spirit of toleration has made little progress in India," the Simon report detailed the plight of the Depressed Classes in particular, which it saw not only as a problem of caste, but as an issue with distinct political overtones.

Based on its assumption that the "true cause of communal conflict...is the struggle for political power and for the opportunities which political power confers," the committee saw the improvement of the Depressed Classes' situation as hinging on increased political influence. Several options emerged, including pursuing a system of nomination, creating separate electorates, and reserving seats in government within a general electorate.

In its consultations, the Simon Commission found that most provincial governments supported a nominating system. The Government of Bihar and Orissa, for example, asserted that a nomination was best since the Depressed Classes were too backward to choose their own representatives. Despite these arguments, the Commission discarded the idea, arguing that the Depressed Classes needed opportunities for training in self-government.

Support for separate electorates was strong among the Depressed Classes. Their representatives proposed combining separate electorates and reserved seats. They also demanded a wider franchise, since property and educational requirements significantly restricted their right to vote and to participate in government. The Bengal Depressed Classes Association, for instance, lobbied for separate electorates with seats reserved according to the proportion of Depressed Class members to the total population as well as for adult franchise. The All-India Depressed Classes Association proposed separate electorates for each of what it termed the four major groups in India: the Brahmins, Muslims, Depressed Classes, and Non-Brahmins. The governments of Assam and Bombay supported similar concepts.

The Simon Commission rejected separate electorates for the Depressed Classes:

> Separate electorates would no doubt be the safest method of securing the return of an adequate number of persons who enjoy the

> confidence of the Depressed Classes, but we are averse from stereotyping the differences oetween the Depressed Classes and the remainder of the Hindus by such a step which we consider would introduce a new and serious bar to their ultimate political amalgamation with others. However, they retained the concept of reserving seats:
>
> The Commission recommends that in all the eight provinces there should be some reservation of seats for the Depressed Classes on a scale which will secure a substantial increase in the number of Members of Legislative Councils drawn from the Depressed Classes.

Seats were to be reserved for the Depressed Classes in general constituencies and these seats would be filled by election, based on a broadened franchise. The Commission also recommended drawing up rules to ensure the competency of candidates for reserved positions. In addition, provincial governors would have the power to nominate or allow non-Depressed Class members to run for election. Competency was of particular concern to the Commission. Members questioned whether enough qualified candidates would be available if seats were reserved according to the proportion of Depressed Classes persons in the population. As a result, the Commission suggested, "the proportion of the number of such reserved seats to the total number of seats in all the Indian general constituencies should be three-quarters of the proportion of the Depressed Classes to the total population of the electoral area of the province." Again, these measures were regarded as strictly temporary, with the goal that an improvement in the Depressed Classes' condition would eventually make reservations unnecessary.

2.1.3. The Round Table Conferences

In 1931, sixth months after the Simon Commission's report was published, a Round Table Conference convened in London to review the Commission's proposals and how they might be incorporated into a new constitution. This time, there were Indian delegates from various interest groups. Ambedkar represented the Depressed Classes, along with Rai Bahadur R. Srinivasan. Gandhi and his Indian National Congress were conspicuously absent, refusing to participate on the grounds that Congress alone represented Indian opinion.

How to treat minorities was a major topic at the conference. Prime Minister Ramsay MacDonald chaired a subcommittee to focus on this problem. Ambedkar and Srinivasan appealed for separate electorates and adult suffrage. Separate electorates were designed to be temporary. After ten years, general electorates with reserved seats would replace separate electorates with the consent of the Depressed Classes and enfranchisement of all adults. In the end, the subcommittee could not reach an agreement, a general reflection of the entire conference, which was inconclusive.

A second Roundtable Conference convened eight months later. Ambedkar and Srinivasan again attended. Gandhi also joined, representing the Congress. Having taken up the cause of the *Harijans* ("children of God," a term the Congress leader coined), Gandhi adamantly opposed separate electorates, especially for the Depressed Classes. Arguing that untouchability was inseparable from Hinduism, he linked creation of separate electorates for the Depressed Classes to alleged British "divide and rule" strategy and asserted that the group should be included in the main body of Hindus. As a result of staunch opposition from Gandhi and the Congress on separate electorates, the second conference was inconclusive and the minority issue remained unresolved.

Ambedkar originally had misgivings about separate electorates as well, but was compelled to ask for them at the second Roundtable conference when he felt the Depressed Classes were in danger of not gaining any concessions. Earlier in the conference, Ambedkar had attempted to compromise with Gandhi on reserved seats in a common electorate, but Gandhi, who had declared himself spokesman for India's oppressed, rejected Ambedkar's proposal, and denounced the other delegates, including Ambedkar, as unrepresentative. At the same time, Gandhi attempted to strike a deal with Muslims, promising to support their demands as long as the Muslims voted against separate electorates for the Depressed Classes. It is apparent that political considerations might have also motivated Gandhi to adopt this position.

Given the failure of the conference to settle minority representation, Prime Minister Ramsay MacDonald, who had chaired the committee on minorities, offered to mediate on the condition that the other members of the committee supported his decision. The product of this mediation was the Communal Award of 1932.

2.1.4. MacDonald's Communal Award and the Poona Pact

MacDonald announced the Communal Award on August 16, 1932. Based on the findings of the Indian Franchise Committee, called the Lothian Committee, the Communal Award established separate electorates and reserved seats for minorities, including the Depressed Classes which were granted seventy-eight, reserved seats. Unlike previous communal electorates set up for Muslims and other communities, the Award provided for the Depressed Classes to vote in both general and special constituencies, essentially granting a "double vote." However, in keeping with earlier special concessions to minorities, MacDonald asserted:

> His Majesty's Government do not consider that these special Depressed Classes constituencies will be required for more than a limited time. They intend that the constitution shall provide that they shall come to an end after 20 years if they have not previously been abolished under the general powers of electoral revision.

Gandhi, who was in the Yeravada Prison in the city of Poona at the time because of his civil disobedience campaign, reacted by declaring a hunger strike "unto death." In his opposition to the Award, he compared the creation of separate electorates for the Depressed Classes to the "injection of a poison that is calculated to destroy Hinduism and do no good whatever." Others were similarly critical of the Award. Ambedkar felt too few seats were reserved for the Depressed Classes. Rajah, another leader of the Depressed Classes, opposed the separation of the community from the Hindu fold.

As a result of widespread disapproval of the Award and Gandhi's hunger strike, a new agreement, the Poona Pact, was reached on September 24, 1932. The Pact called for a single (non-Muslim) general electorate for each of the provinces of British India and for seats in the Central Legislature. At the same time, specified numbers of seats, totalling 148 for the provincial legislatures and to be taken from seats allotted to the general electorate, were reserved for the Depressed Classes. In the Central Legislature, the Depressed Classes were to get eighteen percent of the seats. Voting members of the Depressed Classes in each reserved seat constituency were to form an "electoral college" to select four candidates from among their number. The Pact also called for "every endeavour" to give the Depressed Classes "fair representation" in the public services "subject to such educational qualifications as may be laid down." Like each of its antecedents, the system of representation of Depressed Classes by reservation outlined in the Pact was intended to be temporary, continuing, "until determined by mutual agreement between the communities concerned in the statement."

2.1.5. Gandhi Vs. Ambedkar

The Poona Pact set in motion what one student of caste in India has termed "Ambedkar's qualified victory over Gandhi and the Congress." Although Ambedkar had given in on the common voting roll, he had ensured that specified numbers of Depressed Classes legislators, nominated by members of those Classes, would be included in Indian provincial and national legislative bodies. The number of reserved seats was higher than in the Award. Gandhi and the Congress had little choice. Unless they came to terms with Ambedkar on reserved seats, they risked a break-up of the Hindu electorate with potentially serious political consequences:

> To subtract them [the depressed classes] from the population on which the provinces' Hindu representation was calculated would make a critical difference to the subcontinent's electoral arithmetic, particularly in Bengal and the Punjab where the balance between Hindu and Muslim was so close.

The Poona Pact is significant in that it initiated a pattern of political compromise between "caste" Hindus and the Depressed Classes in the allocation of legislative representation and government jobs. Although much has changed in India, seventy years after the Pact 81 of the 543 members of the Lok Sabha, the lower house of Parliament, are from what were formerly known as the Depressed Classes and 79 of them hold reserved seats.

A by-product of the Pact was the highlighting of the underlying problems between "caste" Hindus and "outcastes." Gandhi initiated a national campaign to eliminate the evils of untouchability. Six days after the Pact, with help from wealthy industrialists like the Birlas, he started the Harijan Sevak Sangh (Servants of the Untouchables Society) and its weekly journal *Harijan.* The serious gulf in Hindu society that continues until now along with the reservations system is evident in an exchange between Gandhi and Ambedkar in the February 11, 1933, issue of *Harijan*. Having asked Ambedkar for a greetings message for the inaugural issue of *Harijan*, Gandhi received a blunt reply:

> ... I feel I cannot give a message. For I believe it will be a most unwarranted presumption on my part to suppose that I have sufficient worth in the eyes of the Hindus which would make them treat any message from me with respect... I am therefore sending you the accompanying statement for publication in your *Harijan*. B.R. Ambedkar
>
> *Statement*
>
> 'The Out-caste is a bye-product of the Caste system. There will be outcastes as long as there are castes. Nothing can emancipate the Out-caste except the destruction of the Caste system. Nothing can help to save Hindus and ensure their survival in the coming struggle except the purging of the Hindu Faith of this odious and vicious dogma.'

In his rejoinder, Gandhi noted: "Dr. Ambedkar is bitter. He has every reason to feel so." Gandhi continued, commenting that Ambedkar's "exterior is as clean as that of the cleanest and proudest Brahmin. Of his interior, the world knows as little as that of any of us." Affecting humility, Gandhi announced that *Harijan* "is not *my* weekly" but belonged to the Servants of Untouchables Society and that Ambedkar should feel "it is as much his as of any other Hindu." Then Gandhi went to the heart of the matter:

> As to the burden of his message, the opinion he holds about the caste system is shared by many educated Hindus. I have not, however, been able to share that opinion. I do not believe the caste system, even as distinguished from Varnashram, to be an 'odious and vicious dogma.' It has its limitations and its defects, but there is nothing sinful about it, as there is about untouchability, and, if it is a bye-product of the caste system it is only in the same sense that an ugly growth is of a body, or weeds of a crop.

Therefore, according to Gandhi, the "joint fight is restricted to the removal of untouchability," a fight into which he invited Ambedkar "and those who think with him to throw themselves, heart and soul..." Ambedkar preferred to carry on the fight through legal and constitutional measures. His legacy is the existing system of reservations. Gandhi, a Hindu traditionalist, sought to inspire Hindus to cleanse the caste system of the evil of untouchability. Judging from his writings, he saw this as an achievable goal.

Gandhi's Harijan Sevak Sangh continues his work throughout India. While the sincerity of the Society's efforts cannot be doubted, some Dalits see the organisation as paternalistic and condescending. At the Society's start, Gandhi opposed having a harijan on the board of directors. Some sense of caste attitude comes from a report in *Harijan* of some early activities. For example:

> Under the auspices of the Valmik Achhut Mandal, Jullundur, Punjab, a well attended meeting of caste Hindus and Harijans was held at Basti Sheikh with Chaudri Daulatram, a Harijan, in the chair. Master Shadiram, a well educated Harijan, exhorted his brother Harijans to keep clean and give up drink and other bad habits.
>
> Bhagat Dhanna Mal, a prominent Congressman of Ferozepur, Punjab, has taken a vow to remove the evil practices of untouchability, as far as it lies in his power to do so. He will gladly respond at his own expense to any call for help from Harijans in any part of India.

2.1.6. The Government of India Act of 1935

The reservation of seats for the Depressed Classes was incorporated into the Government of India Act of 1935, legislation by the British designed to give Indian provinces greater self-rule and set up a national federal structure that would incorporate the princely states. The Act went into force in 1937.

The Act brought the term "scheduled castes," now the Indian Government's official designation, into use, defining the group as including "such castes, races or tribes or parts of or groups within castes, races or tribes, being castes, races, tribes, parts of groups which appear to His Majesty in Council to correspond to the classes of persons formerly known as "the Depressed Classes," as His Majesty in

Council may specify." This vague classification was later clarified in "The Government of India (Scheduled Castes) Order, 1936 which contained a list, or "schedule," of scheduled castes throughout the British provinces.

2.1.7. All-India Depressed Classes Conference at Nagpur, 1942

Efforts by both Indians and British officials encouraged untouchables and the lower castes to form their own organisations to call for more equitable treatment and to demand economic assistance. Ambedkar was at the centre of these activities. Seeking a vehicle to bring pressure to bear on the government to secure more resources for the Depressed Classes he had formed the Independent Labour Party in 1936. Changing tactics, he used a July 1942 All India Depressed Classes Conference in Nagpur to establish an All India Depressed Classes Federation.

Among the group's demands were those for a new constitution with provisions in provincial budgets, specifically in the form of money for education, to support the advancement of the scheduled castes; representation by statute in all legislatures and local bodies; separate electorates; representation on public service commissions; the creation of separate villages for scheduled castes, "away from and independent of the Hindu villages," as well as a government-sponsored "Settlement Commission" to administer the new villages; and the establishment of an All-India Scheduled Castes Federation. When in 1942 Congress Party leaders launched a "Quit India" movement, the British, engaged in a war for survival, rounded up Nehru, Gandhi, and other leaders and jailed them for the duration of the struggle with Germany and Japan. Ambedkar, by contrast, supported the war effort and became a member of the Viceroy's Executive Council. He used his new position to advance the interests of the Scheduled Castes. Ambedkar:

> Submitted a memorandum demanding reservation for the Scheduled Castes in services, and scholarships and financial aid for the promotion of their education. The government accepted the recommendations, and in 1943 reservation in services in favour of the Scheduled Castes became effective.

He had played the situation perfectly. With independence in sight, Congress leaders locked up, and Britain desiring to keep India quiet Ambedkar had successfully expanded the scope of reservations from legislative seats to government jobs and education.

2.2. Independence and of Framing Reservations Policy

On May 16, 1946, the British government released the Cabinet Mission Statement, a set of proposals to guide the framing of a new Indian constitution. By this time, the wheels for India's independence had already been set in motion by Clement Atlee's Labour Party government in London. Among other recommendations, the Cabinet Mission laid out a detailed plan for the Constituent Assembly's composition, such that the body be "as broad-based and accurate a representation of the whole population as possible." Three categories from which to draw delegates were proposed. In addition to divisions for Muslims and Sikhs, the Cabinet Mission suggested a "general" category which would include all others groups—Hindus, Anglo-Indians, Parsis, Indian Christians, the Scheduled Castes and Tribes, and women, among others. Delegates were appointed on the basis of indirect elections in the provincial legislative assemblies.

In March 1947, Britain sent Lord Louis Mountbatten, war hero and royal relative, to New Delhi as the King-Emperor's last Viceroy. His mission was to transfer power to an independent Indian government. In the end, power was transferred to two successor entities, Pakistan on August 14, 1947, and India on August 15, 1947.

Under the Cabinet Mission plan the Constituent Assembly was to consist of 389 seats, 296 of which were filled by delegates elected from the directly-administered provinces of British India and 93 of which were allotted to the princely states. The total number of seats was based on an undivided India, and, overall, represented a cross-section of the population of the country. Given the Muslim League's boycott of the Assembly, the impact of partition and subsequent migration, and the lengthy process of integrating the princely states, the number and distribution of seats continually fluctuated from the time of the first meeting on December 9, 1946. With the 1947 partition, many Muslim delegates left for Pakistan, terminating their membership in the Assembly. As a result, the body was reorganised. By November 26,

1949, it consisted of 324 seats, divided among the provinces and the princely states and representative of all major minority groups.

The make-up of the Constituent Assembly reflected the reality of what groups wield power in India, then and now. An analysis of membership in the most important advisory committees of the Constituent Assembly found that 6.5 percent were SCs. Brahmins made up 45.7 percent. Minority and Scheduled Caste delegates did have some influence during the Assembly proceedings, with several holding significant positions. Dr. H.C. Mookherjee, an Indian Christian, was Vice-President of the Constituent Assembly as well as Chairman of the Sub-Committee on Minorities. However, by far the most important was Dr. Ambedkar.

Jawaharlal Nehru (1889-1964), India's first Prime Minister and dominant political figure until his death, had already selected Ambedkar, an accomplished lawyer, as his Law Minister. A Brahmin himself, Nehru sought to build a secular India free from caste discrimination. He was among the "many educated Hindus" opposed to the caste system as noted by Gandhi in his 1933 *Harijan* exchange with Ambedkar (above). Given Nehru's views and Ambedkar's talents, it is not surprising that Ambedkar became chairman of the drafting committee for India's new constitution. It was also an astute political move for both leaders. For Nehru, it kept the independently minded Ambedkar "on board" with the government at a critical time; for Ambedkar, it was an opportunity to influence preparation of the new constitution and protect Scheduled Caste interests.

From the outset, the Constituent Assembly laid out clearly its objectives and philosophy for the new constitution. Several of the framers' main goals, articulated in the "Objectives Resolution," included guarantees of equality, basic freedoms of expression, as well as "adequate safeguards…for minorities, backward and tribal areas, and depressed and other backward classes." These principles guided the delegates throughout the Constitution-making process.

The Assembly set up a special Advisory Committee to tackle minority rights issues. This committee was further divided into several subcommittees. The Subcommittee on Minorities focused on representation in legislatures (joint versus separate electorates and weightings), reservation of seats for minorities in cabinets, reservation for minorities in the public services, and administrative machinery to ensure the protection of minority rights. After extensive research and debate, the Subcommittee on Minorities drafted a report of its findings for submission to the Advisory Committee. The latter supported most of the Subcommittee's recommendations.

Vallabhbhai Patel (1875-1950), Chairman of the Advisory Committee and the most powerful member of the governing Congress party after Nehru, submitted the Report on Minority Rights to Rajendra Prasad, President of the Assembly, and on August 27, 1947, the Assembly convened to discuss the Report. Patel opened the debate by presenting the Advisory Committee's main recommendations. Rejecting separate electorates—Congress wanted no repeat of the separate electorates granted to the Muslims by the British—and a "weightage" system, the Report endorsed the creation of joint electorates and proportional representation. Reservations were approved for minorities, as long as the reservations were in proportion to the population of the targeted groups. Some minorities, like the Parsis, voluntarily gave up this right.

Treatment of the Scheduled Castes was extensively debated. Efforts by Ambedkar and his allies to craft a provision requiring a "tripwire" 35 percent of Scheduled Caste votes in a constituency reserved for the Scheduled Castes failed. The principle of common voting and reserved seats in legislative bodies throughout the country was retained despite strong opposition from influential Constituent Assembly members like Nehru. However, the colonial-era system of having the Scheduled Castes choose candidates for reserved seats through local "electoral colleges" was dropped. Throughout the debate, caste Hindus permitted nothing that would suggest splitting off the Scheduled Castes in an electoral sense from the Hindu community.

2.3. Reservations Under the Constitution

On January 26, 1950, India ended its "Dominion" status, became a republic, and put in effect its new constitution. With an entire section dedicated to "Fundamental Rights," the Indian Constitution prohibits any discrimination based on religion, race, caste, sex, and place of birth (Article 15[1]). This law extends to all public institutions, such as government-run educational facilities, to access to hotels and restaurants, public employment and public wells, tanks (man-made ponds for water supply and bathing), and roads. The practice of untouchability is declared illegal (Article 17).

Significantly, Article 15, which prohibits discrimination, also contains a clause allowing the union and state governments to make "any special provision for the advancement of any socially and educationally backward classes of citizens or for the Scheduled Castes and Scheduled Tribes." This language was added in 1951 within weeks of a Supreme Court decision outlawing quotas in school admissions. The speed of the amendment is indicative of the strong political support for reservations, Nehru's personal views notwithstanding.

Similarly, Article 16, calling for "equality of opportunity in matters of public employment," contains clauses permitting the "reservation of appointments or posts in favour of any backward class of citizens which, in the opinion of the State, is not adequately represented in the services under the State" and another allowing "reservation in matters of promotion" for Scheduled Castes and Scheduled Tribes.

A separate section of the Constitution, "Special Provisions Relating to Certain Classes," requires the reservation of seats in the "House of the People," or Lok Sabha, and the Legislative Assemblies of the states for the Scheduled Castes and Scheduled Tribes.The numbers of reserved seats are determined by the proportion Scheduled Caste and Scheduled Tribe members to the general population, based on population estimates from the most recent decennial census. The President of India and the Parliament, in consultation with the state governments, determine the list of groups qualifying as Scheduled Castes, Scheduled Tribes, and "backward classes."

Several safeguards accompany these provisions for reservation. First, the Constitution originally required the reservation of seats in the Lokh Sabha and state legislatures to end after ten years. After five amendments, the policy is now set to expire on January 25, 2010. Secondly, regarding the reservation of jobs, Article 335 of the Constitution mandates that the "claims of the members of the Scheduled Castes and Scheduled Tribes shall be taken into consideration, consistently with the maintenance of efficiency of administration." Finally, a National Commission for Scheduled Castes and Scheduled Tribes was created to investigate, monitor, advise, and evaluate the progress of the Scheduled Castes and Scheduled Tribes under the schemes aimed at the socioeconomic development of these groups. Another Commission was also created to investigate the conditions of the socially and educationally backward classes.

It is interesting to note that the Constitution's reservations construct, which explicitly singles out certain castes for special preferential treatment, contradicts the document's prohibition on discrimination based on caste, race, and other such criteria. Furthermore, India's caste system itself, with its strict hierarchy dictated by birth, is at odds with the ideals of equality and social justice.

Despite the creation of centrally based commissions to monitor reservations and other schemes, the Constitution gives great liberties to the individual states to determine the quantity and limits of reservation and what, for example, qualifies as the "maintenance of the efficiency of administration." The clause giving states the authority to formulate and implement policy to facilitate "the advancement of any socially and educationally backward classes of citizens," is also decidedly vague. No concrete definition of "backward" is provided either. In addition, though a specific—if, in practice, flexible—time limit is placed on the reservation of seats in the Lok Sabha and state legislative assemblies, there is no such clause regarding the future termination of reservations of jobs and promotions.

2.4. Other Legal Protections for Dalits

To give teeth to the protections for the Scheduled Castes and Tribes mandated by the Constitution, India's Parliament has passed two major laws. The Untouchability (Offences) Act of 1955 (renamed the Protection of Civil Rights Act in 1976) was intended to provide enforcement of Article 17 of the Constitution, outlawing untouchability. It fell short of expectations. In the words of India's National Commission for Scheduled Castes and Scheduled Tribes, "All the measures taken were not found to be effective enough in curbing the incidents of atrocities on Scheduled Castes and Scheduled Tribes." In 1989 a new law, the Scheduled Castes and Scheduled Tribes (Prevention of Atrocities) Act, came into force. Similar to an American hate crimes statute, it provides heavier penalties than under ordinary law for eighteen specified crimes including forcing the eating of obnoxious substances, bonded labour, and sexual exploitation.

References

Brock, R.W., ed., *The Simon Report on India (An Abridgement)*. London: J.M. Dent & Sons Limited, 1930.

Butler, Harcourt. *India Insistent*. London: William Heinemann Ltd., 1931.

Jaffrelot, Christophe. *India's Silent Revolution*. London: Hurst & Co., in publication.

Khilnani, Sunil. *The Idea of India*. New Delhi: Penguin Books India Pvt. Ltd., 1998.

Mahar, J. Michael, ed. *The Untouchables in Contemporary India*. Tucson: The University of Arizona Press, 1972.

Mandal, Jagadis C. *Poona Pact and Depressed Classes*. Calcutta: Sujan Publications, 1999.

3

Features of Indian Reservation Policy

Government employment in India is widely considered prestigious and a guarantor of security and advancement. Government jobs still account for the majority of jobs in the economy's organised sector. Table 3.1 illustrates that despite serious attempts at liberalisation beginning in 1991, the public sector continues to dominate the Indian economy and serve as the main source of employment.

Table 3.1. Estimated Percent Employment in the Public and Quasi-Public Sectors (in organised sector)

Year	% Employment in Public Sector
1990-91	62.62
1992-93	63.16
1993-94	62.99
1994-95	62.74
1995-96	61.69
1996-97	61.42
1997-98	60.97
1998-99	61.02

As a result, reservations in the coveted area of government services take on increased salience.

Public sector jobs are divided into four levels, distinguished by income and selectivity: Class I (or Group A), Class II (or Group B), Class III (or Group C) and Class IV (or Group D). Table 3.2 shows the distribution of jobs among these four categories based on 1994 estimates:

Table 3.2. Profile of Central Government Employment

Class	% of workforce
I	2.2
II	3.3
III	66.8
IV	27.2
Total	99.5

Class I, the highest-paid level, includes members of the elite Indian Administrative Service (IAS), the Indian Foreign Service (IFS), the Indian Police Service (IPS) and connected Central Government services. In the next income bracket, Class II employees comprise officers of the state civil service cadre. Competitive exams and interviews are usually used to fill these top two tiers, which require highly skilled and well-qualified candidates.

In contrast, the bottom two job categories, Class III and Class IV, include low-skill, low-qualification posts such as primary school teachers, revenue inspectors, constabies, peons, clerks, drivers, and sweepers. These are typically low-income jobs and are not subject to strict selection processes. Additionally, selecting officials exercise a high degree of discretion in filling posts. Influence plays a major role. This is particularly relevant given that Class III and Class IV jobs make up the bulk of public sector employment in the organised economy. According to estimates from 1994, 94 percent of public sector jobs in the Central Government fell into the Class III and Class IV levels. Table 3.3 summarises SC representation in the four classes of central government from 1959 to 1995:

Table 3.3. Percentage of SC Employees in Central Government Services

Class	1959	1965	1974	1984	1995
I	1.18	1.64	3.2	6.92	10.12
II	2.38	2.82	4.6	10.36	12.67
III	6.95	8.88	10.3	13.98	16.15
IV	17.24[a]	17.75	18.6	20.2	21.26[a]

It is clear that there has been a general rise in SC representation in all four categories of employment in central services across time. The SC presence in Class I, for instance, has increased by tenfold, from 1.18 percent in 1959 to 10.12 percent in 1995. The Class II figures show an upward trend from 2.38 percent in 1959 to 12.67 percent in 1995. The lowest class, which initially had more SC employees in 1959 than any of the other classes had in 1995, has had a slower rate of increase.

While these are all good indications that reservations are working, it is difficult to ignore certain realities that detract from this success. First, SC representation in the Classes I and II, after over 50 years, still fall short of the reservations quota of 15 percent for SCs, while the less-prestigious and lower-paid Class III and IV jobs are amply filled. Even prior to 1970, when quotas were set at 12.5 percent, only Class IV met the quota of places allotted to SCs. However, because reservations apply to only current appointments and the average service career is around 30 years, it is a time-consuming process for the percentage of posts held to equal the percentage of positions reserved. The steep increase in Class I and II positions since the 1960s suggests that the percentage of new SC recruits is nearing the SC reservations quota.

Secondly, certain posts are "exempt" from reservation. Under the current policy, reservations do not apply to cases of transfer or deputation; cases of promotion in grades or services in which the element of direct recruitment exceeds 75%; temporary appointments of less than 45 days; work-charged posts required for emergencies (such as relief work in cases of natural disaster); certain scientific and technical posts; single post cadre; upgradation of posts due to cadre restructuring (total or partial); and ad hoc appointments arising out of stop gap arrangements. As far as scientific and technical posts are concerned, reservations do not apply to positions above the lowest grade in Group I services.

Finally, another factor undercutting the positive trends is the prevalence of false caste certification. Non-SCs, whether out of opportunism or desperation, have been known to pose as SCs in order to take advantage of reserved government jobs, in addition to other benefits afforded to SCs, such as relaxation of maximum age limits and waiving of civil service exams and fees. In an attempt to curb the problem, the Karnataka state government considered issuing caste identity cards to SCs, STs, and OBCs in June 2001. However, the plan was shelved when the authorities realised how costly such a policy would be, given that around 90 percent of the state's population could be counted as SC, ST or OBC.

3.1. Reserv. tion of Seats in Legislatures

3.1.1. The Lok Sabha

One of the most explicit constitutional provisions concerns the reservation of seats for SCs in the Union and state legislatures. An analysis of the composition of the current Lok Sabha (the 13th, elected in 1999) indicates adherence to the Constitution's mandate. All seats reserved for SCs are filled, with two states, Maharashtra and Andhra Pradesh, each having an SC Member of Parliament (MP) from a non-reserved constituency (Table 3. 4).

Table 3.4. Distribution of Seats in Thirteenth Lok Sabha (1999) among States with Constituencies Reserved for SCs

State/UT	Total seats	Reserved seats	Seats filled by SCs
Andhra Pradesh	42	6	7
Assam	14	1	1
Bihar	54	8	8
Gujarat	26	2	2
Haryana	10	2	2
Himachal Pradesh	4	1	1
Karnataka	28	4	4
Kerala	20	2	2
Madhya Pradesh	40	6	6
Maharashtra	48	3	4
Orissa	21	3	3
Punjab	13	3	3
Rajasthan	25	4	4
Tamil Nadu	39	7	7
Uttar Pradesh	85	18	18
West Bengal	42	8	8
Delhi	7	1	1
TOTALS	518	79	81

While all seats reserved for SCs are filled, a look at the portfolios and posts held within the 13th Lok Sabha by SCs undercuts the degree of substantive SC representation. Table 3.5 shows all Lok Sabha committees chaired by and Union Cabinet Minister and Minister of State posts held by SCs:

Table 3.5. Posts Held by SC Members of Parliament (MP) in the Council of Ministers and Committees of the Thirteenth Lok Sabha

SC-chaired committees (including departmentally-related standing committees):	
Welfare of SC/ST	Ratilal Kalides Varma (BJP)
Rules Committee	Lok Sabha Speaker Ganti Balayogi (TDP)
General Purposes Committee	Lok Sabha Speaker Ganti Balayogi (TDP)
Business Advisory Committee	Lok Sabha Speaker Ganti Balayogi (TDP)
Labour and Welfare (standing)	Sushil Kumar Indora (INLD)
Union Cabinet Minister:	
Social Justice and Empowerment	Satyanarayan Jatiya (BJP)
Agro and Rural Industries	Kariya Munda (BJP)
Coal Mines	Ram Vilas Paswan (Lok Jan Shakti)
Water Resources	Arjun Charan Sethi (Biju Janata Dal)
Minister of State (non-independent charge):	
Health and Family Welfare	A. Raja (DMK)
Consumer Affairs, Food and Public Distribution	V. Sreenivasa Prasad (J D (Samata))
Public Distribution	Ashok Kumar Pradhan (BJP)
Labour and Employment	Muni Lall (BJP)

Out of a total of 40 Lok Sabha committees, five are chaired by SCs. Ganti Balayogi, an MP from Andhra Pradesh who served as house Speaker until his death in a helicopter crash on March 3, 2002, headed three of these groups—Rules, General Purposes, and Business Advisory—*ex-officio* in addition to presiding over the Lok Sabha. Elected by the Lok Sabha in 1998, Balayogi was the first SC to be Speaker, a post that in the past has been held by such notables as Vallabhbhai Patel. Though the Speaker is mainly responsible for the maintenance of order and the conduct of business in the house, he also can wield considerable influence, especially in cases where a tie vote occurs, and his vote breaks the deadlock.

As a result of the need for governing parties to accommodate party factions with office and to secure representation for certain regions and groups, the Council of Ministers includes 73 ministers. Eight SC MPs currently serve in Union cabinet minister and minister of state positions. Portfolios such as Labour and Employment are not insignificant, but conspicuously absent from the list are such major ministries as Finance, External Affairs, Defense, and Home. There have been other influential SC MPs in past cabinets. Ram Vilas Paswan, a Dalit from Bihar, has held a seat in Parliament since 1977. In addition to serving as Minister for Labour and Welfare in the V. P. Singh Government of 1989-90, Paswan was also Railway Minister, an office considered a "classic source of patronage," from 1996-1998.

Despite not always controlling "heavyweight" portfolios, SC MPs are generally well-qualified. According to Table 3.6, 80.25 percent of SC MPs possess at least an undergraduate degree, compared to 87.5 percent for the entire Lok Sabha. Breaking down these figures by gender brings out some interesting contrasts. All female SC MPs have had, at the minimum, an undergraduate education and 66.67 percent have had postgraduate training. Among the general pool of female MPs, only 74.5 percent had at least an undergraduate degree. The situation for males is the opposite—only 77.78 percent of male SC MPs had undergraduate degrees and higher while the figure for all male MPs was 88.9 percent.

Table 3.6. Educational Attainment of SC MPs in the Thirteenth Lok Sabha

Level of Education	All SC MPs	%age	Male SC MPs	%age	Female SC MPs	%age
Doctorate	6	7.41	5	6.94	1	11.11
Post Graduate	24	29.63	18	25.00	6	66.67
Graduate	14	17.28	13	18.06	1	11.11
Undergraduate	21	25.93	20	27.78	1	11.11
Matriculate	4	4.94	4	5.56	0	0.00
Under Matriculate	5	6.17	5	6.94	0	0.00
Info N/A	2	2.47	2	2.78	0	0.00

Given the last available all-India literacy rate for SCs (37.41 percent according to 1991 estimates), the high educational attainment of the majority of SC MPs resonates with what has been dubbed the "creamy layer" effect. Critics of reservations have often asserted that the policy has had disproportionate effects, benefiting only the most forward of the SCs—those already in a better position to take advantage of reservations—and facilitating the emergence of an SC "elite."

In the case of the female SC MPs, their high educational qualifications might also be an indication of an inherent disadvantage in their ability to seek political influence. Perhaps, the fact that 100 percent of the SC women have higher degrees, compared to 74.5% for all women in the Lok Sabha, is indicative of SC females having to overcome both gender and caste hurdles. In order to obtain office, they need to be even more qualified than non-SC females.

Data to construct an educational profile for an earlier Lok Sabha were not available for the purpose of drawing comparisons. However, information showing the number of reserved constituencies and the distribution of SC MPs among political parties was obtainable. With the intention of finding as much difference in time as possible and avoiding the shuffling of state borders that occurred in the years after Independence, the third Lok Sabha was chosen for analysis.

One of the major differences brought out in the table is the Congress' fall from dominance. This is not only reflected in the total number of seats controlled by the party (366 down to 112), but also in the number of its SC MPs, which has been reduced from 63 to 6. In contrast, the BJP, with 180 seats, has taken Congress' place. The BJP has 24 SC MPs, 17 more than the next highest party. SC MPs also make up nearly 15 percent of the BJP's representatives in the Lok Sabha while Congress' SC MPs are only 5 percent of the total party members in office.

Another change over time has been the significant growth in the number of political parties to which SC MPs belong. SC MPs only represented 12 different parties in the third Lok Sabha. This number has doubled in the current Lok Sabha. Though the BJP has the most SC members of any party, it does not enjoy the same "monopoly" as the Congress party did in the third Lok Sabha.

Finally, an additional important development with the election of the current Lok Sabha has been the emergence of the Bahujan Samaj Party (BSP), the first major party formed to advocate Dalit rights that has achieved electoral success. Ýronically, the BSP's increasing prominence, mainly in northern India has depleted the Congress' traditional vote bank.

3.2. Educational Reservation

Education has long been identified as key to achieving the advancement of the SCs. In line with Article 15(4) of the Constitution, which empowers the State to make special provisions for the educational development of SCs, the Indian government currently allows the reservation of 15 percent of seats for SCs in universities and colleges. This policy covers enrolment in various undergraduate and graduate courses of general, technical, medical and other professional education. Reservations can also extend to the allotment of places in dormitories. State governments observe different rates of reservation, based on the size of their SC populations.

Along with these measures, Central and state governments have also instituted scholarship/stipend programs, as well as initiatives to furnish SCs with special tutoring, books, midday meals, stationery and uniforms. One such scheme, funded entirely by the Central government, provides four years of special and remedial tutoring to select secondary-school students to help SCs gain admission to universities and technical institutions.

Created in 1956 by an Act of Parliament, the University Grants Commission (UCG) oversees the implementation of these policies in institutes of higher education. There are currently 166 central/state universities, 37 "deemed" universities, and 9,278 colleges. The UCG has routinely published guidelines to encourage and aid state governments in filling reservations quotas entirely. For example, SC candidates are normally given a relaxation of marks by five per cent from the minimum qualifying level. Should reserved seats remain vacant, universities are advised to increase relaxation of admission.

In contrast, a look at Table 3.7, which shows the number of SCs in teaching and non-teaching posts in central universities, where reservations should be in operation, reveals a distinct pattern of SC representation:

Table 3.7. Representation of SCs in Teaching/Non-teaching Posts in Central Universities (as on 1/1/93)*

Position	Total Employees	SC Employees	% SC Employees
Professor	1,155	2	0.17
Reader/Associate Professor	1,774	6	0.34
Lecturer/Assistant Professor/ Directors of PhysicalEducation	1,491	35	2.35
Research Associate/ Tutor/ Demonstrator	257	3	1.17
Group A, non-teaching	756	26	3.44
Group B, non-teaching	1,525	49	3.21
Group C, non-teaching	9,001	414	4.60
Group D, non-teaching	10,635	2,368	22.27

Out of eight categories of posts, the reservations quota is met in one, and, as is the case with all central government services, it is the bottom-ranked, lowest-paid group of positions: Group D. None of the remaining job groups has more than five percent SC employees. In all central universities, SCs held two out of a total of 1,155 professorships.

The National Commission for Scheduled Castes and Scheduled Tribes attributed this low level of representation to the "lukewarm attitude of the authorities in the Union Department of Education" which failed to initiate legislation making the implementation of reservations in central universities mandatory. As a result, universities were not instituting reservations because the University Acts contained no legally binding provisions to do so.

Setting the context for the under-representation of SCs in all aspects of university life—learning, teaching, administrating—has been an SC literacy rate lagging behind that of the rest of the Indian population. Table 3.8. compares the literacy rates of SCs and the general population across time and by gender.

In 1991, SCs were trailing the rest of the population by 14.8 percent in literacy, a larger margin of difference than in 1961 when the deficit was 13.75 percent. While SC males have gained some ground over the past decades, now only 14.22 percent versus 17.48 percent behind, SC women are not faring as well. The gap for women has widened from 9.66 percent in 1961 to 15.53 percent in 1991.

Table 3.8. Sex-wise Literacy Trends among SCs and Total Population

	Male	Female	Total	Male	Female	Total
1961	34.44	12.95	24.02	16.96	3.29	10.27
1971	39.45	18.72	29.46	22.36	6.44	14.67
1981	65.5	29.85	43.67	31.12	10.93	21.38
1991	64.13	39.29	52.21	49.91	23.76	37.41
2001	75.85	54.16	65.38			

A state-wise breakdown (Table 3.9) shows that even in states like Kerala, where universal education has been, by and large, achieved, SCs still lag behind by 10 percent.

Table 3.9. State/UT-wise Literacy Rates of SCs (from highest to lowest)

	% Total Literate	% SCs Literate	% Total Literate	% SCs Literate
State/UT	1961	1961	1991	1991
Kerala	46.8	24.44	89.81	79.66
Mizoram			82.27	77.92
Gujarat	30.5	22.46	61.29	61.07
Delhi	52.7	20.86	75.29	57.6
Maharashtra	29.8	15.78	64.87	56.46
Pondicherry	37.4	11.11	74.74	56.26
Assam	21.2	8.47	52.89	53.94
Himachal Pradesh	17.1	8.46	63.86	53.2
Tamil Nadu	31.4	14.66	62.66	46.74
West Bengal	29.3	13.58	57.7	42.21
Punjab	24.2	9.64	58.51	41.09
Haryana	—	—	55.85	39.22
Karnataka	—	—	56.04	38.06
Orissa	21.7	11.57	49.09	36.78
Madhya Pradesh	17.1	7.89	44.2	35.08
Andhra Pradesh	21.2	8.47	44.09	31.59
Uttar Pradesh	17.6	13.58	41.6	26.85
Rajasthan	15.2	6.44	38.55	26.29
Bihar	18.4	5.95	38.48	19.49

However, compared to the disparity in 1961 between the total population and SCs in Kerala (approximately 22 percent), the gap seems to be narrowing. In "Hindi belt" states like Uttar Pradesh, literacy rates among SCs did not clear 30 percent in 1991. At 19.49 percent, SC literacy in Bihar was even lower.

The process of collecting statistics on SCs was frequently complicated by the lack of sufficient information. In addition, when data could be obtained on the representation of SCs in services, legislatures, and educational institutions, there was no guarantee that the figures necessarily reflected whether such representation was due to reservations policy alone. For instance, is the general increase in the SC presence in government services an indication that reservations were helping SCs get jobs or was it that a growing number of SCs were qualified for positions?

Further compounding the problem was the issue of reliability of the figures and tables obtained from government reports. For example, meaningful data regarding the enrolment of SCs in institutes of higher education were scarce. Facing pressure from bodies like the UGC to reserve and fill adequate numbers of seats for SCs, universities have been known to inflate enrolment figures.

Despite such uncertainties and possible distortions of data, the fact that SCs are still underrepresented in government services and educational institutions (in relation to the proportion they make up in the total population) undercuts the goals of the reservations policy.

References

Panandiker, V.A., ed. *The Politics of Backwardness: Reservation Policy in India.* New Delhi: Konark Publishers Pvt Ltd, 1997.

Parikh, Sunita. *The Politics of Preference: Democratic Institutions and Affirmative Action in the United States and India.* Ann Arbor: University of Michigan Press, 1997.

Sharma, Kusum. *Ambedkar and Indian Constitution.* New Delhi: Ashish Publishing House, 1992.

Wadhwa, Kamlesh Kumar. *Minority Safeguards in India: Constitutional Provisions and Their Implementation.* New Delhi: Thomson Press (India) Limited, 1975.

4

Caste and Reservation Politics

The political process of any society is influenced by the nature of the society. India's social structure is best understood in terms of caste system wherein the cast is hierarchically arranged. Over the years, the caste system developed into an elaborate system to maintain socioeconomics inequalities in the society. Individuals born in and belonging to the lower castes and the outcasts suffered from many disadvantages and were oppressed and exploited by the upper castes. The conditions of the outcast is (Dalits) was particularly pathetic. The practice of untouchability epitomised their conditions.

1. In the typical Varna-Vyvastha there are four Varnas: Brahmin (the priest and the intellectual class), Kshatriya (warrior and the ruling class), Vaisyas (the producing class -peasants and artisaas) and Shudra (those who performed menial and 'polluting' jobs. One must note here that the 'varna-vyvastha' provides more the theory than the actuality of the caste. In reality, there are not four but thousands of castes and jatis, in which the caste system is organised. It is possible, nevertheless to classify most of the jatis in accordance with the Varna distinctions, although it is easier to be done at the extreme ends of the social spectrum than at the middle ranges. In other words, Varna system is related to jati in that it gives a holistic framework to which any jati will fit.

2. Caste is a localised group having a traditional association with an occupation. The principle of birth forms the exclusive basis of membership in a caste group. Accordingly, the choice of occupation is not open but is determined on the basis of one's birth in a caste. In addition caste groups have rules governing food

and marriage. The group defines rules of behaviour for its members and exercise some degree of authority over them including the right to expel those who defy its authority.

Caste as group identity, however, got strengthened in the new context of modern ideas and institutions. This happened because it became one of the bases of political mobilisation among the many castes and classes before, during the freedom struggle and afterwords.

The socio-religious movements of the 19th century had made the lower castes conscious of their backward conditions and also of their rights that had been denied to them over the centuries. As a result, many amongst them were no longer prepared to accept their inferior status as divinely ordained. In the backdrop of this awakening, the introduction of democratic principle of governance, the emergence of party-centred politics and the attempt of the British rulers to mobilise the lower and the outcasts along with the Muslims in its support to thwart the growing national movement — all combined to prepare the ground for the politicisation of the castes.

By the time India gained Independence, the Backward classes, because of politicisation, had become a force to reckon with. Their claims and demands could no longer be ignored. At the same time the nationalist leaders were also committed to the task of improving their conditions.

In light of the above, the constitution makers enjoined upon the new state to take positive measures for bringing the backward classes at par with the rest of the society. They realised that without the positive intervention by the state it would not be possible to remove their historically accumulated backwardness. The policy of reservation for the backward classes needs to be understood in this context. Backward classes refer to three categories of the people — the scheduled castes, scheduled tribes and the other backward classes (OBC).

4.1. Cast in Politics

Caste began to play an important role after independence as its involvement in politics increased. The fact that it existed as easily identifiable social cluster of people made it an easy object of political mobilisation by political parties in their quest for political support and votes. While the political parties sought to exploit caste for its own electoral purposes, caste groups by making politics their sphere of activity got a chance to assert their identity and bargain for benefits and position in society. Thus, caste and politics interaction has been a two-way process.

In politicising the castes, the caste associations played a crucial role. Caste associations were quasi-voluntary associations in the sense that its membership was open only to the individuals of the caste community. These associations were formed to secure economic benefits or educational openings or for more clearly political purpose of uniting to fight the hegemony of the upper castes. In either case, involvement in politics was considered necessary for securing the specific purpose for which they were formed. Thus, once formed on the basis of caste identity, caste associations went on to acquire non-caste functions.

In electoral politics the role of the caste in politics has become powerful. This can be seen at all levels of the political process of the country. All political parties tend to give party ticket to candidates for contesting elections from amongst the numerically or otherwise dominant caste in every constituency. Major caste groups get representation in the council of ministers. Be it elections, political appointments or even formation of political parties, caste has been the major consideration.

The influence of caste, however, varies depending upon the level of election and the region. Its influence is far more at the local and state-level political process than at the national level. Caste plays greater role in the rural than in urban areas. In the rural areas and at the local level, the smallness of constituency and the fact that there is greater face to face interactions account for the strong influence of caste in politics.

Since independence two factors have especially brought the issue of caste in Indian politics into sharp focus. These are (1) the introduction of universal adult franchise and (2) the constitutional provisions for protective discrimination in favour of the backward classes. The introduction of universal adult franchise brought a very large section of the populace, who had been hitherto excluded on account of property qualification to vote, into the arena of electoral politics. This made the task of mobilising votes enormously difficult for the political parties. The daunting task was, however, made easy when political parties relied upon castes to get their votes. In the process castes' involvement in politics deepened with every election in India.

In addition to the enlarged arena of electoral politics, the constitutional provisions for protective discrimination also provided the ground for castes to play a significant role in politics.

One may note here that protective discrimination was meant for three categories of people – the Scheduled Castes, the Scheduled Tribes and the OBC — collectively called as the backward classes. Of these three categories, the SCs and STs were easily identifiable and- there was a large measure of consensus on the need and the desireability of having reservations for them. But the case of the OBCs was different.

Since Independence two types of caste politics can be discerned. The first type involved the caste groups clamouring either for being recognised as OBC by the state governments or those already recognised for getting a higher quota in the reservations. The decision of the State governments to appoint Backward classes Commission from time to time provided the occasion for such caste politics to flourish. The second type of caste politics, involved mobilisation of social and political forces for and against reservations for the OBC based solely on caste criteria. The extent of castes involvement in politics can be appreciated by noting a simple fact that over 50% of the populace belong to the category of the OBCs. While the first type of caste politics sought to influence the reservation policy of the state government, the second type of caste politics was aimed to resist the reservation policy of the central government.

The reservation issue thus, provided a fertile ground for castes to play an active role in politics.

4.2. Reservation Politics

Keeping in mind the backward conditions of the backward classes, the constitution makers also made special provisions for the upliftment of the backward classes. The special provisions are in the form of protective discrimination. The policy of reservation is an instance of protective discrimination.

Articles 38 and 46 in the chapter of Directive principles, enjoin upon the state the duty to strive for the welfare of the people in general and the backward classes in particular. Article 38 states: 1) the state shall strive to promote the welfare of the people by securing and promoting as effectively as it may a social order in which Justice — social, economic and political shall form all institutions of national life; 2) the state shall in particular, strive to minimise the inequalities in income, and endeavour to eliminate the inequalities in status, facilities and opportunities not only amongst individuals but also amongst group of people residing in different areas and engaged in different vocations.

Article 46 stipulates: "The state shall promote with special care the educational and the economic interest of the weaker sections of the people and in particular, of the Scheduled Castes and Tribes and shall protect them from injustices and all forms of exploitation."

The policy of reservation is based on the principle of protective discrimination. Protective discrimination in favour of the backward classes was felt necessary by the constitution makers because of the realisation that equality of opportunity alone would not suffice to bring the backward classes at par with the rest of the society. Equality of opportunity in absence of equality of conditions would result in deepening of inequality instead of promoting equality. One must note here that the provision of protective discrimination is not an exception to but integral to the Right to Equality.

4.2.1. Reservations for SCs and STs

The constitution recognises three categories of people as backward classes. In this section we will deal with the provisions relating to the SCs and STs. The constitution provides for three types of reservations for the SCs and STs. These are (1) reservation of jobs in government services and in public sector, (2) reservation in educational institutions, and (3) reservations in legislative representations.

Under Articles 16(A), 320(4) and 333, 15% and 7% of the jobs are reserved at all levels in the public services for the SCs and STs respectively. This reservation however, must as far as it may be, consistent with the maintenance of efficiency of the administration (Article 35).

Article 15(4) deals with the reservation of seats in the educational institutions. Article 15(4) states: "Nothing in Article 15 or clause (2) of Article 29 shall prevent the state from making any special provision for the advancement of any socially and educationally backward classes of citizens or for the Scheduled Castes and Scheduled Tribes." Accordingly, the Union and the State governments have reserved 20% of the seats in all educational institutions maintained by public money. Moreover, qualifications for admission have also been relaxed for the SCs and STs so that they can get access to educational opportunities.

Articles 330 and 332 provide for reservation of seats in the Lok Sabha and State Legislative Assemblies. 78 seats for the SCs and 38 seats for the STs are reserved in the Lok Sabha. In State Legislative Assemblies 540 and 282 seats are reserved for SCs and STs respectively. Moreover seats are also reserved in the Panchayati Raj institutions.

4.2.2. Reservations for the OBCs

The task of specifying and identifying other Backwars Classes (OBCS) was left to the union and state government.

In many States where the backward classes movement was strong, such as in Tamil Nadu, Andhra Pradesh, Kerala, Gujarat, Bihar, to name a few, the state governments have reserved jobs at all levels in the public services and seats in educational institutions.

The Union government, however, took a very long time in deciding to provide reservation to the OBCs in the central services. The Union government had as early as 1953 appointed Kalelkar Commission under Article 340. The Commission submitted its report in 1956, but its recommendations were not implemented by the Union government. The second Commission under Article 340 was appointed by the Janta Party Government in 1978. This Commission known as Mandal Commission submitted its report in 1982. It identified 3943 castes as OBC and recommended 27% reservation in government and semi-government jobs and admission to educational institutions.

On 13th August 1990 the Union Government headed by V.P. Singh issued an office memorandum extending reservation to the OBCs on the lines recommended by the Mandal Commission. Soon thereafter, widespread protests were staged. Writ petitions were filed in Supreme Court and many High Courts questioning this measure. The Supreme Court examined the issue in November 1992 and permitted the Union Government to reserve 27% of the jobs for the OBCs subject to the exclusion of the 'creamy layer' among the OBCs. Ramanand Prasad committee was set up by the Union government to identify the "creamy layer". Once it had done its job, the government executed the order of 13th August 1990 in September 1993.

4.2.3. Woman's Reservation

Women constitute nearly half of the entire Indian population. But condition of women in India is miserable, due to illiteracy, poverty and backward social values. Keeping in view the prevalent circumstances, reservation for the women was started to emancipate the women from the drudgery of household. A debate has been going on to ensure women's reservation at every level of representative system of Indian Democracy and even in the state administrative services. Under the Panchayati Raj system women's seats have been reserved at both the Panchayat level, and the block & district levels. Some political parties are also debating the issue of giving at least 30% tickets to women candidates for contesting elections of state legislative assembly and also for the parliamentary elections but women's reservation bill is still pending in the parliament.

References

Srinivas, M.N. *Caste: Its Twentieth Century Avatar.* New Delhi: Penguin Books India Ltd., 1996.

Steven Ian Wilkinson, "India, Consociational Theory, and Ethnic Violence," *Asian Survey*. Vol. XL, No.5, September/October 2000, 767-791.

Susan Bayly, *Caste, Society and Politics in India.* Cambridge: Cambridge University Press, 1999.

United States Office of Strategic Services, Research and Analysis Branch. *The Depressed Classes of India.* Washington, D.C., 1943.

Venkatesan, V. "The Dalit Cause." *Frontline*, Vol.19:3, February 2-15, 2002.

Wadhwa, Kamlesh Kumar. *Minority Safeguards in India: Constitutional Provisions and Their Implementation.* New Delhi: Thomson Press (India) Limited, 1975.

5

Dalit Women and Reservation Policy

Dalit women are discriminated due to a patriarchic dominated social structure on the one hand and humiliation within them due to caste ridden social system on the other. As such, they have virtually very low access to resources, power and control over their lives than Dalit men and other women in Nepal. Dalit women's families are ultra poor and represent about 80% of the ultra poor in Nepal The situation of the Dalit women is worse even among the general women whose status is very low. They face triple discrimination, because they are women, so-called low caste and discriminated by their male from their own caste groups. Due to triple oppression of class, caste and gender, Dalit women have least of access to opportunities for social and economic nobilities. Their liberation does not lie purely in economic or political terms. The social and cultural liberation is the determining factor for their lives.

The ignorance to the Dalit women by the Government is the common case. On top of that, the political parties and the international aid agencies have ignored them. They are similarly neglected by Nepalese women's movement. Women activists in Nepal never tried to merge Dalit women in their movement. They hardly pay attention towards Dalit women. They advocate for the women in general in their manifestoes and constitutions. But, while the question on Dalit woman is raised, they stay with folding hands. Voiceless Dalit women, therefore, are deprived of their rightful place in the governance process. It is an irony that even the Dalit activists raise the issue of Dalit males and largely overlook the case of Dalit women. It is a fact that no political parties have supported Dalit women by way of associating them at different levels.

In the Nepalese context, gender, caste and ethnicity are the three interlocking institutions or critical fault lines defining social identity. The constitution has enshrined for equality and equal opportunity before the law. But these three groups and communities are subject to exploitation, discrimination and unfair treatment. One Human development and welfare indicators states: Nepali women are almost invisible in the civil service making up only 8% of overall staff and 4% of officers. There is hardly any representation of Dalit women in public services.

Dalit women's literacy rate account for 9% compared to 42.9% on national average (CBS, 2001). Their life expectancy remains the lowest among Nepalese women: 42 years (*Mushar* women) while national average stands for 59.8 years (UNDP Human Development Report, 2001). High rate of infant mortality, child mortality and maternal death amongst the Dalit women are serious problems. A small tribe namely the *Badi* women are still forced to continue the traditional prostitution. They suffer from trafficking and prostitution due to their poverty and ignorance.

Similarly, the Dalits are highly disadvantaged groups. Dalit females have one of the lowest levels of literacy of all groups in Nepal. Their low level of literacy is due to three interrelated factors:

— Continued monopolisation of so-called high caste women and men,

— The stronger influence of casteism in rural areas on Dalit females, and

— The control of Dalit males over Dalit women and girls.

As a consequence, Dalit females' access to even basic literacy education is limited. As mentioned above, Dalit women's literacy rate accounts for 9% compared to 42.9% on national average (CBS, 2001). Close to 95% of Dalit women are rural; most are landless or marginal farmers who live in subject of poverty with grinding labour. Many work as day-to-day manual workers. Wage of the women is less than that of men. Their economic situation has worsened due to the overall deteriorating rural economic conditions over the centuries.

In all cases of caste conflict, the Dalit women are first victims. They are raped, gang raped and even made pregnant showing the temptation of marriage and finally left. Even though these incidences of violence against women are extreme, nevertheless, some of these caste biases exist in schools among Hindu teachers. In addition, Dalit females are invisible in school curriculums and textbooks. There are still various words and sentences hostile to the dignity of Dalit and women.

Malnutrition among Dalit women is high. Controls by men over women starts as a girl child where infant mortality due to neglect and malnutrition is very high. Many Dalit girls and women are used and abused by drunken male relatives. The sexual division of labour, child marriage and restricted mobility also limit Dalit females' access to education.

Most importantly, it must address issues important to Dalit women and be accompanied by other social and economic reforms such as the following; sanitation, health, childcare, credit and loans, land reform, conservation, reservation and scholarship for Dalit women.

5.1. Actions for the Emancipation of Dalit Women

There are about 150 existing positive legal provisions and policies for the substantial change of women at large Though, in general, these provisions were made intentionally to upgrade the status of women, only few from so called high caste and class women have benefited to a larger extent only. No impact on the Dalit women is seen so far.

Here is the details of positive policies for the substantial devlopment of dalit women:

a) *5% candidacy from women for House of Representatives is mandatory to all political parties*. But the practice has shown that only elite women have succeeded and benefited by this provision. Since personal identity of a candidate rather than of political parties is the attraction, the political parties fear to put candidature from Dalit community.

b) *Reservation of Women in National Assembly*: There is also a provision in the constitution for three seats in the National

Assembly of the Parliament. Only the women from so called high caste have got the advantage by this provision. There is not any instance of the Dalit woman as beneficiary of this provision.

c) *Reservation in Local bodies*: In the Local Self-governance Act, there is a provision of the reservation to women for at least one seat in ward Committee. But no Dalit woman benefited by this provision. Similarly there is a provision for the participation of women in the Development Council. Nominal Dalit women have got chance to participate in the Local Councils at the Municipal, Village Development Committee and District levels.

d) *Mandatory Provision for Inclusion of Women*: For the compulsory participation of women in all committees, this provision has been made in various laws i.e. consumer law, local motion pictures, central children welfare, steering committee of local development, breast feeding protection and promotion committee.

e) *Free Education*: The education act obliged all state schools for free education to women. However, Dalit women are not able to have such access due to early marriage and low economic status.

f) *Scholarship*: The scholarship rule has mandated for 20% reservation in scholarship. But none from among the Dalit girls could benefit from this arrangement. Every seat is provided to the so-called higher castes girls and the girls of high economic profile.

g) *Mandatory Plan for a Woman Teacher in Primary School*: The Ninth Plan has obliged every school to nominate a teacher from women, however, no satisfactory impact is seen in favour of Dalit women. This provision is more questionable since the schools are going to be managed locally. But, the social practices inhibit the appointment of a Dalit woman as a teacher to teach children of higher castes.

h) *Relaxation in Age for Civil Service*: The civil service rule (amendment) has relaxed the age limitation for the enrolment for public services to women. Maximum age limit for women to join civil service is 40 years, whereas it is only 35 in case of men. But, there lacks the record of the beneficiary from Dalit women by this provision. Major beneficiaries of this provision of reservation are women from the forward castes.

i) *Women's Bodies to be searched by Women Police*: If the body of woman has to be searched in connection with investigation of a crime, the search has to be conducted by women police without insulting her. Under the existing arrangement, the body of a Badi woman is searched by male police even without prior notice, which is not only objectionable but an insult to the pride of the women folk.

j) *National Commission for Women*: The Commission is established with a view to protecting and promoting the women's rights. But, the composition of this Commission lacks any representation form Dalit women. As such, the Dalit women have not got any positive feeling towards this institution.

Though the government has taken several positive actions for the gender justice Dalit women are considered neither at the time of planning nor in the executing of the policies.

With the transformation of the nature of state structure, it becomes the liability of all state to initiate the welfare programs for the marginalised communities. The motto of democracy itself advocates for the rule of law and wide participation. Wide participation and rule of law will not be meaningful, without giving due respect to the empowerment of all backward and marginalised communities. Various states have included the reservation policy for women, backwards and handicapped. Few examples are:

In South Africa, an Employment Equity Act was promulgated with a view to empowering the blacks. This Act has come for promoting equal opportunity, implementing affirmative action measures to redress disadvantaged in employment experienced by designated groups to ensure their equitable representation in all occupational categories. The Act goes also to elaborate measures that constitute affirmative actions. These measures are to be taken by employers to ensure that members of designated groups are adequately represented in the workforce and equal opportunity to compete for and advance in jobs.

In India serious efforts are being made towards the enhancement of their participation as well as imparting training to the elected women representatives. The members of women elected to the rural and urban bodies in Karnatak exceed the mandatory reserved for them. Districts are selected as the population of Dalit women in the constituency. Under the 1983 Karnatak Act, 25% seats were reserved for women. The reservation for the SC and ST was in the proportion to their population. The new law of 1993 reserves one-third seats for women (from all caste categories) and one-third for backward classes. The amended 1995 Act provides for reservation of seats for the SCs and STs and the OBCs and women on rotation basis. There is a provision for not less than one third of the total no. of seats to be reserved for women, which includes not less than one third of the seats reserved for SCs and STs belonging to these respective categories.

5.2. Demand for Reservation of Dalit Women

Time has come to execute the affirmative action policies and implementation as well. Realising the need of the reservation for bringing the disadvantaged community into the mainstream of the governance process, the government has called for formulation of the reservation policy to the marginalised communities namely; women, *Janajati* and Dalit. Affirmative policy is generally perceived as steps taken to correct historical disadvantages and unfair discrimination by enabling access to full opportunities and benefits. Therefore, the Dalit women should be given specific focus. There should be 10% reservation in Dalit reservation and 10% in reservation for Dalit women. Otherwise only the creamy layer or the forward women will be benefited and rest of the real oppressed women will not be benefited which is not real objective of the reservation policy. Within the women and Dalits, there should specific provision for Dalit women and ensure their participation in policy formulation positions as well. Following measures are recommended in the plan on reservation:

— Specific land reform and allocation programs should be implemented where the population of Dalit women is high. Allocation of state resources for the advancement of women's equality is essential for the fulfilment of the state parties obligations under the ratified international human rights instruments also,

— Skill providing program should be launched and provide them the job as per their skill for their economic survival.

— Specific programs should be planned for exemption of loans to Dalit women.

— There should be provision for compulsory and free education. Mere free education is not enough. The school-going children, particularly from the Dalit communities, should be provided necessary books, bags and school materials as per their needs free-of-cost.

— After increasing the access of Dalit community in education, there should be reservation for their employment in public services. Within the reservation for women, there should be clear percentage for Dalit women.

— For the participation in civil service, the curriculum for examination should be made Dalit women friendly. These women should be provided travel cost, relaxation in fees and extra costs. Provision should be made for preferences to Dalit women in coaching classes. Separate merit list system should be made for encouraging them to be participated in public services.

— Seats should be separated for Dalit women in gazetted class.

— Participation in political and public life has traditionally been regarded as a male dominated sector in Nepal. However, women have been active in various political movements and benefited. But Dalit women are not included within the ambit of political beneficiaries. The factors behind this are their illiteracy, lack of resources and support for their mobility. So, for their political participation, there should be specific provision in the constitution and other laws for the reservation for women. In them Dalit women also should be given special preferences.

— Dalit women are in a disadvantaged position in every sphere of political life. Therefore, 10% seats in constitutional bodies, commissions, committees and mission should be separated from the quotas visualised for women in general.

Other Program oriented activities to be focused are:

— Revise the civil service curriculums and make it Dalit women friendly,

— Create one contact officer in all ministries,
— Family friendly provision should be made for public services like day care, husband and wife in same district, increased maternity mourning leave and paternity protection,
— Gender audit specific reference with Dalit women,
— Dalit women should be given information about the positive policies and provisions and their impact,
— Programs should be framed for the voters' education and for their encouragement in the contest of election.

References

Bob, C. "'Dalit Rights are Human Rights': Caste Discrimination, International Activism, and the Construction of a New Human Rights Issue." *Human Rights Quarterly* 29 (2007) 167-193.

Mary, G. *The Struggle of Dalit Women, Resource Sheet* Paper Presented In Dalit Theology Seminar, Barmingham. 2004.

Michael, S.M., ed. South Asia Edition. *Dalits in Modern India: Vision and Values*. New Delhi: Vistaar Publications. 1999.

Punalekar, S. *On Dalitism and Gender,* edited in Jogadand, *Dalit Women's Issues and Perspectives*, Gyan Prakashan, New Delhi. 1995.

Wax, E. "In an Indian Village, Signs of Loosening Grip of Caste." *The Washington Post*.August 31, 2008.

Zelliot, E. *Dr*. Ambedkar and the Empowerment of Women, edited in Rao *Caste and Gender*, Kali for women, New Delhi. 2003.

6

Educational Problems of Dalit Women

As per the 2001 Census, the population of Scheduled Castes (SCs) is 16.66 crores amounting to 16.2% of the country's total population of 102.86 crores. The male population is 8.61 crores and female population is 8.05 crores which accounts for 16.18% and 16.22% respectively of the country's total population of respective groups.

The population of Scheduled Tribes as per 2001 Census is 8.43 crore accounting for 8.20% of the country's total population. Out of this, males are 4.26 crores and females 4.17 crores, accounting for 8.01% and 8.40% of the total population of respective groups.

6.1. Literacy Status

Despite the fact that there has been an increase in the literacy rates of SCs/STs since independence, the present position is still far from satisfactory. The overall increase in literacy rate in the country during the period 1961-2001 was 36.54 against which increase in literacy rate for SCs and STs during the same period was 44.42 and 38.57 respectively. The female literacy rates among STs continue to remain a serious cause of concern, as it is only 34.76% as against the total female literacy rate of 53.67%.

However, in overall terms, the female literacy rate has increased significantly since independence, the female literacy rate was only 8.86% in 1951. The literacy rate of females is 53.67% as compared to 75.26% among males in 2001. The female literacy rate has risen by 14.38% compared to a corresponding increase of 11.13% in the case of male literacy during the period 1991-2001, which indicates a meaningful narrowing of the gender gap in education.

6.2. Enrolment in Elementary Education

6.2.1. Primary Level

There has been over all increase in the enrolment of children belonging to Scheduled Castes and Scheduled Tribes at all levels after independence. At primary stage, the Scheduled Castes enrolment has increased from 1.1 crore accounting for 14.88% in 1980-81 to 2.31 crore, accounting for 18.03% of the total enrolment at primary stage in 2003-04. The enrolment of Scheduled Caste girls has increased from 13.2% in 1980-81 to 17.3% in 2003-04 while enrolment of Scheduled Caste boys increased from 15.92% in 1980-81 to 18.66% in 2003-04.

The Scheduled Tribes enrolment has increased from 46.60 lakhs in 1980-81 to 125.17 lakhs in 2003-04. The enrolment of Scheduled Tribe girls considerably increased from 15.27 lakhs in 1980-81 to 57.41 lakhs in 2003-04 while the enrolment of Scheduled Tribe boys increased from 31.33 lakhs in 1980-81 to 67.76 lakhs in 2003-04.

6.2.2. Upper Primary Level

About 22 lakhs Scheduled Caste students were enrolled at Upper Primary stage in 1980-81, which increased to 80.77 lakhs in 2003-04 accounting for 10.7% in 1980-81 and 16.58% in 2003-04 of the total enrolment at Upper Primary stage.

Percentage enrolment of Scheduled Caste boys and girls accounting for 11.66% and 8.85% in 1980-81 increased to 17.40% and 15.55% in 2003-04 respectively.

The enrolment of Scheduled Tribes at Upper Primary stage increased from 7.42 lakhs in 1980-81 to 36.62 lakhs in 2003-04 accounting for 3.58% in 1980-81 and 7.51% in 2003-04 of the total enrolment.

While the total enrolment at Primary stage has increased by 6.68 times between 1950-51 and 2003-04, for girls it has shown an increase of about 11 times. The relative share of girls' enrolment in total enrolment at primary level has increased from 28.12% in 1950-51 to 46.68% in 2003-04.

Similarly, at the upper primary level, the relative share of girls' enrolment to total enrolment has gone upto 44.15% in 2003-04 from 16.13% in 1950-51.

6.2.3. High/Higher Secondary Level

About 11.52 lakhs Scheduled Caste students were enrolled at High/ Higher Secondary stage in 1980-81, which increased to 47.60 lakhs in 2003-04 accounting for 10.47% in 1980-81 and 13.6% in 2003-04 of the total enrolment at High/Higher Secondary stage.

Percentage enrolment of Scheduled Caste boys and girls accounting for 11.92% and 7.23% respectively in 1980-81 increased to 14.26% and 12.65% in 2003-04.

The enrolment of Scheduled Tribes at High/Higher Secondary stage increased from 3.29 lakhs in 1980-81 to 19.51 lakhs in 2003-04 accounting for 2.99% in 1980-81 and 5.57% in 2003-04 of the total enrolment.

While the total enrolment at High/Higher Secondary stage has increased by about 23 times from 1950-51 to 2003-04, the relative share of girls' enrolment in total enrolment at High/Higher Secondary stage has increased by about four times only during the same period.

6.3. Gross Enrolment Ratio

6.3.1. Primary Level

The Gross Enrolment Ratio of all categories has increased from 80.5% in 1980-81 to 98.2% in 2003-04 registering an increase of 17.7% at the Primary stage over a period of 24 years. The comparative Gross Enrolment Ratio of Scheduled Castes is 82.2% in 1980-81 and 88.3% in 2003-04 registering an increase of 6.1% and that of Scheduled Tribes from 70% in 1980-81 to 91.3% in 2003-04 registering an increase of 21.3%. There is thus a significant achievement in the Gross Enrolment Ratio of the Scheduled Castes and Scheduled Tribes.

Similarly, the Gross Enrolment Ratio of girls at the primary stage has increased from 24.8% in 1950-51 to 95.6% in 2003-04.

6.3.2. Upper Primary Level

The Gross Enrolment Ratio of all communities has increased from 41.9% in 1980-81 to 62.4% in 2003-04 registering an absolute increase of 20.5% at the Upper Primary stage whereas the Gross Enrolment Ratio of Scheduled Castes has increased from 29.1% in 1980-81 to 71.8% in 2003-04 registering an increase of 42.7% and that of Scheduled Tribes from 19.5% in 1980-81 to 75.7% in 2003-04 registering an increase of 56.2%. The rate of increase of Gross Enrolment Ratio of Scheduled Castes and Scheduled Tribes in a preceding period of 24 years is higher than that for the general categories, though these communities and particularly the Scheduled Tribes are still far behind in terms of literacy.

At the Upper Primary level, the GER of girls has gone up from 4.6% in 1950-51 to 57.6% in 2003-04. However, large disparities exist between the States having lower GER than the all India averages.

6.4. Dropout Rates

At the Primary level, the dropout rate among the Scheduled Castes in 1990-91 was 49.4%, which reduced to 36.6% in 2003-04. At the Upper Primary level the dropout rates have reduced from 67.8% in 1990-91 to 59.4% in 2003-04. At the Primary level, the dropout rate among Scheduled Tribes in 1990-91 was 62.5%, which reduced to 48.9% in 2003-04. At the Upper Primary level the dropout rates, which was 78.6% in 1990-91 reduced to 70.1% in 2003-04. The dropout rates of girls have decreased year after year, in the Primary classes from 64.9 % in 1960-61to 31.47 % in 2003-04. Similarly in the Upper Primary classes, the dropout rates have decreased from 78.3% in 1960-61 to 52.3% in 2003-04.

6.5. Provisions under Existing Schemes for the SC/ST/ Minorities/Girls and other Disadvantaged Groups

6.5.1. Sarva Shiksha Abhiyan (SSA)

SSA is a historic stride towards achieving the long cherished goal of Universalisation of Elementary Education (UEE) through a time bound integrated approach, in partnership with States. SSA, which promises to change the face of Elementary Education Sector of the country, aims to provide useful and quality elementary education to all children in the 6-14 age group by 2010. The main features of the programme are:

— Focus on girls, especially belonging to SC/ST communities and minority groups.
— Back to school camps for out of school girls.
— Free textbooks for girls & SC/ST students.
— Special coaching/remedial classes for girls and a congenial learning environment.
— Teachers' sensitisation programmes to promote equitable learning opportunities.
— Special focus for innovative projects related to girls' education.
— Recruitment of 50% female teachers.

6.5.2. District Primary Education Programme (DPEP)

The thrust of the scheme is on disadvantaged groups like girls, SCs/STs, working children, urban deprived children, disabled children, etc. There are specific strategies for girls and SCs/STs; however, physical targets are fixed, in an integrated manner including coverage of these groups as well. According to a study by NIEPA, 74811 schools in DPEP districts had more than 60% students belonging to SC/ST communities.

6.5.3. Jan Shikshan Sansthan (JSS)

The Scheme of JSS or Institute of People's Education is a polyvalent or multifaceted adult education programme aimed at improving the vocational skill and quality of life of the beneficiaries. The objective of the scheme is educational, vocational and occupational development of the socio-economically backward and educationally disadvantaged groups of urban/rural population particularly neo-literates, semi-literates, SCs, STs, women and girls, slum dwellers, migrant workers etc.

Literacy campaigns have had an enormous impact on other social sectors. The campaigns have served the cause of promoting equity and social justice in society and fostering of a scientific temper and a sense of belonging to India's great composite culture and consciousness of unity in diversity.

6.5.4. Mid-Day Meal scheme

The Mid-Day Meal scheme is a successful incentive programme. It covers all students of primary classes in all Government, local body and Government aided schools in the country with the aim to improve enrolment, attendance and retention while simultaneously impacting on the nutritional status of the children.

6.5.5. Central Institute of Indian Languages (CIIL)

The Central Institute of Indian Languages, Mysore has a scheme of development of Indian Languages through research, developing manpower and production of materials in modern Indian Languages including tribal languages. The Institute has worked in more than 90 tribal and border languages.

6.5.6. Kendriya Vidyalayas (KVs)

15% and 7.5% seats are reserved for SCs and STs respectively in fresh admissions. No tuition fee is charged from Scheduled Caste and Scheduled Tribe students up to class XII.

6.5.7. Navodaya Vidyalayas (NVs)

Reservation of seats in favour of children belonging to SCs and STs is provided in proportion to their population in the concerned district provided that no such reservation will be less than the national average of 22.5% (15% for SCs and 7.50% for STs) and a maximum of 50% for both the categories (SCs & STs) taken together. These reservations are interchangeable and over and above the students selected under open merit.

6.5.8. National Institute of Open Schooling (NIOS)

The SC/ST students are given concession in admission fees to the extent of Rs. 200/- for bridge courses, Rs. 250/- for Secondary courses and Rs. 300/- for Senior Secondary courses.

6.5.9. Strengthening of Boarding and Hostel Facilities for Girl Students of Secondary & Higher Secondary Schools

Cent percent financial assistance is given to Voluntary Organisations to improve enrolment of adolescent girls belonging to rural areas and weaker sections. Preference is given to educationally backward districts, particularly; those predominantly inhabited by SCs/STs and Educationally Backward Minorities.

6.5.10. National Council for Educational Research & Training (NCERT)

NCERT focuses on the development of textbooks, workbooks, teacher guides, supplementary reading materials, evaluation of textbooks, vocational education, educational technology, examination reforms, support to Sarva Shiksha Abhiyan, education of educationally disadvantaged groups.

NCERT operates the National Talent Search Scheme for pursuing courses in Science and Social Science upto doctoral level and in professional courses like Medicine and Engineering upto second-degree level subject to fulfilment of the conditions. Out of 1000 scholarships, 150 scholarships are reserved for SC students and 75 scholarships for ST students.

6.5.11. National Institute of Educational Planning & Administration (NIEPA)

Educational development of Scheduled Castes and Scheduled Tribes is an area of major concern of NIEPA. It carries out a number of studies relating to educational programes and schemes for Scheduled Castes and Scheduled Tribes. It has also been generating material relating to educational institutions and development of Scheduled Caste and Scheduled Tribe students.

6.5.12. University Grants Commission (UGC)

UGC provides financial assistance to Universities/Deemed Universities for the establishment of SC/ST cells in Universities to ensure effective implementation of reservation policy for SCs and STs. The UGC has established SC/ST Cells in about 120 Universities including Central Universities to ensure proper implementation of the reservation policy. The Standing Committee on SCs/STs monitors and reviews the work undertaken by the Universities/Colleges.

As per the reservation policy, UGC has earmarked 15% and 7.50% reservation for SCs and STs respectively in appointments, both in teaching and non-teaching posts, admissions, hostel accommodation, etc. in universities/colleges, professional and technical educational institutions administered by the Central Government. State Universities follow reservation policy as prescribed by respective State Governments. The Commission has been issuing guidelines/directives/instructions from time to time for implementing reservation policy of the Government of India.

— Apart from reservation, there is also relaxation in the minimum qualifying marks for admission for SC/ST candidates.

— UGC has been implementing the programme of Career Orientation to Education (Vocationalisation of Education) to ensure that the graduates have knowledge, skills and attitudes for gainful employment in the wage sector in general, and self-employment in particular for all including SCs/STs.

— UGC provides financial assistance for Remedial Coaching to SC/ST students. It provides financial assistance to the existing coaching centres to prepare SC/ST candidates for the National Eligibility Test (NET) conducted by UGC/CSIR.

— Commission provides financial assistance for extension activities. Under the scheme, all groups of the society are covered including SCs/STs.

— In order to contribute towards social equity and socioeconomics mobility of the under privileged sections of the society, UGC has introduced Remedial Coaching scheme at UG/PG level. The main objectives of the scheme are: (i) to improve the academic skills and linguistic proficiency of the students in various subjects. (ii) To raise the level of comprehension of basic subjects so as to provide a strong foundation for further academic work. (iii) To strengthen their knowledge, skills and attitudes in the subjects where quantitative and qualitative techniques and laboratory work are involved and (iv) To improve the overall performance of these students in the examination.

— Commission has created a Central Pool Database of eligible SC/ST candidates and recommends their candidature for teaching positions in order to fulfil the prescribed reservation quota in Universities and Colleges.
— Periodic meetings of Registrars of Central Universities are organised to review the implementation of reservation policy in the Central Universities.
— Commission has also constituted a Special Monitoring Committee, which reviews the functioning of existing Cells.

6.5.13. Community Polytechnics

The Scheme of Community Polytechnics undertakes rural/community development activities through application of science and technology in its proximity. It provides platforms for transfer of appropriate technologies to rural masses/local communities. Preference is given in training to rural youths, SCs, STs, women, school dropouts and other disadvantaged groups and helps them to obtain need based gainful employment. The scheme of Community Polytechnics has been in operation in selected diploma level institutions since 1978-79. It applies Science and Technology through skill oriented non-formal training, technology transfer and technical support services.

6.5.14. Engineering Colleges

The higher educational institutions administered by the Central Government including IITs, IIMs, Regional Engineering Colleges, etc. provide reservation to the extent of 15% and 7.5% for SCs and STs students respectively. Apart from reservation, there is also relaxation in the minimum qualifying marks for admission for SC/ST students. Seats are also reserved in hostels. However, in institutions run by the State Governments, the reservation percentages varies as per the State Government's policy.

6.5.15. Scheduled Caste Sub-Plan & Tribal Sub-Plan

The SCP for SCs and the Special Central Assistance (SCA) to SCP are two innovative strategies to ensure additional flow of funds/benefits for SCs. The SCP, introduced in 1979-80, involves earmarking population-proportionate funds from the general development sectors for the overall development of SCs to raise them above the poverty line. The SCA to SCP is extended to states as 100 per cent grant to fill the critical gaps in family-based income-generating schemes with supporting infrastructure development. So far 14 Central Ministries/ Departments and 27 States/UTs have been earmarking funds under SCP. States/UTs have been advised to prepare specific project reports for utilisation of SCA, linking it with the loan component under NSFDC for helping the BPL SC families in an intensive manner. The Central Standing Tripartite Committee (CSTC) reviews the implementation of SCP and Tribal Sub-Plan (TSP) and guides the nodal Ministries of Social Justice and Empowerment and Tribal Affairs in ensuring earmarking of funds by the service-oriented Ministries have been identified: regulatory Ministries, Ministries whose services are divisible in nature and Ministries/Departments whose services are not divisible in nature. Presently the SCP has been renamed as Scheduled Caste Sub-Plan (SCSP).

From the allotted budgets of the Departments of School Education & Literacy, and Higher Education, 16.20% and 8.00% are allocated under the Scheduled Caste Sub-Plan and the Tribal Sub-Plan for Scheduled Castes and Scheduled Tribes respectively.

6.6. Scheme for Minority Education

The National Policy on Education (NPE) –1986 and updated Programme of Action in 1992 (POA-1992) spells out the concept of a national system of education, in which all students irrespective of caste, creed, location or sex have access to education of comparable quality. The Policy lays special emphasis on the removal of disparities and seeks to equalise educational opportunities by attending to the specific needs of those who have remained educationally backward so far. Suitable incentives, therefore, have to be provided to educationally backward sections of society. Government has always shown concern for the education of these groups in the interest of equality and social justice. In order to attain the stated objective, the following two central schemes were launched in 1993: -

6.6.1. Scheme of Area Intensive Programme for Educationally Backward Minorities

The basic objective of the scheme is to provide basic educational infrastructure in the primary/upper primary and Secondary Education where such a need is felt and viability established on the basis of a school mapping exercise.

6.6.2. Target Areas

— For this purpose 325 blocks and 4 districts of Assam have been identified as having concentration of such Minorities. This scheme was restricted to these areas only.

— Under this component, only 4 districts of Assam of the North Eastern Region are covered.

6.6.3. Scheme of Financial Assistance for Modernisation of Madarasa Education

— Salary to two teachers per Madarasa @ Rs. 3000/- per month per teacher for study of modern subjects like Science, Mathematics, English and Social Studies;

— One time grant of Rs. 7,000/- for purchase of Science/ Mathematics kits per Madarasa; and

— Another one time grant of Rs.7,000/- for book banks and strengthening of libraries.

This component is spread all over the country including the NER.

From the Tenth Five Year Plan, the two major schemes relating to Minorities i.e., i) Scheme of Area Intensive Programme for Educationally Backward Minorities and ii) the Scheme of Financial Assistance for the Modernisation of Madarasa Education have been clubbed together with their old components in a unified programme of the Area Intensive and Madarasa Modernisation Programme (AIMMP) devising two Components i.e.: -i) Infrastructural Development; and i) Madarasa Modernisation Development.

The expenditures during the years 2003-04, 2004-05 & 2005-06 was Rs.29.00 crores, Rs.22.06 crores and Rs.26.46 crores respectively. The anticipated expenditure for 2006-07 is Rs. 50.00 crores.

In the existing set up of SSA, Madarasas are being assisted in states like Bihar. However in many states the Madarasas are not being benefited much due to the fact that State Governments have to take the initiative. The Madarasas are having, in several States, good infrastructure, which could be utilised to universalise primary education especially when the State Governments are facing difficulties in locating suitable land and constructing school buildings. In several states like West Bengal, students from other communities are being enrolled in Madarasas. This not only enables the minority communities to modernise their education system but also bring it in line with the national mainstream.

From the Eleventh Five Year Plan, the scheme of AIMMP is being revised to give more scope for the educational development of Madarasas by way of modernisation of education to bring the madarasas in the main stream of education without interfering in their traditional religious education. The scheme is being renamed as 'Scheme for Providing Quality Elementary Education in Madarasas (SPQUEEM)'.

Besides, the scheme to provide financial grants for girls hostels, school building, auditorium etc., in the minority concentrated areas in the private unaided institutions managed by different Non-Government Organisations is also being formulated. For both the schemes, the financial requirement will have to be increased in the Eleventh Five Year Plan.

6.6.4.National Monitoring Committee for Minorities Education

A National Monitoring Committee for Minorities Education has been constituted on 7.8.2004 under the Chairmanship of Minister of Human Resource Development. Two meetings have so far been held i.e. first on 27.08.2004 and second on 17.11.2005. A Standing Committee of this Committee also been constituted on 3rd September, 2004. Its Chairperson is Sh. Jafar Ali Naqvi. The Standing Committee had held a number of meetings and had visited Uttar Pradesh, Maharashtra, Andhra Pradesh, Karnataka and Kerala in the first year of its constitution and submitted its report in the second meeting of the NMCME held on 17.11.2005. The Committee considered the report of the Standing Committee. Action points which emerged from the Standing Committee report have been circulated to all the states and concerned departments/organisations for their comments/views. In the next phase, the Standing Committee had visited West Bengal and Assam, Haryana, Punjab and Chandigarh Administration, Tamil Nadu and Pondicherry.

6.6.5.National Commission for Minority Educational Institutions

A Commission with the name of "National Commission for Minority Educational Institutions – 2004" has been established through an Act of Parliament.

The functions of the Commission would be as follows:

1) Advise the Central Government or any State Government on any question relating to the education of minorities, that may be referred to it;
2) Look into specific complaints regarding deprivation or violation of the rights of minorities to establish and administer educational institutions of their choice, and any dispute regarding affiliation to a Scheduled University and report its findings to the Central Government for implementation; and 3) To do such acts and things as may be necessary, incidental or conducive to the attainment of all or any of the objects of the Commission.

6.7. Girls' Education

The extant National Policy on Education, 1986 envisages the use of education as an instrument of basic change in the status of women and provides for a well conceived edge in favour of women in order to neutralise the cumulative distortions of the past. The removal of women's illiteracy and obstacles inhibiting their access to and retention in elementary education will receive over riding priority through provision of special support services, setting of time targets and effective monitoring. The Policy also lays emphasis on women's participation in vocational, technical and professional education at different levels.

The Constitution of India grants equality to women and forbids any discrimination based on religion, race, caste, sex or place of birth. It also empowers the State to practice protective discrimination in favour of women.

In the first three Five Year Plans, girl's education was shown as a special component with earmarked allocations but was discontinued subsequently. In pursuance of the provisions contained in the National Policy on Education, 1986 and the Programme of Action, 1992, several strategies were adopted to promote education of girls. All formal and non-formal education and training programes are open to women. In addition, the provision exists for opening separate institutions or separate wings exclusively for women/girls. Education is free for girls up to the higher secondary stage and in fact, several States have made education free for girls right up to the university level. Besides free education for all children up to the age of 14, there are incentive schemes like free midday meals, free books, free uniforms and attendance scholarships for girls and children from disadvantaged groups. Overall, the initiatives taken by the Government have resulted in significant progress in women's education.

6.8. Early Childhood Care and Education

Early childhood care and education (ECCE) is of critical importance as a major programme in the country where more than half the children are born and live in dire poverty. ECCE provides for the holistic development of the child catering to the health, nutrition, physical, mental, social and emotional needs of every child. There are several programes of ECCE which includes ICDS, Crèches, Balwadis, ECE centers, Pre-Primary Schools run by the State and the private sector and many experimental and innovative projects like child-to-child programme, child media laboratory, mobile Creches and Vikaswadis.

6.9. Schemes/Programmes Exclusively for Women

The following schemes of Department of School Education & Literacy and Department of Higher Education are exclusively meant for women and under these schemes the entire funds are targeted for benefiting women:

6.9.1. National Programme for Education of Girls at Elementary Level (NPEGEL)

The NPEGEL under the existing scheme of Sarva Shiksha Abhiyan (SSA) provides additional components for education of girls, underprivileged/disadvantaged at the elementary level. The Scheme is being implemented in Educationally Backward Blocks (EBBs) where the level of rural female literacy is less than the national average and the gender gap is above the national average, as well as in blocks of districts that have at least 5% SC/ST population and where SC/ST female literacy is below 10% based on 1991.

6.9.2. Mahila Samakhya (MS)

The Mahila Samakhya Programme is a women's education and empowerment project.Currently it is operating in 59 districts, covering more than 12,000 villages. The programme strategy is to mobilise and organise women in the collectives called "Sanghas" and in this process develop their capacity to play a pro-active role in their community. The outcome of the process has been that the women now demand literacy for themselves and want to ensure educational opportunity for their children especially girls and this has resulted in their taking decisions including the postponement of the age of marriage. The Sangha women have been equipped with information and skills whereby they are actively involved in local bodies, like Panchayati Raj Institutions and Village Education Committees and play a role in ensuring the proper delivery of Government Services and preventing violence against women and girls.

6.9.3. Kasturba Gandhi Balika Vidyalaya

The Government of India has approved a scheme called Kasturba Gandhi Balika Vidyalaya (KGBV) for setting up residential schools with boarding facilities at Upper Primary level for the girls belonging to the SC, ST, OBC and Minorities in difficult areas. The scheme will be coordinated with the scheme of Sarva Shiksha Abhiyan, National Programme for Education of Girls at Upper Primary level and Mahila Samakhya (MS). The KGBV scheme would cover those hard to reach girls, belonging predominantly to the SC, ST, OBC and Minorities in difficult areas, those who cannot attend regular primary schools.

It is proposed to provide incentive to the girl child belonging to SC, ST, OBC and who passes VIII Standard examination and enrols in secondary schools. A sum of Rs. 3000/- will be deposited in her name and she would be entitled to withdraw the amount on reaching 18 years of age. Following this proposal by Finance Minister, this Department has sent a concept paper to the Planning Commission for 'in principle' approval of the proposed scheme of Incentive to the girl child who passes class VIII standard examination and enrols in a Secondary School.

6.9.4. Access with Equity

This scheme is taken up during Tenth Five Year Plan on the recommendations of the Working Group on Secondary Education for Tenth Five Year Plan. Under the scheme the following two initiatives are proposed.

— Strengthening of existing scheme of girls' hostels managed by NGOs.

— One time assistance to reputed NGOs, trusts, societies, and State Governments, etc. for setting up secondary schools.

Under the component – I of the scheme, financial assistance is provided to the NGOs for running hostels for girl students of Classes VI-XII. Recurring grant of Rs.10, 000/- per girl boarder per annum and a one-time non-recurring grant of Rs.3,000/- per girl boarder is provided under the scheme. During 2004-05, a sum of Rs.5.4 crore was released to 89 NGOs benefiting approximately 5400 girl boarders.

6.9.5. Women's Hostel Scheme of UGC

The University Grants Commission provides financial assistance to Universities and Colleges for the construction of hostels for women with a view to provide a safe environment and to encourage the enrolment of women students pursuing higher studies in universities of their choices.

6.9.6. Infrastructure for Women Students, Teachers and Non-Teaching Staff in Universities

The objective of the scheme is to provide assistance for creating and strengthening infrastructure for women students, teachers and non-teaching staff members in universities. Under the scheme, a maximum of Rs.10.00 lakh is provided as one time grant in the Plan period to a university for creation and up gradation of infrastructure.

6.10. Other Schemes/Programmes

The other schemes of Departments of School Education & Literacy and Higher Education are not amenable to gender segregation.

For some major schemes, however, of the Department of SE&L, the proportion of the provisions targeted at benefiting the women have been worked out on the basis of a reasonable proportion of Males/ Females benefiting under the schemes.

The schemes of Department of HE which are not exclusively meant for girls can be group under three categories (a) The Schemes of Secondary and Higher Education, where enrolment for women is taken as 40% (b) in respect of Technical Education the flow of funds for women benefit is taken as 20% (c) in remaining sectors the enrolment for women is taken as 33%.

6.10.1. Integrated Education for the Disabled Children (IEDC)

This Scheme of Integrated Education for the Disabled Children (IEDC) was started with the objective of providing educational opportunities to all children with disabilities under the general school system. The ultimate objective is to integrate children with disabilities in the general education system and to eliminate disparities and equalise educational opportunities to enable them to become equally contributing members of society.

IEDC scheme was launched in 1974 by the then Department of Social Welfare and was transferred to the then Department of Education in 1982. Under the scheme, financial assistance on 100 per cent basis is provided to State Governments and NGOs towards facilities extended to disabled children such as books and stationery, uniforms, transport allowance, escort allowance, readers allowance for blind children, equipments. In addition to the above, the grant is also provided for the salary of teachers recruited for teaching the disabled children and for officials manning the IEDC Cell in State Governments to implement and monitor the Scheme. The Scheme also has a component for free school training for disabled children and counselling for their parents. Assistance is also provided for setting up of resource room, survey and assessment of disabled children, purchase and production of instructional material, training and orientation of general teachers to take care of the educational need of the disabled children.

6.11. Recommendations

There is a need for overall expansion of education facilities in the country. Lack of expansion in educational facilities in the country during last few decades has hurt the disadvantaged sections most. In order to expand the educational facilities larger allocation of funds is required. National Common Minimum Programme (NCMP) has also committed a minimum of 6% of GDP to be spent on education of which at least half should be spent on Elementary Education. Accordingly, therefore, the Group strongly recommends that allocation for education should be raised to 6% of GDP on priority basis. This Group also recommends that Central Government should bear the major share of this expenditure on education, as the States will not be able to share this expenditure uniformly in view of their variable financial situations. This should be accompanied by the devolution of controls of management to local levels for ensuring efficiency of the institutions.

The Right to Education Bill should be passed on priority basis and should be implemented, as this will help the disadvantaged groups. The Group noted that privileged sections of the society have already adequate access to education and the institutional support in education will go to help the disadvantaged sections that are otherwise deprived of adequate access to the quality education. The Group, therefore, recommends for the quick implementation of Right to Education Bill.

At present there are large variations in the standards of education in various schools. The disadvantaged sections therefore have no access to good quality education. It is therefore utmost necessary that Government should adopt common school system imparting same quality of education throughout the country. The community control coupled with the adequate training of teachers and provision of infrastructure development should be ensured to improve the efficiency of the schools from the point of view of equality in access and quality of education.

During last decade the expansion in higher and technical education has taken place mostly in private sector institutions charging high fees. The group recommends that there should be substantial expansion in higher and technical education in the public sector. The private sector institutions should also be brought within the reservation policy by suitable legislative enactment so that the disadvantaged sections can benefit from quality education by cross subsidisation.

Some of the institutions under the education sector are run on commercial basis. This deprives the disadvantaged section of the society from access to the courses run by such organisations. It was noted that even some Central and State Universities have been allowed to organise self-financed courses in new emerging sunrise sectors. This should be discouraged and all existing self-financing courses should also be made available to disadvantaged sections on the regulated fee structure as applicable in other fields of education.

Considerable expansion of KVs and NVs should be taken up during Eleventh Plan period. In order to reach the disadvantaged groups it is necessary that all new KVs and NVs should be opened in areas inhabited by these groups.

The fees charged both for technical and management training is on the high side. The students from disadvantaged groups find it difficult to finance such courses from their own resources. Hence, it is recommended that no fees should be charged from the disadvantaged groups at all levels of education.

In order to increase the enrolment of Muslims in education, Urdu medium schools may be opened in the districts where there are large concentrations of Urdu speaking Muslim population.

Education Policy should be sensitive towards cultural and linguistic diversity of tribal society, and therefore uniform standards should not be applied.

There should be increased access of Minorities in all non-minority institutions. While minority institutions are kept out of the purview of reservation of SCs, STs and OBCs in general, these institutions should be obligated to reserve certain seats for members of their own minority community who belong to SCs, STs and OBCs.

Nomadic groups and de-notified tribes should also be grouped along with disadvantaged groups and should be given special focus.

Majority of the people in country are not aware of the Plan Schemes/Programes, which are targeted to benefit them. In view of this Equal Opportunities Cells may be set up at Central/State/University and Institution levels. Officers who would manage these Equal Opportunities Cells should be made responsible to widely circulate information brochures and pamphlets and also to educate people in the target groups and take remedial steps. The officer so appointed should act like a single window operator who can be approached by the applicant and should also act as anti discrimination officer (Ombudsman). It is very important to ensure that these cells function properly.

Registrar General of India (Census) may be directed to ensure availability of disaggregated data for OBCs, Backward Caste amongst Minorities and other disadvantaged groups. Data relating to all the disadvantaged groups should be collected and published so that they should become a point of reference to general public and for formulation of perspective planning. Data gaps on the students of SC/ST/Minorities/Girls/Disadvantaged Groups need to be filled at each stage of education.

6.11.1. Elementary Education

— Disaggregated data about Minorities, OBCs and Backward Castes among Minorities should be made available to assess the impact of SSA.

— The street children, children of convicts, sex workers should have a special focus under SSA.

— The local needs and also the community requirement should be a predominant factor under SSA.

— Educational incentives like free uniforms, footwear may be supplied to SC & ST children especially girls to offset economic cost of education. Cash incentives may be provided to SC & ST children to offset hidden cost of education.

— Funds may be earmarked for remedial teaching of SC/ST and other disadvantaged children at district level.

— More Minority concentration districts should be identified so that more children from Minority groups get facilities under SSA. More NGOs may be involved in opening of the schools.

— Out-of-school children in urban slum areas should be given focused attention under SSA.

— Use of primers in tribal languages should be extended to all the schools in tribal areas.

— Recognised Madarasas should be brought under SSA and facilities extended to them.

— SSA should enlarge support for hostels for boys also and girls on the same lines as Kasturba Gandhi Balika Vidyalayas with 75% minimum reservation for SC/ST/OBC and Disadvantaged Groups.

— Schools should develop disabled friendly structures within 3-4 years. Special attention should be given for this aspect coupled with adequate fund allocation.

6.11.2. Adult Literacy

— Keeping in view the unique socioeconomic and cultural characteristics of various disadvantaged groups various strategies like area approach, functional approach, camp based approach, convergence with other departments and specific attention to disabled may be adopted for improving adult literacy with an emphasis for Disadvantaged Groups.

— More Special Literacy Programes may be taken up in areas predominantly inhabited by Disadvantaged Groups.

— Innovative measures, especially of local content, may be introduced in all the literacy programes.

— Upgradation of skill competence may be provided through vocational training.

— Literacy camps may be organised taking into account the lean periods in agricultural activities.

— Neo-literate women themselves should become literacy trainers in adult literacy programes.

— Depending on the need there should be more of camp approach followed by campaign approach.

— Short duration full time literacy camps may be organised in Gram Panchayats and also in urban slum areas.

— Training in personality development, skill development and issues of local governance may also be covered in the adult literacy campaigns/camps.

— An accelerated programme of inclusion of more and more low literacy districts especially low female literacy areas may be covered in all districts in all States.

— The Local Self Government Institutes, Panchayati Raj Functionaries, Voluntary Women Teachers and also Women Self Help Groups should be involved in all the camps under the adult literacy programes.

— Periodical evaluation may be done by external evaluating agencies to understand the weaknesses in the programme.

— The weaknesses in the prógramme identified by evaluating agencies should be rectified at the earliest.

— The aim of reaching 100% literacy at the earliest should have a sustainable level of achievement on a year to year basis.

— The Neo-literates may be retrained after 2-3 years to upgrade their skill in functional literacy and levels of reading, writing and numerical comprehensions. The Neo-literate women should themselves become Trainers in Adult Education programes.

— The financial parameters under the adult literacy programes should be increased substantially.

— An integrated approach along with other programes of Government - health, nutrition, sanitation, employment potential etc. should be inbuilt in the system.

6.11.3. Secondary Education

— The existing Kasturba Gandhi Balika Vidyalaya Scheme should be extended up to class XII.

— Dropout rates of disadvantaged groups are noticed to be going up as the level of education goes up. To reduce the rate of dropouts amongst disadvantaged should become the focus of the Eleventh Five Year Plan.

— More special schools focusing on the needs of the disadvantaged should be opened nearer to the habitations of these groups.

— More hostels especially for girls may be opened nearer to the schools, which the girls attend.

— All schools should have basic facilities like drinking water, toilets and common rooms for girls.

— There should be schemes and programes in schools, which make value addition in the mental and intellectual growth of the children.

— Inclusive Education should become the idea of every school located in villages taking care of SCs/STs/OBCs/ Handicapped. All schools should develop disabled friendly structures within 3-4 years for which adequate funding should be ensured. Private schools should also ensure this through CBSC/State Boards.

— Every block headquarter should have a hostel facility for school children especially for those belonging to disabled and STs.

— A comprehensive scheme of establishing hostels at district level for the mentally retarded should be conceived and implemented.

6.11.4. Vocational Education

— Vocational education should be expanded to cover more skilled jobs.

— Employment potential should be gauged by the type of industries that are available in a locality and vocational education should be based on such specific industries.

— Interaction with industry should be enhanced to reduce the mismatch between demand and supply of skilled manpower.

— Upgradation of skills or learning of a new skill should become a part of vocational education.

— The interaction between the Directorate of School Education and the industries should be strengthened.

— State Governments should appoint full time teachers in all the vocational education centers.

— Textbooks and workbooks and also raw materials and equipments should be made available at subsidised rates in vocational institutions.

— Evaluation and certification of every skill should be made periodical and standardised.

— Evaluation and monitoring of the implementation of vocational education programes should be done periodically and corrective steps taken.

— Apprenticeship programes should be enlarged to cover a large number of trades.

— A total revamping and a re-look at the existing scheme may be done at the earliest with a special focus on disadvantaged groups.

6.11.5. Higher Education

— Hostel facilities for girls/women should be increased and made available in and around the existing educational institutions. There should be a special scheme for construction of hostels, especially for girls.

— More colleges and institutions of higher learning should be opened in rural areas.

— The existing institutions of higher learning exclusively for boys should also admit girls/women wherever possible.

— There should be barrier free facilities provided for SCs, STs, Girls and Disabled in all the institutions.

— Every institution should have women study centres.

— Day Care Centers should be made available in all the institutions especially in institutions where girls/women are studying/ employed.

— With the increasing number of private institutions entering in the field of higher education, the fees payable are observed to be too high for the disadvantaged groups. In view of this more freeships, scholarships, free textbooks, free hostels, subsidised facilities in institutions/hostels should be extended to this group.

— There should be subsidised loan facilities for the fees/hostel expenditure from the financial institutions like banks etc.

— An inbuilt system of upgrading the educational needs of the disadvantaged groups should be provided in all institutions through coaching classes for them.

— Institutions of higher learning may have their own autonomy but at the same time provide protection under the law in relation to the reservation etc.

— Disabled friendly facilities should be provided in all institutions within a time frame of 3-5 years for which adequate funds should be made available. Every university should have a Disability Coordinator to look into the facilities provided and complaints etc. so that the institutional bias and discrimination are eliminated.

— To avoid private sector from shirking its responsibility in Higher Education, Government should regulate their activities through appropriate interventions. Government should regulate the fee structure and pay the fees etc. of disadvantaged groups.

— UGC should make strict rules and regulations to fill in the post of reserved category. Defaulting universities or affiliated colleges should not be granted financial support or any grants. Imposition of some kind of penalties may be considered and impose penalties, if required even cancellation of their recognition/ accreditation of such universities/institutions, which fail in implementing the reservation policy, may also be considered, if required.

— The teaching and other posts in the universities and other institutions should be filled as per the reservation policy without any dilution.

— All the universities/institutions should establish Women Study Centres.

— More scholarships should be extended to girls/women for taking up professional courses.

— 30% of the financial allocation for an Educational Institution should be earmarked for girls/women.

— Special coaching should be provided to reserved category candidates for successfully clearing SET or NET examination. The high quality of this coaching should be ensured.

— UGC should prepare norms and guidelines to allocate students for Ph.D. courses. The Professors guiding these Ph.D. students should be sensitive to their backgrounds. This should be mandatory to all universities. A monitoring mechanism should be devised to ensure its compliance. Defaulters should be heavily punished.

6.11.6. Technical Education

— In the absence of any available dependable data, the statement that enrolment of girls is about 10-15% in technical education may be inappropriate. In view of this data relating to all categories of children including girls under different communities have to be collected and correlated.

— The fees payable for technical education are generally high. In view of this freeships, scholarships, subsidised fees and loan facilities especially to girls should be extended to all disadvantaged groups.

— Norms for Ph.Ds should be relaxed for IITs.

— A reservation of not less than 33% should be made for girls in all technical education institutions.

— A programme of gender sensitisation and plan to tackle cultural bias should be implemented with sufficient financial support.

— The quality of Coaching under the coaching schemes for SCs/STs should be of really high quality to be really useful.

— Fair financial allocation should be given to all the educational schemes especially to the disadvantaged groups.

— Discrimination Officer should be appointed to look into various issues and to take remedial action.

— The quota for Ph.D. in technology for reserved category candidates should be increased. They should be provided with required technical equipments, residential and financial support alongwith recognised guide.

6.11.7. Recommendations for the Disabled

— Inclusive Education should become the objective of every school taking care of SCs/STs/OBCs & Handicapped.

— There is need for expansion of the Integrated Education for Disabled Children (IEDC) Scheme to cover higher and technical also. The proposed revision of IEDC Scheme should have practical applicability and concentrate on teacher training and pedagogy.

— Allocation of Rs.3000/- per child per annum under the revised IEDC Scheme appears too low and hence should be enhanced. The Group recommends a recurring provision of about Rs.10,000/- per student per annum, besides a non-recurring provision of about Rs.8 crore per district assuming about 7200 disabled children per district. A pilot scheme may be run for testing and confirming the norms.

— The kind of disabilities should be defined and graded.

— The Neighbourhood Schools should become disabled friendly and a policy of Inclusive System of Education imbibed.

— A comprehensive scheme of establishing hostels at district level for the mentally retarded children studying at secondary level should be conceived and implemented.

— Financial commitment of the Government in any new scheme/ programme should at least be for two Five Year Plan periods.

— Teachers and teacher trainers should be given special training especially in managing the children with disabilities.

— Teachers and teacher trainers should develop a better relationship with Community, NGO and Government.

— National Council for Teacher Education (NCTE) should be actively involved in finalisation of a revised curriculum framework for teacher training with Disabled children.

— There should be barrier free facilities provided for SCs, STs, Girls and Disabled in all the institutions.

— With increasing number of private institutions entering in the field of higher education, the fees payable are observed to be too high for the disadvantaged groups. In view of this more freeships, scholarships, free textbooks, free hostels, subsidised facilities in institutions/hostels should be extended to this group.

— There should be subsidised loan facilities for the fees/hostel expenditure from the financial institutions like banks etc.

— Every University should have a Disability Coordinator to look into the facilities provided and complaints etc. so that the institutional bias and discrimination are eliminated.

— Disabled friendly facilities should be provided in all educational institutions within a time frame of 3-5 years. There should be substantial increases in the funds allocation to make the infrastructure in universities and other institutes disabled friendly. UGC should start a Disability Cell and this should be extended to all the universities. There should be an anti-discriminatory authority/Ombudsman, and institutionalised system for checks and balances and corrections required in the system.

References

Bandhu, P. Dalit Women's cry for Liberation: My Rights Are Rising like the Sun, will you deny this sunrise"? Edited in Rao. *Caste and Gender, Kali For Women*, New Delhi.2003.

Chakravati, V *Reconceptualising Gender*; *Phule, Brahmanisam and Brahminial Patriarchy,* edited in Rao. *Caste and Gender*, Kali for women, New Delhi. 2003.

Chitnis, V *Human Rights of the vulnerable groups*, Futuristic Digital, Pune. 2005.

Dietrich, G . *Dalit Movement and Women's Movement*, Edited in Rao 2003 *Caste and Gender*, Kali for women, New Delhi. 2003

Jogdand, P *Dalit Women, Issues and Perspectives*, Gyan Publication, New Delhi. 1995.

7

Empowerment of Tribal Women

The tribal population is an integral part of india's social fabric and has the second largest concentration after that of the african continent. It is more than the total population of france and britain and four times that of australia. The population of tribal communities scheduled in the constitution of india and known as scheduled tribes (STs) was 8.43 crore as per 2001 census and accounts for 8.2% of the total population. 4.26 crores are man and 4.17 crores are women, accounting for 8.01% and 8.40% respectively. They are scattered over all the states/UTs, except punjab, haryana, delhi and the UTs of pondicherry and chandigarh.

Tribals have traditionally lived in about 15% of the country's geographical areas, mainly forests, hills and undulating inaccessible terrain in plateau areas, rich in natural resources. They have lived as isolated entities for centuries, largely untouched by the society around them. This seclusion has been responsible for the slower growth, dissimilar pattern of their socioeconomics and cultural development and inability to negotiate and cope with the consequences of their involuntary integration into mainstream society and economy. Tribals continue to be socio-economically backward.

7.1. Status of Tribal Women

The status of women in a society is a significant reflection of the level of social justice in that society. Women's status is often described in terms of their level of income, employment, education, health and fertility as well as their roles within the family, the community and society. In tribal communities, the role of women is substantial and crucial. They constitute about half the total population but in tribal society women are more important than in other social groups, because they work harder and the family economy and management depends on them. Even after industrialization and the resultant commercialization swamped the tribal economy, women continued to play a significant role. Collection of minor forest produce is done mostly by women and children. Many also work as labourers in industries, households and construction, contributing to their family income. Despite exploitation by contractors and managers, tribals are more sincere and honest than non tribals.

However, tribal women face problems and challenges in getting a sustainable livelihood and a decent life due to environmental degradation and the interference of outsiders. The strategy for tribal development, and specially women, needs improvement, betterment, development and upliftment to effect their Empowerment. Tribal women have Adjusted themselves to live a traditional Life style in the local environment and Follow occupations based on natural Resources. Undoubtedly, the programmes, Oriented towards the empowerment of Tribals, particularly women, have improved Their socioeconomics conditions and Status. However, there are wide variations across regions and tribes in terms of work Participation, sex ratio, economic Productivity and social life. The impact of development planning needs to be Evaluated in terms of desired and Unanticipated consequences. The development process should be perceived as an involvement and reorganization mechanism of not only the socioeconomics system but the entire ecosystem.

7.1.1. Gender Equity of Tribal Women

For the accelerated socioeconomic development of any community, the active participation of women is essential. In a social set up like india's,.their participation has to be ensured through tangible measures, taken at various levels, which result in their empowerment in the real sense. Empowerment of women is one of the concepts that has developed in connection with improving their status. Empowerment includes higher literacy levels, education, better healthcare, equal ownership of productive resources, increased participation in economic and commercial sectors, awareness of rights and responsibilities, improved standards of living, self-reliance, self-esteem and self-confidence.

Raising the status of tribal women is not Just a moral imperative but also a strategic one. Within the framework of a democratic Policy, our laws, development policies, plans and programmes have aimed at Women's advancement in different Spheres. In recent years, the empowerment of women has been recognized as a central issue in determining their status.

Tribal women, while being a disadvantaged and vulnerable group are, nevertheless, better placed, in many respects, than their counter parts in the general population and are, in certain areas, more empowered. They do not suffer segregation or lower status. This is reflected in their higher sex-ratio vis-à-vis the general population (977 as compared To 933–2001 census). The child sex-ratio for tribal women also compares favourably Vis-à-vis the general population, being 972 as against 919 for the general population –2001 census. However, the negative practices of the mainstream population seem to have started percolating to the tribal population as well. The child female to male sex ratio shows a decline from 985 (per thousand males) in 1991 to 972 in 2001 while in areas such as education and health tribal women lag behind significantly.

7.1.2. Tribal Women in Agriculture

Over 80% of tribals work in the primary sector against 53% of the general population. About 45% are cultivators against 32.5% of the general population. According to available data, the number of tribal who were cultivators, declined from over 68% to 45% in 2001, whereas agricultural labourers increased from about 20% to 37%, an indication that tribals are steadily losing their lands. Unlike other communities, among tribals there are no restrictions on women's participation in the cultivation process. A tribal woman can participate actively in all agricultural operations including, ploughing, digging, sowing, manuring, transplanting, weeding, harvesting, preparing the granary, threshing, winnowing and storing food grains. In agriculturally back ward areas, tribal women are forbidden to touch a plough and can not dig the ground but in all other agricultural operations, women participate actively and traditionally these are a female's job. Processing of food grain is exclusively a woman's job. Every morning tribal women dehusk millet and paddy in husking levers and then clean the grains and cooks them. They not only save money, but also earn it, unlike females of other communities.

Tribal women work as men's partners in agriculture, yet their status remains the same. Tribal women work very hard for the livelihood of the family but live a poor life, in spite of their many contributions in the house and on the farm. Tribal women are important for the improvement and progress of tribals. They are the pivot of tribal agriculture, performing many household and agricultural jobs. Without them, tribal welfare in agriculture is meaningless.

7.1.3. Tribal Women in Ecological Development

Environment and sustainable development are firmly on the global agenda. Ecofeminism is to be viewed in this context. The movement began in the U.S., and sherry ortner was among the first to point out that women's interests coincide with nature's while man's with culture. Ecofeminism considers that:

1. There is a distinct relationship between women and the environment,
2. Women have certain responsibilities which make them dependent on nature and women have an extensive knowledge of natural resources.

Eco-feminism points to the need for an integrated view of nature, culture and gender issues. An appropriate strategy of development would be one which is not only ecologically sustainable but takes the interests of women into consideration. The problems of ecological distress and climatic changes require immediate attention with a specific formula to achieve ecological safety. All the initiatives taken under unep, biosphere programmes, various governmental and non-governmental actions lag behind since none was specifically empowered to achieve eco-equilibrium and ecological security. Women provide sustenance to the family and community by their judicious use and management of natural resources. Women are consumers, producers, educators and caretakers of their families, playing an important role for a sustainable ecosystem in the present and future. However, environmental deterioration has a negative effect on the health and quality of life especially of girls and women. A policy of conservation of natural resources will be successful only if women are integrated into all programmes and policy making.

Tribal habitations are facing environmental hazards everywhere due to careless, unplanned and faulty development policies followed by government's skipping the necessary environmental safeguards in development projects. Most development activities impinge upon the environment and adversely affect the ecological balance. The large scale cutting of forest trees in tribal habitats has led to a shortage of fuel, fodder, foliage and forest produce which form the economy of tribals. In the changed context of development, environment protection and sustainable development with a human centred approach must be ensured. Since tribal women are engaged in ecological movements, environmental protection and conservation, their role may be enhanced through capacity building and empowerment in the context of ecological development.

7.1.4. Tribal Women and Forests

Tribals have been residing in forest areas for generations, cultivating land and collecting non-timber forest produce. As per the forest survey of india report, 2003, 60.04% of the 63% forest cover of the country and 63% of dense forests lie in 187 tribal districts, though the geographical area of these districts is just 33.6% of the country's geographical area. Out of 58 districts, which have more than 67% of their area under forest cover, 51 are tribal districts. A comparison of the 2001 and 2003 assessments of forest cover in tribal districts shows a net increase of 321,100 hectares underscoring a very strong symbiotic relationship between tribals and forests and of tribals being at the forefront of conservation regimes.

While tribal women have more say in family decisions than their non-tribal counterparts, they also share more responsibilities. Preparing food and providing for drinking water is solely their responsibility so they operate closely with the forests from where they get water, fuel and minor products including edible fruits, tubers, flowers, vegetables and berries.

Minor forest produce plays an important part in the tribal economy. Its collection and marketing is a major source of livelihood for most tribal families contributing around 70% of their total income. The different varieties are classified as plants for use in tanning, natural gums, resins and balsams, plants and seeds used in pharmacy and perfumery and *tendu* leaves.

Firewood is also provided by forests. Since firewood gathering is done mainly by women, the interaction between forests and women gets further enhanced. Since all the duties of tribal women are connected with the forests and they look towards the forest for nature's gifts, dependence on forests is strong and intrinsic.

7.1.5. Tribal Women in Education

Tribal women play a significant role in the economic development of tribals as they contribute in various economic activities and education is one of the them. Education is a crucial requirement for the sustained growth of a developing society and lack of it is largely responsible for the exploitation and pitiable plight of the tribals. The literacy rate of tribals was 8.53 in 1961 and steadily increased to 47.10 in 2001, yet it is far below the national rate of 64.84 (2001 census).

Table 7.1. Literacy in STs

Year	Total Population			STs		
	Male	Female	Total	Male	Female	Total
1961	40.40	15.35	28.30	13.83	3.16	8.53
1971	45.96	21.97	34.45	17.63	4.85	11.30
1981	56.38	29.76	43.57	24.52	8.04	16.35
1991	64.13	39.29	52.21	40.65	18.19	29.60
2001	75.26	53.67	64.84	59.17	34.76	47.10

There has been an overall increase in the enrolment of children belonging to STs. At the primary stage, against an overall increase of 15%, st enrolment increased by 25%, whereas that of st girls increased by 36% against overall increases of 23% from 2000 to 2004.

At the upper primary level against an overall increase of 20%, st enrolment increased by 35%, whereas that of st girls increased by 47% against girls' overall increase of 30%.

Table7. 2. Enrolment of ST students in schools (in 000)

Year	Primary (i-v)			Upper Primary/Middle (vi-viii)		
	Boys	Girls	Total	Boys	Girls	Total
2000-01	6330	4665	10995	1879	1205	3084
2001-02	6691	5040	11731	2054	1306	3360
2002-03	6422	5408	11830	1930	1320	3250
2003-04	6776	5741	12517	2136	1526	3662
2004-05	7367	6369	13737	2395	1776	4171

The dropout rate among tribal school children is alarming. Various steps taken by state governments to check dropouts, including free distribution of books and stationery, scholarships, reimbursement of examination fees, free bus travel, midday meals, etc. Have had an impact but still fall short. The performance of certain states in providing matching grants, maintenance of service and management of hostels is not encouraging. The pace of construction of hostels has been very slow and the basic amenities provided therein are substandard.

Low literacy especially among tribal girls and high dropout rates at elementary and higher levels are areas of serious concern. The main causes are:

1. Poverty,
2. Contents of the education,
3. Inadequate educational institutions and supporting services in tribal areas,
4. Absenteeism,
5. Medium of instruction and
6. Education policy.

7.1.6. Health

Healthcare is a major problem in far flung isolated tribal areas. Lack of food security, sanitation, and safe drinking water, poor nutrition and high poverty levels aggravate their poor health status. The problem of malnutrition is multidimensional and intergenerational. Health institutions are few and far between. Till recently, an abundance of fruits, tubers, roots and leaves in forests on the one hand and indigenous health-care systems on the other, contributed positively to tribal health. Tribal people have over the centuries developed their own medicinal system based on herbs and other items collected from nature and processed locally. They have their own system of diagnosis and cure. But the skills and natural resources are fast disappearing. Moreover, the traditional systems can not treat or prevent many diseases that modern medicine can.

Some health indicators of tribals, SCs and others (per thousand persons) are given below to establish their poor state of health:

Table 7.3. Health Iindicators

	Infant mortality rate	Under 5 mortality rate	Under nutrition
SC	83.0	119.3	535
ST	84.2	126.6	559
All	70.0	94.9	470

7.1.7. Money Lending and Indebtedness

Despite legal and protective measures to curb money lending in scheduled areas and provisions for debt relief, enforcement has been weak and ineffective. The non recognition of the consumption needs of tribals and the non-availability of Institutional consumption credit makes tribal people fall easy victim to money lenders and leads to dependence on them. The enormous rates of interest keep tribals in perpetual debt, resulting in the mortgage and ultimate loss of land and property.Positive measures to improve the flow of institutional credit for consumption through self help groups must be taken. The andhra pradesh model for food security and consumption credit would be worth emulating in other states.

7.1.8. Traditional Knowledge and Intellectual Property Rights

Dwelling amidst hills, forests, coastal areas and deserts, tribals have gained vast experience in combating environmental hardships and leading sustainable livelihoods. Their wisdom is reflected in their water harvesting techniques, agricultural practices, irrigation systems, construction of cane bridges, adaptation to desert life, utilization of forest species like herbs and plants for medicinal purposes and meteorological assessment. This invaluable knowledge needs to be properly documented and preserved to prevent it getting lost as a result of modernization and the passage of time.

Tribal communities have a close dependence on biological resources related to *flora* and *fauna*. Their livelihood and lifestyle depends upon and is shaped by these resources. Their survival and sustenance is intricately linked to conservation and utilization of these resources. Corporate protectionism in terms of patents and intellectual property rights arising out of various international treaties/instruments on trade and common property resources such as TRIPs and WTO represent a real threat to their economic livelihood and a source of potential exploitation of their resource base as bio-diversity expressed in life forms and knowledge is sought to be converted into private property and treated as an open access system for free exploitation by those who want to privatize and patent it. There is an urgent need to provide appropriate legal and institutional arrangements for acknowledging the rights of tribals to such resources and knowledge.

7.1.9. Information and Communication Technology

Tribals live in far-flung areas often outside the reach of modern means of information and communication technology. They are thus deprived of crucial information regarding development initiatives, employment programmes etc. Use of it could help women to improve agricultural productivity and become entrepreneurs and information intermediaries. It could provide tribal women with farm-related information such as best package of practices, weather forecasting, access to credit, price and availability of farm inputs, market information etc.

7.2. Tribal Empowerment Policies

The need for empowerment of tribals hardly needs justification. Their primitive way of life, economic and social backwardness, low level of literacy, outdated system of production, absence of value systems, sparse physical infrastructure in backward tribal areas and demographic quality of tribal areas make the development of tribals and tribal areas essential.

7.2.1. Tribal Sub-Plan Strategy

The tribal sub plan was adopted for the first time at the beginning of the 5th five year plan in 1974-75. It applies, at present, to 21 states and two union territories, where tribals constitute a sizeable population and provides for the allocation of funds in proportion to the tribal population in the country by each of the concerned central ministries/ departments in proportion to the tribal population of that state.

The TSP as originally conceived had a two prolonged strategy: promotion of development activities to raise the living standards of tribals, and protection of their interests through legal and administrative support. The tsp mechanism has however become routine and humdrum in most states with little awareness of its original objectives. Tsp has become a loose agglomeration of schemes prepared by line departments and driven more by departmental priorities than by any broad philosophy or thrust on development of tribals and tribal areas.

After the adoption of this approach, since fifth five year plan, the flow of funds to tsp areas has significantly increased. Tsp expenditure which came down to poor 0.51% during the 4th five year plan increased to 9.47% during the 8th five year plan. The objective of the tenth plan was to empower STs through their educational, economic and social development. An outlay of rs. 1,719.71 crore was provided in the annual plan for 2007-08, which is 3.79% higher than the outlay of rs. 1,656.90 crore for 2006-07 (RE). The outlay includes rs. 816.71 crore provided as special central assistance (SCA) to tribal-sub plan (TSP) which includes rs. 220.00 crore for development of forest villages and rs. 150 crore for minor irrigation of tribal lands. SCA to tribal sub–plan is a 100% grant extended to states as an additional funding to undertake developmental, family–oriented, income–generating schemes, the creation of critical infrastructure, the extension of financial assistance to self help groups (SHGs) for community–based activities, and the development of primitive tribal groups (PTGs) and forest villages. Grantin-aid under article 275(1) is also being provided to the states to promote the welfare of STs, improve administration and take up special welfare and development programmes which are not included in the plan.

Under the TSP strategy, a number of development schemes have been evolved to bring scheduled tribes up on the ladder of development. One strategy has been the attempt to earmark funds for the TSP in TSP states/UTs which are equal in proportion to the ST population in the state/UT. Pooling of funds has been envisaged from various sources like central schemes, state plan and institutional funds. The strategy has been largely successful in garnering more funds for the TSP.

7.2.2. PESA

The provisions of the panchayats (extension to the scheduled areas) act, 1996 (PESA) came into force on 24th December, 1996 with the objective of Safeguarding and preserving the traditions and customs of people living in scheduled areas, their social, religious and cultural identities and traditional management practices of community resources.

PESA is an instrument for tribals' empowerment of tribals. To make it effective, it is necessary to:

1. Endow panchayats at the appropriate level and gram sabhas with ownership of minor forest produce (MFP),
2. Empower gram sabhas to approve beneficiaries under poverty alleviation programmes and the provisions relating to minor forest produce, minor minerals and settlement of land rights in forest,
3. Make prior consultation with gram sabha or panchayats at the appropriate level mandatory before acquisition of land for development projects,
4. Make the recommendation of gram sabha or panchayat at the appropriate level mandatory for granting prospecting licences or mining leases for minor minerals and

5. Get state governments to change their existing laws whenever they are inconsistent with central legislation.

For the PESA act to be more meaningful, provisions relating to gram sabhas as per the constitutional amendment and the amended panchayat raj act have to be translated into local tribal dialects and made available to all gram panchayats in scheduled areas. Training programmes should be organized so that all gram sabhas members including tribal women are aware of the function, responsibilities and powers of gram sabhas.

In reality, PESA has not become part of mainstream policy. Many state governments have passed laws not fully in conformity with the central law. While PESA remains unimplemented, tribal areas are increasingly being opened up by state governments for commercial exploitation by national and multinational corporate bodies.

7.2.3. State/UT Minor Forest Produce Act 2005

The tribals are in need of forest-based sustainable livelihoods for which ownership of forest resources and management of the ecology are crucial. The government of india has come out with the minor forest produce act (MFPA) 2005 whereby forest dependent communities should be endowed with collection, processing and trade in minor forest produce on the principle of "share and care". Other provisions include coverage of a minimum 1/3 of area under trees, demarcation of area under biological diversity act 2002 and safeguarding forest area covered under wild life (protection) act 1972. If these initiatives are effectively implemented, the ecological balance will be restored and tribals will have safe livelihoods with assured participation and ownership.

7.2.4. Development and Employment Programmes

The government has implemented various programmes which encourage tribals to take up new ventures. The assistance for the poor households of SCs/STs under the major programmes is as follows:

7.2.4.1. National Rural Employment Guarantee Act (NAREGA)

Narega guarantees 100 days household whose adult members are willing to do unskilled manual work. The Act came into force in 200 selected districts on 2nd february, 2006, and an additional 130 districts from 2007-08. The sampoorna grameen rozgar yojana (SGRY) have been subsumed into NAREGA in these 330 districts. All districts will be included from april, 2008. Narega is a demand-driven scheme so separate earmarking of employment/resources for SCs/STs has not been provided. However, the reports of physical achievements during 2006-07 reveal that more than 61% of the total man days of employment generated were for SC/ST households. During 2007-08 (up to dec. 2007) total employment of 8557.97 lakh man days was generated out of which employment for SCs and STs was 2330.36 lakh man days (27.2%) and 2648.02 lakh (30.94%) man days respectively.

7.2.4.2. Sampoorna Grameen Rozgar Yojana (SGRY)

While the SGRY is open to all rural poor who are in need of wage employment, preference is given to SCs/STs and parents of child labourers withdrawn from hazardous occupations, who are below the poverty line. 22.5% of the annual allocation (inclusive of food grains) at district and intermediate panchayat level is earmarked for individual/group beneficiary schemes of SC/ST families living below the poverty line. A minimum 50% of the village panchayat allocation (inclusive of food grains) is for the creation of need based village infrastructure in sc/st habitations/wards. A total employment of 1170.75 lakh man days was created during 2007-2008 (up to dec. 2007) out of which there were 435.49 (37.2%) lakh man days for SCs and 151.31 (12.9%) lakh man days for STs.

7.2.4.3. Swarnjayanti Gram Swarozgar Yojana (SGSY)

The SGSY is a major self employment Programme being implemented all over The country. Its guidelines stipulate that at least 50% of the swarozgaris will be SCs/STs, 40% women and 3% persons With disability. Subsidies will be uniform at 30% of the project cost, subject to a maximum of Rs. 7500. For SCs/STs and The disabled, the subsidy limit is 50% of the project cost subject to a maximum of rs. 10,000 respectively.

The number of swarozgaris assisted under This scheme during 2007-08 (up to dec. 2007) was 776408. This includes the Swarozgaris of SHGS and individual Swarozgaris out of which the sc Swarozgaris assisted were 267740 (34.4%) and ST swarozgaris 113215 (14.58%).

7.2.4.4. Indira Awas Yojana (IAY)

The Indira Awaas Yojana (IAY) is being Implemented at national level to provide dwelling units to people below the poverty line living in rural areas. Preference is given to BPL families belonging to SCs/STs. 60% of the total allocation during a financial year is for construction of dwelling units for SCs and STs.

The guideline provides for allotting houses In the name of the female member of Household or in the joint names of Husband and wife. 3% of the funds are Reserved for the disabled below the Poverty line in rural areas. Homes completed during 2007-08 (up to dec. 2007) were 1063920 out of which 462273(43.4%) were allotted in the name of SCs and 188247 (17.69%) in the name of STs.

7.2.5. National Rural Health Mission (2005-2012)

The government of india launched the National rural health mission (NRHM) in April 2005 to provide effective healthcare To the rural population throughout the Country with special focus on 18 states, With weak public health infrastructure and Poor performance in demographic and Health indicators. Those states are Arunachal pradesh, assam, bihar, Chhattisgarh, himachal pradesh, Jharkhand, j & k, manipur, mizoram, Meghalaya, madhya pradesh, nagaland, orissa, rajasthan, sikkim, tripura, uttarakhand and uttar pradesh.

The NRHM will cover all villages through approximately 2.5 lakh village-based "accredited social health activities" (ASHA) which will act as a link between villagers and health centers. One ASHA will be formed in every village or cluster of villages to advise villagers about sanitation, hygiene, contraception and immunization. Rs. 67 billion was provided in the budget in 2005-06. A national health insurance scheme has also been launched for bpl families to ensure annual health coverage of rs. 30,000 for families or individuals. Rs. 100,000 will be paid to the families of those who die in accidents and in cases of disability. Rs. 50,000 is paid in case of partial disability.

7.3. Recommendations

The role of tribal women is important but their socioeconomics development is poor. More needs to be done. The problems of tribal women and tribals are largely common. Suggestions and recommendations to strengthen and empower tribals as well as tribal women are:

1. Increase agricultural production. Through conservation to settled agriculture, where possible, with linkage to easy credit and markets and assured irrigation.
2. Undertake a comprehensive survey of water resources, including surface water and ground-water, in tribal areas with the help of remote sensing to prepare land use maps. Where water levels have gone down, an Integrated watershed management approach must be adopted. Ponds and tanks should be increased and renovated for optimum use.
3. Promote the diversification of agriculture and non-farm sectors to create job opportunities. Train tribal women in kitchen gardening, childcare, food preservation, handicrafts and other housebased activities.
4. Form and stabilize tribal women's co-operatives to take up dairy, sericulture, fisheries, handicrafts, horticulture agri-food processing And post harvest technologies. .
5. Impart practical knowledge and training in modern techniques to all tribal women regularly so that their work becomes easier and crop production increases.
6. Undertake research and extension to improve current practices, increase output and incomes and eliminate adverse ecological effects.
7. As per the PESA 1996, the gram sabha enjoys the authority to decide the natural resources which include non-timber forest produce (NTFP). The monopoly restrictions over NTFP should be immediately removed while ensuring social protection through provision of support prices to tribals who should be allowed to collect, process, transport and market the NTFP.
8. Low literacy especially among tribal girls and high dropout rates at elementary and higher levels are areas of serious concern.

Focus on girls' education, inclusive of context-specific traditional and innovative interventions.

9. Teach tribal children in their mother tongue at least at primary level. Prepare textbooks in tribal languages.
10. To prevent teacher absenteeism in tribal areas, give preference to local and tribal teachers from local panchayats, and place the teaching and non-teaching staff of primary schools under the control of the village management committee.
11. Devise new systems to improve the access of tribals to modern healthcare.
12. Promote the synthesis of indian systems of medicine like ayurveda, sidha and unani with the tribal system.
13. Provide good drinking water facilities in tribal areas.
14. Strengthen the tsp strategy with an institutionalized mechanism for compliance and monitoring. Make TSP funds non-divertible and nonlapsable develop a workable system.
15. Take measures through community efforts to eliminate pernicious practices which result in the torture and oppression of women e.g. witchcraft and superstitions.
16. Discourage the migration of tribal women to urban areas, to take low paid, domestic and mental work by providing an enabling regulatory framework.
17. Train tribal women to take up their responsibilities and sensitize the gram sabha about the new provisions.
18. Inform all gram sabha members, Including tribal women, of the Functions, responsibilities and powers of gram sabhas.
19. Encourage women's organizations working among tribals and ensure the formation, stabilization and bank linkages of SHGS to promote viable micro-economic activities with substantial support in terms of credit and market.

These strategies would empower tribal women and bring them mainstream development.

Tribal women play a major role in the comanagement of their natural, social, economic resources and agricultural development including crop production, livestock production, horticulture and post harvest operations but they remain backward due to traditional values, illiteracy, superstitions, dominant roles in decision making, social evils and many other cultural factors. The participatory role of tribals in improving their living conditions by fully exploring natural endowments and alternative uses must find an appropriate place in the strategic approach. The social dynamics of tribal welfare and development is such that effective strategies to protect tribals and their livelihood imply negotiating some kind of social consensus about criteria concerning tribal development and values of the society that evolves from such programmes. This also implies a broad social consensus about the basic rights and opportunities that tribals should enjoy and the responsibilities that should be taken by different individual and social groups.

REFERENCES

Aiyar, Mani Shankar, "Recognising the Rights of Forest Dependents", *Yojana*, Vol. 52, September, pp. 59. 2008.

Bano, Zenab, "Tribal Women : The Gender Issues", *SAJOSPS*, Vol. 3, No. 1, July-December, pp. 24-28. 2002.

Gaur, K.D. and Rani, Poonam, "Women Empowerment in India : Socio and Economic" in *Women Empowerment*, (ed.) Agarwal, Meenu, Mahamaya Publishing House, New Delhi, pp. 33-46.2007.

Joseph, Vinod, "Tribal Development during the Five Year Plans", *Kurukshetra*, Vol. 51, NO. 8, pp. 23-28. 2003.

Pandey, G.S. "Environment and Development" in *Tribal Development: Options* (ed.), Samal, P.K. Gyanodaya Prakashan, Nainital.1998.

Sinha, Archana, "Economic Empowerment and Amelioration of Tribals in India", *Kurukshetra*, Vol. 54, No. 9, July, pp. 3-13. 2006.

8

Impact of Economic Liberalisation on Dalits

Since 1991 India's economic liberalisation has generated a lively debate, with opposition from both the left and the right. There is a widespread demand for reform of the previous economic regime of quotas and controls but the consensus over the need for reforms is not to be mistaken for consensus over reforms. Responses are mostly based on subjective considerations rather than ideology: entrepreneurs often oppose reforms which may deny them concessions or protection and newspapers which may regularly denounce 'subsidies' and 'dole-outs' are unlikely to support the removal of subsidies on newsprint or the government cutting back on its practice of advertising in the media. The reform debate then boils down to the specific question of what liberalisation offers a particular segment or sector.

It is relatively easy to gauge responses of the organised sector: both trade associations and trade unions routinely respond to policy changes that affect them. However, the unorganised sector and social groups such as Dalits have has no way of articulating their responses except at elections. Electoral preferences, though, cannot simply be attributed to attitudes towards liberalisation. At the same time, for many Dalits the response to liberalisation transcends the narrow confines of economic reforms and includes social and political concerns as well.

8.1. Economic Reforms

India's economic reform process started in response to the 1990-1991 balance of payments crisis. As a result, the response had to be quick, with little deliberation of the pros and cons. But the BoP crisis was only the trigger for reforms. Jayati Ghosh records that, prior to the crisis, "there was already a significant lobby within India, and even within the Indian government, in favour of decontrol and more market-friendly policies." Moreover, the reforms were outward looking in the sense the response was meant to instil confidence among international financial institutions and other lenders. The process was driven by a newly-elected government which did not have to worry about adverse electoral fallout and did not attempt to gain popular support (and legitimacy) for the reforms. This has continued under subsequent governments. First, economic reform is still a top-down process. Second, after more than a decade, the reform process have continued in a piecemeal manner. Third, the tone and tenor of economic reforms have been delinked from constitutional requirements. Fourth, the reform process is reminiscent of the 1960s belief in 'trickle-down'. Jos Mooij and S. Mahendra Dev explain how this assumption informed economic policy making in India:

> Throughout the period 1991-2002, there was a great belief in the 'trickle down' mechanism. Even though initially the poor could be negatively affected, there was an explicit assertion that in the end economic growth would help them. This belief in 'trickle down' was not new in Indian development. In the first decades after Independence, there was a strong belief that the benefits of industrialisation and agricultural growth would trickle down to the poor... In the course of the 1960s and 1970s, however, the assumption had come under attack and additional interventions were introduced. The 1990 budget speech was still very critical of the 'trickle down' mechanism, but from 1991 onwards [the] belief... became again prominent in the thinking of the subsequent Finance Ministers.

These characteristics have implications for the poor, a predominant number of which are Dalits and tribals.

The 1990s started with the Congress Party losing its electoral base. Though upper castes had always dominated its leadership, Congress' success had stemmed from a coalition of Dalits, Tribals, minorities, Brahmins and a few other groups. How far the party worked for the betterment of its core constituency may be debatable but the coalition helped introduce the political idioms of equality, justice and empowerment into the national discourse. Poverty and discrimination were explained as aberrations which occurred despite, rather than because of, Congress. The loss of its support-base coupled with the intolerance triggered off by the Mandal controversy created an environment by 1991 in which the commitment to the welfare of weaker sections was treated as outdated. Christophe Jaffrelot explains how the upper castes saw in liberalisation a new opportunity where they alone can succeed:

> The upper castes are losing ground in the political sphere and in the administration but the liberalisation of the economy—which coincided with the implementation of the Mandal Commission Report—has opened new opportunities for the upper castes in the private sector, and hence they may no longer regret their traditional monopoly over the bureaucracy being challenged.

Though there is no evidence to suggest that the upper castes opted for liberalisation after becoming disillusioned with the Mandal episode, liberalisation clearly provided them with a new avenue to maintain their dominance. Many Dalits believe either that liberalisation represents the upper castes trying to escape the mess they themselves created or that it exemplifies, especially given the urban bias of the reforms, the upper castes' lack of concern for the pocr. Either way the rural poor tend to regard liberalisation with disappointment, insofar as it has not benefited them, and resentment, as it reflects a lack of concern for them.

The reforms are still characterised by a crisis-management approach. All the changes so far do not amount to a coherent and comprehensive approach to tackle the problems facing the economy. The same zeal and single-mindedness evident in trade and financial sector reform is conspicuous by its absence in attempts to revive the rural economy; to increase non-agricultural employment; to integrate the vast mass of wage labourers into the economy; and to ensure social security. A reform process that does not touch nearly two-thirds of the population cannot be expected to succeed unless a way is found to insulate the privileged from the rest. "Economic logic alone cannot explain," writes Ashutosh Varshney, "the selectivity and rhythm of reforms" and adds:

> Reforms that touch, directly or primarily, elite politics have gone the farthest; a large devaluation of the currency, a restructuration (sic) of capital markets, a liberalisation of the trade regime, and a simplification of investment rules. Reforms that are economically desirable but concern mass politics have been of two types: those that have positive political consequences in mass politics (for example inflation control) and those that have potentially negative or highly uncertain consequences in mass politics (labour laws, privatisation of public sector, agriculture). The former have been implemented with single-minded determination; the latter have either been completely ignored or pursued with less than exemplary policy resolve (fiscal balances).

Another complication is that there are glaring contradictions between the liberalisation process and the Constitution of India. A honest approach would have necessitated amending the constitution to delete all vestiges of the bygone era such as references to Socialism, some of the Directive Principles in part IV and inconvenient items in the Seventh Schedule. But this is not expedient politically. Liberalisation has aggravated the mismatch between the resource-base and responsibilities between the central and state governments. While states are saddled with responsibilities in areas that directly affect people—such as sanitation, drinking water, roads, power, education (excluding higher education), public health—the centre is content with financial centralisation. It can impose structural changes affecting states without taking their views into consideration. In practice, the centre can impose a burden on states, for instance by raising employees' salaries through pay commission awards. The additional financial burden due to the implementation of the fifth pay commission recently might have neutralised any savings on account of the freeze in fresh recruitment in the public sector.

As Varshney mentions, the reformers have so far concentrated exclusively on what is practicable in the organised sector rather than what is needed everywhere. Whether there are any elements in liberalisation that can solve problems in the unorganised sector is a moot point because no serious effort has been made to include rural economy in the economic reforms. Nearly three-quarters of the population of Dalits and tribals live in the countryside. Moreover, the slow pace of human development since 1950, particularly relating to education, has limited their mobility away from villages. The failure to tackle rural issues has resulted in increasing anti-incumbency in state and central government elections. Since Indira Gandhi, no ruling party or prime minister has managed to hold power in a general election after completing a five-year term. Is increasing political instability connected to economic reforms?

The 1990s witnessed the collapse of political process as a means of 'interest aggregation'—the art of balancing competing interests. It may be noted that the crisis in the nation's polity started before economic reforms began. But the reforms have in no way helped redefine politics because economic policies before and after 1991 suffer from a narrow base, catering to metropolitan and upper-caste interests. According to the National Human Development Report 2001, published by the Planning Commission,

> "The attainment levels for the Scheduled Castes and the Scheduled Tribes are also lower than others on the available indicators. This aspect of the development process has been captured both in the individual indicators, as well as in the composite indices."

8.2. Impact on Dalits

Dalits have traditionally worked as artisans and wage labourers, regarding economic mobility as possible only through education and employment. They lack an entrepreneurial culture and their inferior social position has discouraged them from entering professions. Though many were dissatisfied with pre-1991 policies, earlier policies had symbolised a certain commitment on the part of national leaders to social justice and equality. While most Dalits were poor and illiterate, affirmative action policies provided them with some mobility and, until the 1980s, the few who could acquire education could gain employment in the public sector. Liberalisation was a bolt from the blue, which they saw as an anti-Dalit upper-caste process. In a seminar organised on the topic at the University of Pune in 1996, most participants broadly agreed on this view:

> The policy marks a significant departure from the past. The much cherished principles of growth with justice, social responsibility and accountability, equity and self-reliance have been rendered obsolete

> with the new slogans of 'liberalisation', 'privatisation', 'efficiency' and 'competitiveness.'

One participant predicted that "the position of Dalits would deteriorate further" due to reforms and another said, "the free market ethos... can neither conform to the democratic spirit of the Indian Constitution... nor can it coexist with the system of positive discrimination..." With a couple of exceptions, most participants at the Pune seminar—probably the first major attempt to articulate Dalits' concerns after reforms were introduced—could not see much hope for the community in the new dispensation.

It is useful to understand here the nature of Dalit movements and the way the community articulates its demands. Apart from reports of, and comments on, atrocities, hardly any debate takes place on Dalit issues in the media. Even academic works, for instance on rural development or social sector spending, rarely treat Dalits as a subject matter. Political parties have stopped the earlier practice of treating Dalits as a target group in their programmes and policies. At the same time, Dalit activists and politicians remain divided on sub-caste, regional and religious lines. Whatever discourse that takes place among the community is emotive to begin with, primarily because it is often in response to incidents of discrimination and denial, but this idiom of protest cannot be appealing to the non-Dalits whom they are attempting to influence. Unsurprisingly, many books or articles by Dalits in the 1990s focussed entirely on caste discrimination and did not pay attention to the economic changes taking place around them. What areas of liberalisation may adversely affect Dalits?

8.2.1. Retreat of the State

Dalits repose their faith in the Indian state for two reasons: the association of Dr. Ambedkar with the Indian constitution and the nature of the Indian state, which personifies the constitution. Being the victims of caste system for centuries, Dalits tend to view society with suspicion and resentment. A common stream in Ambedkar's writings is that Indian society is incapable of imbibing universalist ideals of liberty, equality and fraternity and he rejected the arguments that the country could construct a nation state based solely on its civilisational ethos. Consequently, the constitution adopted the individual as the unit, rejecting the age-old varnashramdharma. Furthermore, Dalits' rights to equality and claims for protection through affirmative action are embodied in the constitution.

Therefore, when the state withdraws from some spheres, Dalits feel apprehensive since they view the market as an extension of society. This raises four key concerns:

1. That their constitutionally guaranteed rights of affirmative action will be eroded;
2. That there will be less stress on poverty alleviation and developmental activities;
3. That the emasculation of the state will mean less protection for their human rights;
4. That without the state as their guardian, the market will discriminate against them.

Affirmative action: Dalits have benefited from the extensive schemes of affirmative action under the constitution. The system gives them representation in legislative bodies and guarantees reservations (quotas) in employment in the public sector. Furthermore, there are many other features, from the abolition of untouchability to provisions for their socioeconomic and educational advancement, that make affirmative action a comprehensive regime.

Liberalisation does not deprive Dalits of political representation. But it has already affected job reservations to some extent and is likely to reduce avenues for public sector employment. As the following table shows, there has been a steady decline in the number of jobs in the government, which means reduced employment opportunities for educated Dalits.

Table 8.1. Employment in the Public Sector

(Million persons as on March 31st)

By Branch	1997	1998	1999	2000	2001
Central Government	3.30	3.25	3.31	3.27	3.26
State Governments	7.49	7.46	7.46	7.46	7.43
Quasi-Governments	6.54	6.46	6.35	6.33	6.19
Local Bodies	2.24	2.25	2.26	2.26	2.26
Total	19.56	19.42	19.42	19.31	19.14

Employment reservation is inherently a narrow instrument. Quotas are often unfilled and many departments and areas, such as the armed forces and scientific institutions, have been excluded from the purview of reservations. The implementation of reservations is also not uniform—there is a marked reluctance to fill quotas in the upper echelons of the government while more than the required number of Dalits and tribals are accepted into lower positions. Moreover, even assuming that the entire quota is filled, the total number of beneficiaries and their dependent will be too small a proportion to have any impact on the community. Commenting on the 1999 figure of 19.42m jobs in the public sector, Chandra Bhan Prasad argues, "if the SC/STs' total existing quota of 22.5% is given to them, the total number of their employees cannot go beyond 45 lakh, which, if multiplied by five (assuming that every SC/ST employed caters to a family of five), the benefits cannot reach beyond a population of 2.25 crore." Therefore, the total number of beneficiaries (22.5m) is just 10% of their total population (around 250m). Although job quotas cannot solve the problem, liberalisation will reduce these opportunities.

8.2.2. Human Development

A much larger problem associated with liberalisation is the decreasing ability or political will of the state to ensure human development. That affects not only Dalits but the poor in general and the rural poor in particular. Until now, no policy maker has asserted that economic reforms or liberalisation prevents the state from discharging its responsibilities to ensure, for instance public health and education. Every finance minister since reforms began has justified them in the name of the poor: "throughout the 1990s, the issue of poverty has played an important role in the justification of the economic reform policies."

Ironically, the so-called reforms for the poor have not been translated into more expenditure in areas that directly benefit them. Low-spending on the social sector is a chronic Indian problem and cannot entirely be attributed to liberalisation. For example, the government accepted more than three decades ago the need to spend 6% of GDP on education. By the early 1990s, the country was spending 3.6% on education, and this fell to 3.4% in 1996/97. Since 1991 an already weak commitment to human development has fallen further.

Table 8.2. Average Annual Development Expenditure

(% of total development expenditure)

Sectors	Eighth Plan (1992-1997)	Ninth Plan (1997-2002)
Education, art and culture	7.1	9.3
Medical, public health, sanitation & water supply	2.7	3.3
Labour & employment	1.1	1.0
Public works	1.0	0.8
Foreign trade & export promotion	1.6	0.9
Irrigation (including major, medium and minor sources)	0.3	0.3
Rural development	7.7	6.6
Rural water supply schemes	1.2	1.2
Welfare of backward classes	0.8	0.7
Special central assistance for Scheduled Castes	0.6	0.5

On the other hand, it is difficult to attribute claims that poverty has fallen to economic reforms. Reforms or no reforms, states traditionally doing better economically, such as Punjab and Gujarat, have continued to do so. It is correct to credit reforms for the growth in services, industry and urban employment and infrastructure but no such claim can be made with regard to rural development.

What is particularly relevant with regard to the poor is the fact that the so-called direct action on poverty eradication seems to have lost its appeal with policy makers, with ramifications for political economy. In the 1970s and 1980s, direct action in the form of employment generation and other developmental schemes had created a sense of belonging among the poor. With all other excesses typical of India, these direct interventions were expanded into hundreds of 'schemes' and 'programmes' most of which emanated from, and were sponsored by, the central government. These 'Centrally Sponsored Schemes' number around 250 (though some estimates suggest as many as 327) and range from the provision of drinking water, housing, welfare of scavengers to Malaria eradication and AIDS control. One reason the central government sponsors these schemes in sectors that come under the jurisdiction of the states is that it is reluctant to decentralise financial powers to states, many of which routinely divert central funds to other schemes.

Though the direct action schemes may not have had a spectacular impact, they did help legitimise the overall development strategy, as well as the political establishment. Such a bonding and communication between government and citizen has been less conspicuous since 1991. Too much duplication, administrative apathy and delivery failures have discredited the direct action approach. Recent efforts to streamline and rationalise developmental policies at the centre have not yielded any tangible results. Placed in this context, the policies of the new United Progressive Alliance government towards poverty alleviation, such as 'food for work' programme, may be seen as a return to direct action. The ineffectiveness of programmes to help the poor and the lack of transparency involved in policy-making is at the core of the Dalit alienation today.

8.2.3. Human Rights

Dalits fear that the smaller role for the state will mean that they will receive less protection, though the state has had little success in protecting the human rights of Dalits in the past. The community remains subject to myriad violations and atrocities. S.K. Thorat says, "the data between 1981 and 1997 showed that on average annually about 508 formerly untouchable persons were murdered, about 2,343 were hurt, 847 were subjected to arson, 754 women were raped and about 12,000 were subjected to other offences. With 513 murdered every year we cannot say that the formerly untouchable persons enjoy an unequivocal right to life." A more indirect impact of the retreat of the state from economic activity is in the erosion of social and political norms evolved as a result of the constitution against denial and discrimination. The recent revitalisation of local self-government through the 93rd and 94th constitutional amendments resulted in elections in most states for panchayats (village councils). Across the country, Dalits suffered social and economic boycotts and violence. While unconnected to economic reform, the redistribution of power from central government, perceived as more benevolent, to local councils from which they feel ostracised, is a further cause of pessimism in the Dalit community.

8.2.4. Market Neutrality

Can the market ensure balanced development across regions and social groups? According to Pratap Bhanu Mehta:

> A system of private ownership of industry, and the market as a system of allocation, in almost all societies, needs social legitimation. Part of this legitimation comes from its performance as an economic system; it just is palpably superior to its rivals. But part of the process of legitimation is also tied to its connection to other values that a society collectively decides are important. In this instance, it is an important social goal that the occupational structure of the economy does not represent a caste system as it were.

In a country like India, where people are divided into castes and communities, the market is unlikely to ensure the welfare of all. Dalits are not inherently incapable of economic progress but the social prejudice they face puts innumerable hurdles in their way. Dalits regard the market as an extension of the society in which they have little faith. Oliver Mendelsohn and Marika Vicziany describe the market's attitude towards Dalits:

> Given a choice, it would seem that employers [in private sector] will ordinarily opt for a caste Hindu over a Scheduled Caste person. It might be argued that the caste Hindu is likely to have a stronger record of academic achievement and greater social presence as a result of the usual disparity in family background. But it is highly doubtful that this is a sufficient explanation. There are now considerable numbers of Dalits who can compete equally with high-caste people for at least middle-level positions. As yet, private employment in the white-collar sector is only a relatively minor source of overall employment in India. But India is to prosper, it will become perhaps the most important sector. Unless attitudes change, or unless reservation is extended to the private sector, the lack of a Dalit presence there will reinforce their lowly social position.

In a decade of reforms India has failed to introduce safety nets or to channel more resources into human development such as better educational facilities and better health care. Dalit criticisms echo those of Ambedkar's comments, made in 1925, on the economic management of British India:

> All the revenue that was collected was spent on Services such as Police, Military and Administration which are calculated to maintain order. Such services as Education, State aid to industries, hardly found any place in the scheme of public expenditure as managed by this irresponsible Executive. But it may be asked as to why the Executive, sovereign as it was, should have stood for order and against progress?
>
> ...so far as the moral and social life of the people was concerned, the change of government by the Moghuls to a government by the British was only a change of rulers rather than a change of system.
>
> ...That there was some advancement in material progress is not to be denied. But no people in the world can long remain contended with the benefits of peace and order, for they are not dumb brutes... Any people, however patient, will sooner or later demand a government that will be more than a mere engine of efficiency.

Unlike British India, which Ambedkar identifies with 'irresponsible executive', the Indian state is entrusted with a constitutional mandate to introduce radical socioeconomic changes within a democratic order. That the state is unwilling to own that responsibility is at the core of the Dalit problem. In fact, it is at the core of the failure to introduce any socially-redeeming features in the reform process. The crucial difference between earlier, elite-driven, pro-poor policies and current elite-driven liberalisation policies appears to be that whereas earlier the elite was influenced by the ethos of Independence struggle and by the constitution, the liberalisation elite is unencumbered by such sentiments. To appreciate why the elite may not care for Dalits, it is essential to understand who are these elite. According to Naomi Hossain and Mike Moore:

> They are the people who make or shape the main political and economic decisions:ministers and legislators; owners and controllers of TV and radio stations and major business enterprises and activities; large property owners; upper-level public servants; senior members of the armed forces, police and intelligence services; editors of major newspapers; publicly prominent intellectuals, lawyers and doctors; and – more variably –influential socialites and heads of large trades unions, religious establishments and movements, universities and development NGOs.

The absence of Dalits among the elite means their interests are not taken care of. Of the above list, Dalits can be said to have adequate representation among ministers and legislators, a negligible presence among upper-level public servants, and lawyers and doctors. The adequate representation in numbers of Dalits among ministers and legislators—the lawmakers and rulers—has been rendered ineffective by virtue of their dependence everywhere on non-Dalits to get elected.

8.3. Solution from the Bhopal Conference

The Bhopal Conference of Dalit intellectuals and activists, held in January 2002, is perhaps the first attempt at mass level (more than 250 people attended from all over the country) to address the problems of the Dalit community in the changing economic situation. It was policy-oriented and aimed at influencing public opinion. The conference was conceived and organised by second or third generation English-speaking Dalits. In fact, with few exceptions, the working language of the conference was English. Mid-career Dalit academics and researchers along with sympathetic non-Dalit scholars and journalists participated. The basic assumption of the conference was that the economic reform process was irreversible no matter what Dalits thought of it. The stand is similar to that of a participant, Gail Omvedt, at the Pune Conference:

> A healthy market-oriented economy (liberalisation) is necessary for the economic growth which will alone provide the basis for reducing poverty... Dalits and other progressive forces should press for an alternative new economic policy in their interest, an 'open economy' oriented to sustainable development that includes liberalisation with social justice.

Having acknowledged the irreversibility of the process, the participants confronted the obvious challenge: How to realise 'liberalisation with social justice'? As part of the exercise, the Bhopal Conference issued a pre-conference book, The Bhopal Document: Charting a New Course for Dalits for the 21st Century32, and a unanimous declaration at the end of the conference. These two documents record a policy-oriented approach for Dalits under liberalisation.

The conference drew inspiration from the Civil Rights Movement in the US and the Anti-Apartheid struggle in South Africa. Reduced to one word, the Civil Rights Movement's accomplishment was 'Diversity'—the ideal that public institutions, be they government or private, should reflect societal diversity in their workforce and contracts. The crucial difference between India's quota system of reservations and Diversity is that while the former is mandatory the latter is voluntary. Backed by 'equal opportunity' clauses in the law, the US model of Diversity does not require lowering of the standards but prohibits discrimination based on extraneous considerations.

While commenting on the limitations of public-sector reservations, the Bhopal Document's author, Chandra Bhan Prasad, argues that as the private sector in India employs less people (8.69m) than the government, "reservations cannot uplift the community from its existing economic conditions." For the Bhopal Conference, private-sector reservations are not an issue. Instead, the conference concentrated on how best Dalits could be prepared or helped to enter a liberalised economy. There is a need to look beyond jobs which are incapable of having any transformative impact because their number is too small while the state still has a major role to play in areas within its jurisdiction.

Therefore the conference explored avenues within the state to which affirmative action could be extended. Historically, affirmative action under the constitution has been defined in a narrow manner, reduced to the provision of reserved employment. What about other economic activities undertaken by the state? The Bhopal Declaration demanded a proportionate share for Dalits and tribals in government purchases, dealerships and contracts. This would not necessitate any additional financial burden on the exchequer, but would enable the community to come out of the present jobs-only mindset and help it to imbibe a more entrepreneurial culture. The Bhopal Conference had three significant successes. First, it prevailed on the Madhya Pradesh state government to accept and implement dealership Diversity. It is too early to predict how far the new government in Madhya Pradesh, which came to power in the first week of December 2003, will continue with the programmes which emanated from the Bhopal Conference. Second, the conference succeeded in mainstreaming the Dalit question as well as making the issue of economic empowerment a part of Dalit discourse. Since the conference, media commentary and academic research have taken note of the development.

Third, the Congress Party adopted 'Diversity' (though in vague terms) in its election manifesto for the 2004 parliamentary elections. The manifesto said:

> "Determined efforts will be made to promote a culture of entrepreneurship among the dalits and adivasis by providing businesses run by them with preferential treatment in government procurement and by extending bank credit at affordable terms."

Congress also promised that it would "create a national consensus on the issue of dalits and adivasis getting a reasonable share of jobs in the private sector." After coming to power, however, the Congress party committed an 'oversight' – the promise of creating national consensus over job quotas in private sector became initiating 'a national dialogue' in the government's Common Minimum Programme (CMP). More significantly, the CMP is silent on the promise of giving preferential treatment in government procurement. When asked about the discrepancy between the manifesto and the CMP, a senior Congress leader who didn't want to be named pleaded 'oversight' and promised "to bring this to [Congress President] Sonia Gandhi's notice."

8.4. Liberalisation and Social Justice

Experiences in other liberalised countries suggest that liberalisation is compatible with social justice, but it is not automatic. Democracy remains the only hope to inject social justice component into liberalisation. Continued anti-incumbency will force politicians to re-evaluate their approach to economic reforms. Experience so far suggests some lessons that the elite ought to learn.

1. Economic growth and prosperity does not automatically ensure social justice or 'balanced' growth across social groups. India can continue to enjoy GDP growth of 7% or more but will remain poor. There is something fundamentally wrong with a system in which a population of over one billion is called a market of 250m. The state should attend to the problem of why three-fourths of the population are not even 'consumers'.

2. The Indian state has failed to discharge its police functions to defend the human rights of Dalits. The state's equanimity in implementing law of the land and some activism to ensure capacity-building among discriminated sections will help create an enabling environment for liberalisation to flourish.
3. Social justice should be implemented within the state before requiring the market to do so. As the Bhopal Conference experience showed, the state could become pro–active, not just in providing employment but in several economic activities it undertakes. What prevents the state, for example, from setting aside a proportion of its dealerships and contracts for entrepreneurs among Dalits and other marginalised sections?
4. Social justice can be implemented even in the private sector. India urgently requires equal employment clauses in its laws to ensure gender equality and social justice. A clear definition of 'public institutions', distinct from entirely private-owned ones, has to be evolved. A private firm which receives investment or loans from public financial institutions or public sector banks can be made to implement social justice. In fact, the financial resources at the command of the state can be utilised to promote social justice.

India's pitiable performance in the social sector has more to do with the elite's lack of concern for the poor and is unrelated to liberalisation or earlier 'socialist' development models.

There is something deceptive about the terminology of liberalisation. Liberalisation in the present context only means 'economic' liberalisation. Even the seemingly neutral usage, 'economic reforms' also hides more than it reveals. In popular perception liberalisation may be associated with 'liberalism' but it does not contain any of liberal elements such as individual liberty, tolerance, rule of law and equality. None can be taken for granted in a country in which caste and communal divisions and discrimination are commonplace. The trouble with India is that at Independence, as Ambedkar mentioned, political democracy did not contain social democracy. Now, during economic liberalisation, there is no parallel process trying to free society from obscurantism, narrow mindedness and caste prejudice—the inhumane features of the society that keep Dalits in poverty and denial.

Negligence or unwillingness to reform society was responsible for the failure of past attempts to economically empower Dalits. Now, economic reform is being undertaken without paying attention to social reform. The result will be the same. Dalits' apprehension about being left behind is turning into despondency. Economic reform without social change will not solve the problems faced by Dalits, and will ensure continued political instability.

References

Aditya Nigam, "In Search of a Bourgeoisie: Dalit Politics Enters a New Phase," *Economic and Political Weekly* (Bombay), Vol. XXXVII (13), March 30, 2002

"Cong takes up quota issue with pvt sector," *Hindustan Times* (New Delhi), September 3, 2003

"Dalits must get their full rights: Digvijay", *The Hindu* (New Delhi), January 6, 2002

Javed Anand, "Dalit Drishti: Dateline Bhopal", *Communalism Combat* (Mumbai), N0. 75-76, January-February 2002

Pratap Bhanu Mehta, " New agenda for Dalits — I", *The Hindu* (New Delhi), February 14, 2002

Rajesh Ramachandran, "Private sector for Dalit cause: Party", *The Times of India* (New Delhi), July 10, 2003

"Reserved Signs: Politicians can only offer job quotas but no actual jobs," *The Times of India* (New Delhi), June 2, 2003

Swaminathan S Anklesaria Aiyar, "Diversity doesn't mean reservations", *The Economic Times* (New Delhi), July 23, 2003.

9

Dalit Emancipation in India

In India there are approximately 16 million Dalit (which means "oppressed people"). They are defined as "untouchables" by the caste system and occupy the lowest level of society. Dalit people's use of water wells is limited, they face restrictions on entering temples or residences of higher caste people, their ability to own land is limited, and their residences are frequently isolated and sequestered from the rest of the population. In addition to this social discrimination, Dalit people also face physical violence and murder. Dalit live in abject poverty and are forced into such jobs as street cleaning, disposal of excrement and animal carcasses, and leather tanning; sometimes they are also forced to work as indentured servants. Within the group, Dalit women occupy the lowest caste, class, and gender position, and have long been the object of oppression and violence in all parts of their daily lives.

The Constitution of India formally abolished "untouchability" when it went into effect in 1950 and there have been subsequent laws prohibiting brutality and protecting civil rights, which was to function as a Dalit protection law. However, due to resistance on the part of higher castes these laws do not function as they were intended.

In order to empower to its and socio-economically deprived sections of the society, the Ministry of welfare constituted on 25 September 1985 was renamed as Ministry of Social Justice and empowerment on 25 may 1998. The Ministry of Social Justice and empowerment undertakes programs aimed at ensuring social justice to and empowerment of the disadvantaged sections of the society such as scheduled castes, scheduled tribes, backward classes, minorities, persons with disabilities and other victims of alcolism and drug abuse, children in need of care and other persons.

The Ministry of tribal Affaires set up in October 1999 is the nodal ministry for the overall policy, planning and co-ordination of programs for the development of scheduled tribes. The National Commission for Scheduled Castes, a constitutional body monitors the safeguards provided for issues concerning their power. According to 2001 census, the population of the scheduled castes is 16.16 crore constituting 16.23% of the countries population, which as 102.64 crore. Persons belonging to this category are regarded socially and economically backward sections of the society. The tribal people of India, who come under the category of Scheduled tribes. According to the 2001 census, the population of scheduled tribes in the country was 8.43 crore. i.e. constituting 8.2 % of the total population of the country. Other backward classes constitute largest percentage of population in the country as per estimates given in the Mandal report. This social group got recognition after the Mandal judgment 1992.The government of India and the state governments have been taken a number of measurements over the years to improve the conditions of the scheduled castes and tribes and other backward classes. However, we could not achieve the goals of education, health care. environment and sustainable development for socio-economically disadvantages groups of the society. Let's discuss the concepts of empowerment and sustainable development.

9.1. Concept of Empowerment

From the women empowerment point of view, some studies have explained the concept of empowerment. According to Dhamija and Panda, the concept of women empowerment was introduced at the international women conference at Nairobi in 1985. The term empowerment was defined as a distribution of social power and control of resources in favour of women. Empowerment actually is a process that addresses all sources and structures of power. It is not enough to provide only education to women but they require access, to the labor market and employment also. Therefore the term empowerment refers to give power or authority to person or group for development. Empowerment is related to social justice and equality. Equality in social system is necessary condition for empowerment of men, women. However it is not sufficient for their development, as development and empowerment are not synonymous. Development refers to progress of an individual or group in economic, social, political and cultural context. Where as empowerment is defined as distribution of social power and resources in favor of women, men, groups, communities, societies etc.

In the 21st century, human society faces the various problems. The new relationship is the best defined by "Sustainability" a question that has been emerged from analysis of the regional and global trends in population, development and the environment .Sustainability implies meeting current human needs while preserving the environment and natural resources needed by future generations. The world's human population has recorded 6 billion and by 2050 is expected to reach nearly nine billion. Hence reducing hunger and poverty will be the primary challenge.

It is necessary to use science and sustainable technologies for ensuring food security for the future. The concept of dictionary meaning of sustainability is the amount or degree to which the earth's resources may be exploited without deleterious effects. Sustainable development requires that population resources and environment and development be fully recognized and brought into harmonious, dynamic balance. It is interesting to note that the millennium declaration 2000 by heads of states of 189 countries in the millennium Development goals stressed on eight dimensions. The goals are to be achieved by 2015 and give on education, environment, health care and sustainable development.

9.2. Position of Dalits

Dalits narrowly defined and commonly understood as backward people of India, In short, those persons, who belong to scheduled castes in India, they constitute 16 % of the Indian population. The Dalits indeed are one of the earliest settlers or indigenous communities of India, whose today's problems have a history over 3500 years. Dalits in their history have been addressed by their opponents with many names such as Dasa (Slave) or Awarna (without caste or identity) or achut (untouchables).but those who belong to this group, have preferred to address as Dalits. Dalit is not a caste; Dalit is a symbol of change and revolution. The Dalit believes in humanism. Mahatma Jyotiba Phule in his writings wrote, the title shudra, atishudra for Dalits. Dr. Babasaheb Ambedkar in his writings describes the untouchables for Dalits. Besides, according to Dalit Panthers Manifesto 1973, Dalit means members of scheduled castes and tribes, neo- Buddhists, the working people, the landless and poor peasants, women and all those are being exploited politically, economically and in the name of religion.

Therefore, Dalit is a broad concept which includes most deprived persons of the society. Such as rural poor, the working people and others. What is the present position of Dalits in India Today? Some studies have pointed out real facts of Dalits in India. According to Thorat,In 2000, the Sample Survey(NSS) data on livelihoods indicated that only 16 percent of the total SC rural house holds occupied cultivation, while the similar figures for the STs and OBCs stood at 35 %.The proportion of house holds involved in business was 12 % for SCs, 5%for the STs and 15 % for the OBCs .Also, the percentages of casual labors was the highest for the SCs & STs (25%),followed by the OBCs (17 %)and others 7.4%.Studies also suggest that SCs faced discrimination in various markets in rural areas. Thus, the Cumulative impact of the exclusion of lower castes is clearly visible in their lack of ownership of assets and low education. Besides, scheduled caste workers seem to suffer from possible discrimination both in employment and wage earning in the labor market.

A common misconception is that Dalits are less educated and they are less meritorious. The social disadvantages faced by the scheduled castes with particular reference to the practice of untouchability, discrimination in public spheres and atrocities covered under the protection of civil rights Act,1955 and preventation of atrocities Act 1989. During the period 1981 to 2000,a total of 3,57,945 cases of crimes committed against the scheduled castes were registered .Ramvilas Paswan says that fifty six years after independence not much has changed for the Dalit community.

In India today, scheduled castes and scheduled tribes form about 25 percent of the population. Accordingly, 25 % of the seats in the parliament and in the state legislatures should be reserved for these communities.The presences of scheduled castes and tribes in exports and imports, other business, and trade and industry are negligible. Besides, most of the states and union territories have not implemented land reforms. As a result, the Dalits still have limited assets in terms of land ownership .Most of the Dalits do not even have permanent houses and continue to live in poverty and misery. Most of the Dalits still do not have even basic amenities such as electricity, sanitation and safe drinking water.

An examination of the socio-economic profile of the scheduled castes and scheduled tribes shows that there has been no marked improvement in their social condition ever after five decades of implementation of reservation policies. It would be shocked by this fact that even the stipulated 15 % &7.5% jobs for SCs and STs are not filled. Many of these prescribed posts are filled by the dominant castes. There is a need to set up an equal opportunity commission office in order to implement the reservation policy and advice the government on a regular basis.

The Government has introduced several Department programmes and policies under five years plans, with special budgetary allocations to help the under privileged sections ,including an extensive scheme of "affirmative action" encompassing reservations in education, public sector employment as well as legislative bodies.

Even after state intervention, Dalits and (trials) remain at the bottom of most human development indictors. They face an additional handicap of cast discrimination and violence. Even today, Dalits are struggling for there human rights. In regard to dalit women, "Dalit women have always been victims of family feuds with the upper castes. In most cases, men from the upper caste rape the women of their rival communities. The dominant caste has a traditional mildest ,wherein they think themselves to be superior than Dalits" says Martin Macwan ,a dalit human rights activists in Ahmadabad of Gujarat state.

During last few years many provisions have been made to safeguard Dalit representatives from any type of encroachment. However, the socio-economic environment in the villages are still particularistic and not necessary in favor of the Dalits empowerment.It has been realized that though several creative programs were initiated by the planning commission of India, they could not be fully implemented during prescribed time because of the failure involving our people. The planning commission is the topmost think tank of the country. It should advice the country to accept new direction for sustainable development.

The planning commission is now prepared the draft of 11th five year plan 2007-2012. In view of future sustainable development, the planning commission should have focused on the new direction for the country and suggested urgently required time bound programs to render economic and social justice to millions of our people. The planning commission should consider that our huge masses are our capital and gainful assets. The most deprived are rural poor and socio-economically disadvantaged groups, which are marginalized and excluded from enjoying the present exceptional economic resurgence taking place in India.

In order to empower Dalits, we need not only to give them more economic power but also bring changes in the entire, social, political and legal systems and policies of the country because these are responsible for Dalits lower states in society and the main hindrances in their progress.

9.3. Empowerment of Dalits in Tamil Nadu

In this section, we shall address the issue of oppression and emancipation by paying attention to the Dalits from Tamilnadu, the southeastern Indian state known for its vigorous identity politics articulated by the Dravidian movement.

Before considering the Dalit movement in Tamilnadu in the 1990s, it would be useful to draw from the narrative of an humble illiterate Tamil woman — let us call her Viramma — who, through the 1980s, once mutual trust was established, narrated her life story and philosophy in great detail using the most vivid and simple words. Her story is of great interest not only for its vividness and frankness, but also for its gusto. It certainly provides a first-hand account of what was and still is, to a large extent, the daily life, the joys and sorrow, beliefs and the psyche of millions who share the life and the views of this mother of twelve children — only three of whom have survived —

residing in a village amongst paddy fields, in an enclave of former French Pondicherry territory hemmed in by Tamilnadu, a four hour coach drive from Chennai (formerly Madras). But Viramma's story also sheds light on what is discussed here: the dialectics of oppression and emancipation of those who for ages have been subjected to the scourge of untouchability. She conveys the views of the older generation, and offers an image of those sometimes libelled "the Subalterns," not always in line with the "subaltern" school of historians of India — who emphasise that behind the established history, there is another history to decipher: the mute or the open struggles of the dominated classes. They are right: there is a mute history to discover and recover, but it is not always a history of protest. Like Viramma, most of the "subalterns" have probably had to balance an aspiration for a better life with the strong consciousness of what their *dharma* of submission is supposed to be, all the while ex periencing the full force of the dominant classes and the state power machinery eager to crush even the most incipient forms of protest. This does not prevent struggles, but it does reduce their occurrence.

Let us forget for a moment the new vocabulary — in 1996 Viramma was still ignoring the word "dalit" — and call Viramma by the caste name she uses for herself: Paraiyar, the caste of funeral drummers who play the *parai* drum and whose name, in a slightly altered form, was diffused throughout the world by the French and the British during the time of the East India Companies. From the most numerous local "untouchable" caste name, Paraiyar, they coined a generic word: pariah.

Viramma is a Paraiyar whose daily life revolves around her family, hard work and caste culture. But as "one has to fill one's belly," Viramma's life also centers on the patronage of the main local landlord to whom she has become attached under the traditional bondage link between the master and his *adimai*. Viramma sees this status as one combining dependence and a degree of protection, for the master is her usual recourse in case of necessity, particularly when money has to be borrowed to meet the costs of important social occasions: funerals, weddings or other ceremonies in the family. This pattern of personal relations between the dominant and the dominated is extremely important, for it acts as a considerable obstacle preventing Viramma and others like her from joining a caste or class line of struggle to better their situation. Like many older Untouchables, Viramma appreciates the few improvements she has seen in her lifetime. Still she clings to the traditional perception of what the Pariah's *dharma* is: a sense of submission combined with a sense of duty. The internalisation of the dominant paradigm of submission does not, however, prevent her from either joking about Brahmins (for she depends on Reddiars landlords, not on Brahmin masters) or from identifying herself completely with the Paraiyar culture, which distinguishes itself from upper caste norms in numerous ways, including a much freer speech, a much greater non-religious inspiration, and a strong sense of humour. Though not blind to the domination she faces, lamenting and complaining occasionally, she does not dwell on her misery. Her strength, her capacity to face terrible hardships, the way her culture sustains her moorings — she is a singer with a large repertoire and a born storyteller — are impressive.

Few of the theoretical interpretations by foreign scholars on Dalits in Tamilnadu fully highlight the complexity of Viramma's life. She shares, as Michael Moffatt underlines,the consensus that places the Dalits at the bottom of the caste hierarchy and accepts the rationale of a system based on "purity," a system that orders the hierarchy among the different Dalit castes as much as it does between them and the rest of Hindu society. However, Viramma also illustrates the view of Katherine Gough, who stressed the distinctive features of the Dalit sociocultural world, freer than the inhibited brahminical model, and based on an admixture of less authoritarian family structure and a greater caste solidarity. Contrary to Mencher's analysis, Viramma does not basically challenge the dominant values. She accepts the concepts of *karma* and *dharma*. Mencher's finding is, however, much more prevalent amongst the younger generation, which Viramma finds disturbing. She thus tries to calm her son who questions the rationality of God's discrimination, and condemns the exploitation of Dalits by the dominant castes. Believing that things are better "when everyone is in his own place," Viramma, like many elders, is afraid of the militancy of the younger generation, which dismisses the legitimacy of the ritual duties of the Paraiyars and which silently asserts itself in such aspects of daily life as the way to dress after fieldwork, the way to walk in the main village street, or the manner in which to speak. While Viramma takes pride in adhering to the Pariah's *dharma*, her son, exposed to the modern reformist political discourses, wishes to uphold his self-respect. Viramma fears this aspiration to full emancipation and believes that controversy and protest are risky because power remains in the hands of the dominant castes.

9.3.1. Dominance and Protest

Bare statistics might underline the size of the problem of untouchability. Scheduled Castes accounted for almost 11 million people in Tamilnadu — 19 percent of the state's population — and in several districts these castes account for as much as 25 percent, higher than the all-India average of 16.5 percent (in 1991, there were 138 million Dalits in India). Such figures, however, give no indication of the extent to which untouchability is still practiced. While some change is noticeable in this regard, traditional patterns of contempt and submission have not disappeared. In Tamilnadu, the old *paraceri* where the Paraiyars have to live has always been built away from the *ur*, the main quarter of the village where high castes as well as "backward castes" (another denomination for OBCs) reside. Worse, even the new "colonies" (the local modern euphemism for Dalit quarters) built up by the government for Scheduled Castes are still generally erected apart. Temple entry is still prohibited in the *ur* for the *ceri* dwellers, and the age-old compulsions concerning funerals and rituals calling for the *paraimelam* (the "Pariah orchestra") are still expected to be fulfilled. Tea stalls and arak shops do serve Dalit patrons, but usually keep two sets of glasses so that Untouchables may not "pollute" the glasses used by others. Despite recent changes, the usual perception of Dalits amongst high castes and even backward classes remains derogatory: village Paraiyars continue to be stereotyped as ritually impure, "uncivilised," uncultured, unsophisticated and quarrelsome. Mixed marriages of Dalits with other castes are rare in town. They would not be accepted in the villages.

The socioeconomic status of most Dalits is still very depressed. Most of them (72 percent) are landless agricultural labourers. Dalits account for 23 percent of the rural population in Tamilnadu, but own only seven percent of the land, and even those who do own land have, for the most part, very small plots. In terms of access to amenities, they are well below the state average. Ninety percent of rural Dalits are still illiterate; the figure for non-Dalits is 10 percent. With the diffusion of capitalism in rural India, agricultural labourers are progressively less attached to the landlord families as *adimai*, and try to make a living as day wage labourers or contract for a specific operation such as the peanut harvest, paddy transplantation, cutting sugarcane and so on. That does not necessarily signify a total break with landlord families. But this emerging proletariat has to pay for its relative freedom by losing whatever protection the master previously bestowed on his attached labourers. The extent of this "protection" varied according to the master's benevolence, but was also, for the most part, a result of two non-competing rationales: on the one hand the "established wisdom" ruled by the *swadharma* paradigm, defining the duty of everyone according to his/her caste (the dharmic landlord thus has a duty vis-à-vis his *adimai*); and on the other hand, what there is has been called the iron law of wages, such as granting the workers only just enough to reproduce the workforce or making loans to impoverished labourers thereby strengthening the bond of dependancy on their creditor.

Dalits are not only experiencing poverty; they are also victims of violence. The official registries of violence do not tell the whole story, for all acts of violence are not reported to the courts. If murders are somewhat difficult to conceal, rapes and beatings (including in police stations) are clearly underestimated. The press covers and comments on big events, but not all acts of violence are reported. On the other hand, the increased number of reports and registrations does not necessarily express an aggravation of the situation: they may testify to the fact that more and more victims, or more and more concerned militants and support groups, make public what was previously concealed. For each tragedy that draws national attention, such as the burning alive in 1969 in Kilvenmani (Thanjavur district) of 42 Dalits, including children, as a response to a strike for better wages, how many cases are forgotten, or ignored? Besides raw brutality and open murders, one must not forget the silent violence of everyday life, the violence of poverty, debt and bondage, the violence of discrimination, the humiliation Dalit men, women, and children experience. Even if practices associated with untouchability recede to some extent, the "change of hearts" that Gandhi called for is still largely unrealised.

The *bhakti* movement launched in South India around the VIIIth century A.D. personalised the relationship between God and the devotee, beyond the hierachy of castes and without the esoteric knowledge and the ritualistic intercession of Brahmin priests. However, the movement quickly became part of mainstream Hinduism, and did not result in the disappearance of untouchability. In the ranks of the Saivite Nayanmar saints we find an "untouchable," Nandanar, just as we find Tiruppanalvar in the ranks of the Vais hnava Alvars. Both could approach God, but only after a purifying ordeal: the *bhakti* movement, after all, gave everyone an avenue to approach God personally, whatever his or her rank in the caste hierarchy. Its goal was not to dismantle the caste system.

From the 19th century onwards, a number of social reformers emerged in Tamilnadu, as in other parts of India, with a discourse against caste prejudices. Different trends can be noted in this connection: the *siddhar* mystico-ascetic tradition as rejunevated by Ramalingaswami (1823-1874), the nationalist humanism represented by Subramanian Bharati (1882-1921) and Bharatidacan (1891-1964), and the Marxist approaches of novelists such as Jayakanthan or Pavannan.

Tamilnadu, like other parts of India, has a neglected history of petitioning by the most oppressed, starting with a petition sent to the British in 1799 by Untouchables facing eviction from their huts close to Fort Saint George in Madras. More significant was the creation of the Adi-Dravida Mahajana Sabha in 1857. Petitions for using the term Adi-dravida and prohibiting the word "paraiah," for reservations in scholarships, government jobs, seats in village panchayats and municipal councils started in the last decades of the 19th century. Journals and magasines multiplied, including *Tamilan* in 1907, whose editor, Ayoti Das, converted to Buddhism in 1898 and founded the Indian Buddhist Association in Madras two years later.

But much larger moves against the impact of a rigid caste system were brewing at that time. They were launched not by the Panchamas, but by those who would call themselves the non-Brahmins, a designation which could well have been complemented by an additional attribute: non-Dalits. The Non-Brahmin Movement, founded in 1916, fought against the disproportionate Brahmin hegemony in administrative services and professional circles. Soon after, its political arm, the Justice Party, gained provincial power in the Madras Presidency under British rule. But this awakening of the well-off Non-Brahmins was mainly the surge of a bourgeois group of rich entrepreneurs, lawyers, bankers and *zamindars*, most of them from castes of "fair" status, for the expansion of their economic interests, better social recognition and a due share in political power. The fate of the "depressed classes" in general, and of the "Untouchables" in particular, was not their concern. On the other hand, the Self-Respect Movement, founded in 1925 by E.V. Ramaswami Naicker, had a much stronger impact. Periyar ("The Great One" as Naicker was later named) explicitely combined his struggle for the Dravidians (an ethnic concept excluding the Brahmins supposedly from the Aryan North from the rest of the South Indian population) with a frontal attack against Hinduism and its ideological justification for the caste system and gender inequality. To a large extent, the Self-Respect Movement was an immediate consequence of the 1924 Vaikom agitation in Travancore that Naicker had been drawn into. Naicker was by then a prominent Congress leader, but had become utterly disappointed by the response of the Congress to the Vaikom agitation. Naicker left the Congress Party, presaging a radicalisation of his sociopolitical views, which discarded the viability of a democratic electoral process in fighting either untouchability or, more generally, "the evil of caste."

To summarise, the 1920s and the 1930s saw three distinct trends in the ideological attack on untouchability: the first embodied in Gandhi, a Hindu not opposed to caste, but actively condemning untouchability as a shameful perversion of Hinduism; the second in Ambedkar, a Dalit struggling for political rights of the Untouchables through reservation and already thinking about taking the Dalits away from the clutches of Hinduism through conversion to Buddhism; and the third in Periyar, who simultaneously attacked caste and religion, linking the liberation of man — and woman — with a militant atheism. In the 1940s Periyar assumed the mantle of the ailing Justice Party, and transformed it into the Dravidar Kajagam (the Association of Dravidians). His aim was to use the D.K. as a platform for waging an ideological struggle against brahminical views and for mobilising thinkers and agitators who opposed in the stultifying effects of religion and brahminical paradigms on the otherwise great Tamil culture and society.

In 1949 the D.K. experienced a split when C.N. Annadurai broke away to launch the Dravida Munnetra Kajagam (Association for the Emancipation of the Dravidians). Annadurai's main point of departure from Periyar was his acceptance of the electoral process. He thus discarded the extremist atheist militancy of the D.K. while keeping many of its goals. The Dravidian movement cannot thus be reduced to a mere chauvinist anti-Hindi, anti-Brahmin, anti-North regionalism, driven by ethnic secessionism. In its early years the DMK, under the leadership of C.N. Annadurai and M. Karunanidhi, had a strong social reformist dimension. It is precisely this combination of a social agenda with an ethnic card which pushed the DMK to power in 1967. Since then, the Dravidian parties, either the DMK, which split in 1972 or its AnnaDMK rival, have been continually in power in Tamilnadu.

Dravidian parties have consistently implemented a strong reservation policy in favour of the Scheduled Castes. In addition to positive discrimination, they have strongly contributed (particularly the DMK in its pre-electoral speeches) to the dissemination of an anti-caste discourse calling for equality down to the remotest village. We must not underestimate the impact of what some might discard as mere rhetoric: words, even if not always followed by acts, are not innocuous, and help to change the mindset, particularly of the young generations born under the DMK or the AnnaDMK rules. But this rhetoric was neither adequate for improving dramatically the socioeconomics status of most of the Dalits, nor did it prevent the Dravidian parties from using the caste labels for gaining electoral constituencies. Despite Periyar and the atheist Dravida Kajagam, religion is as alive in Tamilnadu as it is in the rest of India.

This does not mean, however, that nothing has changed in the life of the Dalits since the 1940s. As in other states, a set of policies has slightly improved the fate of the Scheduled Castes, especially through the distribution of housing sites, street water taps and electricity, access to schools, specific subsidies or benefits in the implementation of rural development programs. However, land reforms and poverty alleviation programs have not made a breakthrough, which perhaps explains why there was no radical change in the status of most of the rural Scheduled Castes landless agricultural labourers who constitute most of the Tamil Dalits.

Dalits today are certainly more aware of their rights than before. But the weight of the Dravidian parties whose resilience was founded on a large sociopolitical base encompassing the Scheduled Castes and the Backward Classes (all supposed to benefit from the 69 percent reservation of seats in colleges, universities and government jobs) did not leave much space for an autonomous Dalit political party until recently. One has also to appreciate how, after the ADMK assumed power in 1977, the Dravidian movement came to be linked with the extraordinary charisma of the two successive film stars turned chief ministers, M.G. Ramachandran and J. Jayalalitha, whose politics banked on populism to win elections and foreclosed any radical move.

Limited emancipation was therefore perceived by many Dalits — and by Viramma — as the result of two processes, quite often linked together: the benevolence of the masters on one hand and, on the other, the result of decisions taken at the State level and implemented within the existing structure of political power relations from the top to the bottom through the dual network of the bureaucracy and party representatives.

9.3.2. Need for Emancipation

The emancipation of Dalits of course requires much more than their material progress, no matter how necessary this first step may be. The social and developmental policies of the central or state governments, despite their limitations and shortcomings, have brought changes in the Dalit "colonies," and quite a number of higher castes people are apprehensive about the implications. Such resentful villagers can be both high caste landlords who think that decidely too much is being given to those "Untouchables," as well as people of modest means and status who feel aggrieved that the Scheduled Castes can receive government loans at better rates than themselves or stipends for going to college. Rural Dalits now also have access to symbolic and practical sites, although village temples where other castes go are still barred to them. They can, however, enter the village school, a decisive change, notwithstanding the continuing prejudice of some teachers and a high dropout rate. For some OBCs living a difficult life, those below them, though stigmatised, are still seen as unwanted competitors. We must therefore distinguish two, not necessarily mutually exclusive, types of reactions inside and outside the Dalit fold. On the one hand, attention is simply directed towards the material improvement of Dalit life. On the other, physical destitution and ideological submission have been so linked together for so long that any material improvement is interpreted as triggering a new emancipative thinking amongst the Dalit. In a world where everything is a sign, to wear a fashionable nylon sari, to smoke a cigarette in the village street, to take a request to the bureaucracy is to testify to changing attitudes.

This is a key issue. For the Virammas, any sign of material improvement confirms their views that positive changes can be obtained from within the existing social structure. Maintaining the traditional humility while accepting whatever benefits come from the government is thus seen as the best path to follow, since it does not directly oppose the powerful and thus reduces the risk of reprisal. Many Dalits from the younger generation, however, assert themselves and object, even publicly, to the rationale behind the discrimination. They are better aware of their rights, and keener to use their vote and the political process for articulating their aspirations, their sense of self-respect and their dignity.

Emancipation is thus firstly an internal process. It involves a process of liberation of the self from the old internalised prejudices. But what are the goals? Generally, the model for emancipation is set (even if unwillingly) by the upper castes themselves. For many Dalits, emancipation is tantamount to an adoption of mainstream behaviour. The ultimate goal, in this process, is a dissolution of the "pariahhood" or "dalitness." To free oneself from the traditional bonds and enter a free labour market is just a first step. To speak and wear clothes as others do, to have access to what they enjoy, whether in the village space, in the sphere of power, in the professions, or in the religious world — these are the many tests of the real possibilities of not just improving one's material life but more generally, and as importantly, breaking the old discrimination barriers enclosing Dalits in their multifaceted submissive status. Such a model of successful emancipation implies integration of at least some Dalits in the mainstream society. Confirmation of emancipation through assimilation comes when honours are bestowed upon a Dalit by members of upper castes themselves. This is true all over India when a Dalit is elected or nominated at a post of high responsibility. The most significant case in this regard was the almost unanimous election in 1997 of the first Dalit Indian President, K.R. Narayanan.

In Tamil Nadu, where, as in other states, no government is formed without at least one or two Dalit ministers. One case, at least, illustrates that such recognition is not limited to politics but can also occur in the mainstream cultural sphere: Ilayaraja, the music composer, is enjoying success not only in the film world but is also donating money for the renovation of the prestigious Ranganathaswami temple at Srirangam, one of the most sacred of

Hindu sites in South India, and has even won the blessings of the senior *jagadguru* of Kanchipuram, the most eminent Brahmin pontiff of Tamil Nadu.

This is only one side of the picture. To enjoy the same rights of justice and equality — concepts embodied in the preamble of the Indian Constitution — is of paramount importance. But the question remains for the Dalits: are they just ideally free to do as others do, or do they have other ways open to them for charting the route to emancipation? There is now an assertive trend among the Dalits which refuses to incorporate the dominant cultural values as a modus operandi of emancipation. Dalit cultural associations, groups such as the Forum for Dalit Culture (*Dalit panpattu peravai*) and Dalit journals are trying to open new ways in this regard. A new Tamil Dalit literature — varied in style and ideological content — portrays Dalit life and denounces the existing order. While the beginnings of this literature can be traced to the Christian Sri Lankan novelist Daniel, its major exponents today are the novelist Poomani, the short-story writers Idhayavendan and Devibharati, the writer Bama and the playwright Gunasekharan, to mention only the most prominent examples. The rejection of the dominant cultural values is multifaceted, and of course does draw on outside influence such as other Dalit literary or political experiences (leading Marathi Dalit author Arjun Dangle, for example, has been translated into Tamil), or the works of revolutionary Marxist intellectuals. On a much larger scale, the influence of Ambedkar, whose writings have been extensively translated in Tamil recently, is beginning to rival that of Marx and Periyar.

Symbolically, the three of them appear on the cover of K. Manokaran's *Varalarruppor,* where they are portrayed as being attacked by a Brahmin and an orthodox Marwari (a regional group of merchant castes from Rajasthan, whose members have established themselves in bazaars all over India, many also being moneylenders). At a more theoretical level, the writings of Raj Gautamam reassess completely the cultural history of Tamil Nadu. Gautamam traces the roots of the age-old oppression afflicting the Dalits to the perverted values of the caste system "imported" from the North. In such a radical analysis, the cultural values of the high castes are no longer a recognised model to adopt for joining the mainstream: they are the definite sources of inhumanity. Dalitness may sometimes join hands with those pleading for the greatness of the Tamils. With Gautamam, however, Dalitness defies established Tamilness, calling for a new culture on which freedom may be based. Emancipation, then, is not only a liberation from social bondage but also a construction of cultural tools required for alternative modes of thinking. Amongst such tools, urban Dalit intellectuals have created, beyond the established publishing houses, numerous small literary and ideological journals and poetry magasines. Although often with modest circulations and short-lived, such publications have repeatedly reappeared. These *ciruppattirikai* have long been a resource for hundreds of groups moving new ideas, and not just in Dalit circles in Tamilnadu.

In addition to words, images also convey a part of the new message. It could be plain drawings, such as those adorning some recent publications. Some of them are explicitly militant, and contest the dominant Hindu paradigm: on the cover of *Yuttam Totarum,* a collection of Subbaiya's revolutionary poems, Ambedkar is seen trampling a copy of Manu's laws, the ancient Hindu code. There are also unusual cover photographs which go one step further by showing objects that refer, either directly or indirectly, to what the Hindu purity criteria derogatorily associate with the "Untouchables": a large bloody piece of beef hanging at a butcher's stall on the cover of Kurusu Sacrats' *Navval*, or a rotten mummy in a fetal position on the cover of a collective "metafictional novel." Such images are not just a pale copy of western surrealism, although in both instances their deliberate intent was to shock the conformists. More deeply, those images of beef and blood, of birth and death, express strongly the reappropriation by authors of the symbols of pollution, and hence untouchability. The use of such symbols clearly sends a new message: Dalits are not to be ashamed of the "polluted" images traditionally ascribed to them.

For the moment, those images on book covers have a limited circulation, even amongst literate Dalits. There is, however, a much more prevalent symbol around which Dalit identity is expressing itself: the portraits and the statues of Ambedkar. The Ambedkarite Republican Party and the Ambedkar People Movement are still not very widespread, but they are now much more visible than before. Ambedkar's statues are to be seen in large numbers, blue flags flutter in towns and villages. Ambedkar is very much present these days in intellectual debates, bookshops, newspaper columns, academic conferences and so on. He is now regularly referred to in political discourses of all shades, even by BJP politicians. This sudden importance of a hitherto-neglected political personality who died in 1956 is an apt testimony to the growing strength of Dalit consciousness. Skeptics might contend that sheer opportunism drives all sorts of orators and politicians to pay tribute to the new hero as a means of cornering the Dalit vote. Yet empty though it might be, the rhetoric is itself both a testimony to and an instrument of change among those without voice. It shows that, like other groups, they have a figure revered by the establishment, a highly educated Dalit, a key redactor of the Indian Constitution who rejected Hindu domination and converted to Buddhism, a modern-day Dalit saint complete with his suit and tie. An attack on a statue of Ambedkar, a not uncommon occurrence, is seen as a desecration.

It is not by chance that Bhim Rao Ambedkar has become an icon. His contribution to the emancipation of the Dalits—combining theoretical work and official responsibility in the service of the nation with a constant concern for the emancipation of his brethen—is unparalleled. The Republican Party he founded has not met with his expectations, but his example and his motto, "Educate, organise and agitate," is still the guideline for many NGOs who believe that dignity and justice are not just bestowed from above but have to be gained through struggle.

9.3.3. Paths of Militancy

Dalit liberation movement today pursues three main lines of action. The first seems to equip the Dalits with confidence; the second resorts to militant action; and the third raises the issue of the appropriate political tools.

The first two lines of action can be combined to a certain extent. The example of the Dalit Liberation Education Trust is significant. As the name suggests, this Madras NGO, run by Christian Dalits, identifies education as a powerful tool for social change, though without denying the need for action. It helps to rethink the conditions for liberation and, like other NGOs, tries to place the traditional oppression and the quest for justice in a broader framework with large implications in the field of civil and human rights. This helps both to question the limitation of Indian democracy, tainted by untouchability, and to raise the Dalit liberation issue in international forums. To equip Dalits with a better knowledge of their rights helps to bridge the gap between theory and practice.

A second line of struggle resorts to spectacular militant action. Sometimes the goal is symbolic — important for recognition, pride, confidence — and the figure of Ambedkar as an icon of Dalit emancipation is often privileged in such actions. The best known has been the long struggle by Dalit groups from Maharashtra to have the Marathwada University renamed Dr. Babasaheb Ambedkar University. Protest or revendicative marches, or celebrations of Ambedkar's anniversary, not to mention the collective reaction to attacks on Ambedkar statues, offer opportunities for public expressions of Dalit identity and aspirations which are sometimes serious enough to attract national attention. Such was the case with the protest agitation in suburban Bombay in July 1997, a protest marked by the killing of 10 Dalits.

But action can also have economic goals, taking the protest beyond identity symbols, as the agitation for *panchami* lands shows. *Panchama* is a very old term for those beyond the pale of the four varnas (*panch* in sanskrit means five), i.e., those defined by the Laws of Manu as Untouchables, barred both from education and land ownership. In 1890 the British regime in the then Madras Presidency passed a law assigning land to the Dalits. It took more than 50 years for 650 acres of uncultivated land to be distributed to about 500 Dalits families in seven villages of Chingleput district, south of Madras. Despite the law prohibiting the sale of such lands to non-Dalits, other castes were able to gain control of them in the 1950s. In 1989 a movement for the reappropriation of these lands began in Chingleput. It expanded in 1994, when village police fired on a crowd in Karanai protesting the forcible removal of a statue of Ambedkar installed just hours earlier on claimed lands. The incident, in which two Dalits died, had a profound impact in the state, and resulted in the consolidation of the Panchami Land Committee. In 1996 the Committee, with the support of 127 Dalit organisations, launched a march of about 100,000 claiming their land rights.

The emergence of such large movements raises two distinct issues. The first relates to the structure of the Dalit movement itself, which is riven by internal divisions. The more radical groups are close to the Communist Party of India (Marxist-Leninist), which is marginal politically but plays an important ideological role. Other radical Dalit groups combine an ultra-left ideology with a concern for Tamilness as articulated by the Liberation Panthers, a Southern Dalit group supporting the Tamil Tigers in nearby Sri Lanka. Christian Dalits are much more important in struggle than their small numbers might suggest, and include Protestants like Rt. Rev. M. Azariah, Bishop of Madras, Church of South India, and Catholics. A number of Dalit priests complain about the persistence of caste prejudices in the community and the Church hierarchy. The most militant follow Liberation theology, which finds in Dalit emancipation an obvious field of action and theorisation. Militant groups can sometimes bridge religious and philosophical differences. At other times, differences result from competition between concurrent groups, and more fundamentally from disagreements about strategies and perceptions of the transformed Dalit identity.

The second issue is political. Before independence, Gandhi persuaded Ambedkar to renounce the separate Dalit electorate the British were ready to concede (a good opportunity to weaken the National Congress, as the British saw it). After 1947, for decades the Dalit vote was not autonomous. Most rural Dalits have, for long, "voted for the master," i.e., for the landlord. The rise of the DMK introduced, as already noted, a new rhetoric and progressive actions. But Dalits were not seen as a special entity needing more than specific reservations and development programs offered to the Scheduled Castes. Like the Congress Party at the national level, the DMK saw itself as an umbrella organisation, able to muster votes from everybody (with the exception of the Brahmin in the early stages), from the Dalit agricultural labourer to his landlord. The Communist parties have certainly had an impact in some areas, particularly with labour movements among agricultural labourers. But the established communists of the CPI and CPI-M, faithful to the doctrine, could not emphasise caste differences in their organising. The Marxist-Leninists of the CPI-ML are certainly much more engaged in the Dalit struggle for land, and may even believe in the revolutionary potential of a Dalit mass movement, but they are a very small minority. The major parties in the state — the DMK and AnnaDMK — are now perceived by many Dalit groups and NGOs as mainstream structures, paying mere lip service to the Dalits without offering them sufficient room in the leadership or adequate support to make a real difference. Hence the renewed quest for the best political instrument: should the Dalits conduct political struggle in larger formations, or should they set up their own parties?

The caste movement reappeared in Tamilnadu with a bang in 1987 when the Vanniyars — a numerous caste of small peasants, classified as OBCs — launched an agitation in the northern districts to highlight their problems, at the cost of numerous lives. Shortly thereafter, their organisation, the Vanniyar Sangam, set up a political party, the Pattali Makkal Katchi (PMK), the Workers Party, which failed in successive elections to attract sufficient Vanniyar votes to elect representatives who could air their grievances in the Legislature. Subsequently the PMK, under its Vanniar founder leader C. Ramadoss, developed a new and inclusive strategy, presenting itself as the party of the OBCs, Muslims and Dalits, and adopting the North Indian concept of *bahujan*—the masses—which extends the definition of the oppressed far beyond the Scheduled Castes. This strategy seeks to overcome the fact that, in the field, OBCs have been as violent adversaries of the Dalits as the high castes, exemplified by the history of clashes between the Vanniyars and the Paraiyars in Northern Tamilnadu and even more so by the violent confrontations between Pallars, a Dalit caste renamed Devendra Kular Velalar (Velalar is a high caste of landlord origin) and Thevars. Alliance building and the arithmetic of electoral politics may help Dalits and OBCs gain access to power, through coalition if necessary. This is the story of the Bahujan Samaj Party in Uttar Pradesh, the most populous Indian state, where Mayawati had the distinction of being, albeit briefly, the first Dalit Chief Minister in India, first with the support of the Samajwadi Party, backed largely by OBCs, and then paradoxically with the support of the Bharatiya Janata Party, which, whatever its present policy of wooing Dalit voters and offering party seats to Dalits and Tribals, still has a high caste image.

Having learned from the tactics of the Bahujan Samaj Party, the PMK leader, not without some debate in the party, decided to back the apparently disgraced leader of the AnnaDMK, Jayalalitha, who had allied herself with the BJP during the 1998 general election. The AnnaDMK made an unexpected comeback (partly due to the weak support extended to the DMK by disappointed Dalits), and for the first time the PMK won four seats to the Indian Parliament. In the fluid political situation prevailing in an uncertain coalition, the PMK even got one ministerial appointment in the BJP-led Vajpayee Government. The happy nominee, it must be noted, was not a Vanniyar, but a Dalit, publicising his identity in his very name: Dalit Ezhilmalai. Neither in Tamilnadu nor in Uttar Pradesh is the alliance between Dalits and the BJP fortuitous. It may sound strange that Dalits should ally with the political arm of the hard core Rashtriya Swayamsevak Sangh, whose religious sister organisation, the Vishva Hindu Parishad, pretends to embody the eternal values of Hinduism. Two observations might explain this unexpected alliance. First, despite a high caste leadership, the strategy of the Sangh Parivar, the coalition of organisations that propagate Hindutva, is to try to accommodate all Hindus in its fold, including Dalits and Tribals (and the BJP plays the same card). Second, in the very fluid situation that has followed the decline of the Congress Party, political risks, including odd and unstable alliances, are sometimes the necessary precondition for political power. Dalit political parties are caught in this general predicament. Caught between this drift and the bane of division which has so weakened the Ambedkarite Republican Party, the road is not an easy one. Clearly enough, new formations will emerge, the last one in Tamilnadu being the "New Tamil Country" (Pudiya Tamilagam) founded in 1998 by a noted Dalit militant, K. Krishnasami, Chairman of the Devendra Kula Velalar Federation, the association of the main Dalit caste of South Tamilnadu. Whether such Dalit parties succeed or fail is not the issue; their very appearance is significant. Certainly, the progress of the PMK and the appearence of a Tamil Dalit party point to the fragmentation of the established Tamil polity: caste parties are now challenging the traditional hegemony of the Dravidian non-Brahmin parties, but they are also unwilling to portray themselves as exclusively Dalit for fear of losing the electoral support of other castes.

As a matter of fact, the Pudiya Tamilagam appears in a context marked by deep conflicts. In 1997 the relationship between the OBC Thevar caste and the Devendra Kula Velalars (DKV) took a turn for the worse. With the higher castes migrating to urban areas, the Thevars have become landowners, and rely upon the DKV for agricultural labour. But the social equation has changed, and the Dalits aspire to more than mere survival. They are not satisfied with whatever little (and poor) land the state has given them. While elders like Viramma point out that their situation has improved in the last fifty years, the younger generation expects a lot more, including jobs and respect. As V.S. Sambadan has observed, the sparks of violence which disturbed the southern districts in 1997 have been symbolic: desecrations of Ambedkar statues, changes in the names of districts or public transport corporations. But behind the sparks basic issues continue to divide "backward caste" like the Thevars from the Dalit Pallars: based on economic competition, social assertion and political access to power. Politics and symbols met unfortunately in the gruesome murder of six Dalits from Melavalavu village, in Madurai district, on June 30, 1997. This included Murugesan, the new president, and Mookan, the new vicepresident of the village *panchayat,* that had for the first time a constituency reserved for Dalit candidates.

In a number of reserved constituencies, no Dalit had dared to contest. Murugesan was convinced to do so, despite severe obstruction by the local dominant castes to "reversed" constituencies. He was elected, but prevented from taking office, and finally murdered, and even beheaded. Two weeks later, far from Melavalavu, the Indian Parliament and Members of the States Assemblies chose another Dalit as President of India.

The divergent fates of the two Presidents is not just paradoxical. It emphasises that much is still to change, and that what is possible and even celebrated at the national level is not necessarily accepted at the ground level of the village. George Matthew, Director of the Institute of Social Sciences, has rightly pointed out that the Melavalavu murders are not just "one more instance of caste tension. It was a serious attack on the institution of the *panchayati raj* (the village government) which has the potential of changing the powerful rural groups."

Since the recent administrative reforms, the *panchayat* is not just an honourable body of elected villagers, without much say on real issues. It now has control of local resources, and its president enjoys both status and power. Hence the reluctance of many established castes — including OBCs, which may be locally dominant — to accept a Dalit leadership, which offends them on both accounts, status and power. The necessary change of mind is not just a matter of Dalit consciousness. Change is needed as well among those high castes or OBCs who believe they are born leaders. As Mathew notes, the murders call into question the kind of political and social education that has taken place in Indian villages since Independence: "while empowerment of the weaker sections, organising them to fight for their rights, was happening as a natural reaction to oppression, there was no concomitant move to educate the dominant caste about the changing times, the values of democracy, social justice and equity."

While all tensions do not result in murder, the difficulties faced in expanding democracy and the slow pace of real change at the local level have resulted in a feeling of "broken promises" among the Dalits. Could a Dalit political party offer a way out? Several choices are open to Pudiya Tamilagam. The first would be the way it plans its expansion. Will it become not just the party of the Devendra Kula Velalar but also encompass the Dalit castes from northern Tamilnadu? But should it stop there? If it succeeds in attracting most of the Dalit vote in Tamilnadu (and not just the two percent it got during its first electoral test in 1998), it may hope to play a major role in the political life of the state, and be strong enough to join a governing coalition. It could follow the PMK's lead and try to build an alliance with OBCs and Muslims. The PMK and the new Dalit party would therefore compete on the same field. Once a party chooses to contest elections, this must sooner or later result in dialogue with other groups and parties. The very names of the two formations open perspectives larger than caste: workers, in the case of the PMK, and a renovated Tamilness in the case of the Pudiya Tamilagam. The key question remains: Is the concept of *bahujan* a myth, or a hopeful anticipation? Or does such a hope result from a simplistic reading of the power distribution in Indian society, separating the "high caste oppressors" from all the other groups? In the field, to say the least, "other backward classes" and Dalits do not necessarily share the same views or the same interests, and the union with the Muslims supposes that Dalits do not fall prey to the strategy of Hindu communalists who have attempted with some success to subordinate the Dalit caste identity to a larger "Hinduness" affiliation.

This brings us to the basic question of caste. Faced with "broken promises," Dalits have to consider conducting their struggle in a specific caste frame—either as a group of Scheduled Castes or through their own political party— to implement specific actions linked with reservation and human and civil rights. But how to reconcile such a choice with the Ambedkarite concept of the annihilation of caste? What is needed is not just the political tool of a caste party, and even the hypothetical all-India confederation of Dalit regional parties, however necessary that might be at this moment. The need of the times is also to carry on a cultural revolution.

9.4. Dalit Empowerment in Modern India

Whatever interpretation is given to the interaction between castes of different status in the old *jajmani* relationship, caste culture is hierarchical and divisive. With the weakening of the caste *system*, the interplay of unequal but regulated relations between castes is bound to collapse, except on the new level of political alliances. But neither political tools nor the new National Human Rights Commission and its state counterparts that help to implement the existing legislation are enough. Many Dalit groups and intellectuals believe that an alternative culture has to emerge as well, culture being understood broadly. In most cases, the goal is to free the Dalits from the dominant Hindu paradigm.

Conversion has sometimes been seen as the best opportunity, be it to Buddhism (particularly in Maharashtra after Ambedkar), Christianity or Islam. But conversion does not solve all problems on the ground or in the larger social context: converts may also be discriminated against, in or/and outside their new community. Furthermore many Dalits are not ready to convert, and conversion can hardly be a precondition for change. The problem is therefore to be able to go beyond the filter of religious persuasions. The program for action published in Madras by Katti Padma Rao, a Dalit leader from Andhra Pradesh, is an attempt to address the challenge of emancipation in all fields. A mix of strong anti-Hinduism, socialism and radical opposition to the caste logic, it is certainly not credible and practical on all points. But it illustrates the difficulties faced by militants who believe that the overarching reality of untouchability calls for an equally overarching emancipation strategy, one that is attentive not only to socioeconomic contexts and political tools but also emphasises a radical rethinking of attitudes, ideas, daily practices. Trying to build an alternative culture is a process which asks for constant efforts at rejecting the legacy of the dominant past.

Padma Rao's first point is certainly too radical to be implemented. Impracticable and as much of a restraint on freedom as the old system, though in different ways, it goes to the core of the caste problem, that is, endogamy: "intra-caste marriage must be banned. Inter-caste marriage must become mandatory." A second line of action recommends alternatives to the dominant culture in terms of names (dropping the caste titles, giving to children or to houses names choosen outside the Hindu fold) and celebrating festivals honouring Dalit leaders instead of Hindu gods. A third line of action addresses the "reconstruction of rural culture," banning caste titles from villages names or village streets, stopping construction of specific Dalit "colonies" in favour of mixed settlements, in addition to eliminating illiteracy, establishing health centers and rural libraries and opening community halls for meetings. The fourth proposal calls for the propagation of people's art and culture through a revalorisation of popular art forms and, simultaneously, new creations celebrating Dalit life and Dalit heroes. The fifth proposal addresses the spread of education and calls for the multiplication of village schools, educational institutions and research centers, not to mention the revision of curriculum and text books. The sixth recommendation focuses on the necessity to spread alternative culture among women in order "to encourage them to resist the pressure of patriarchal domination" brought by Hindu culture. Padma Rao also calls for economic reorganisation (on socialist lines) and political reorganisation (building a political organisation for all the oppressed classes, with the goal of Dalit rule in mind).

The radicalism of such a program limits its practicability, but the attempt to build up a detailed line of action at least identifies clearly the fields where change is needed and defines one line of thinking. The resolute denunciation of the dominant Hindu culture supposes profound changes in the daily life and in the "empire of signs" which governs its semiology. Politically and socially, Padma Rao suggests a blue and red perspective where the blue (the Dalit colour) emancipation calls for a class (red) alliance with "backward and minority classes" against the upper castes Hindu ruling classes.

The question remains whether an alternative Dalit culture and Dalit activism is enough, or does Dalit emancipation also require a change in the mainstream culture? S.K. Thorat, in a paper on "Dalit and Human Rights" has seen the Dalits today as "a part of the whole, but a part apart." One can hardly find a better formulation of the present dilemma facing Dalit militants and all those struggling for Dalit emancipation. "A part apart" could be the motto of some Dalit intellectuals who believe that only Dalits can emancipate themselves, and that non-Dalits cannot really understand the Dalit experience, nor be fully trusted. "A part apart" could also convey the mixed feelings of a large part of the 80 percent non-Dalit Indians who do not see themselves as oppressors but still believe that the former "Untouchables" are not really fit for integration into the mainstream.

Let us consider the thoughts of a noted fellow-traveller of the Dalit movement, D.N. Nagaraj, on the dialectics of Dalit oppression and emancipation in a small but very dense book: *The Flaming Feet.* His experience is largely drawn from the Dalit movement in Karnataka, and combines themes in cultural politics with motifs and metaphors in literature. But Nagaraj offers clues and raises issues which are of much larger value, in space as well as in content. His parallel between Gandhi and Ambedkar brings us back to the point raised earlier: the need for a change in the self-perception of the Dalits, but also in the self-perception of the non-Dalits. What history shows in this regard is that what is needed is not the Gandhian emphasis on Dalit quest for self-purification as a precondition for the eradication of untouchability. Against Gandhi's self-purification need, Ambedkar posits a quest for Dalit self-respect, which raises immediately the question of identity and the need for the emergence of an alternative culture which could eliminate the stigma of untouchability and stand in opposition to the established logic and psychology of the caste system. Ambedkar went so far as to leave the Hindu fold in his quest for a new collective identity. But while his neo-Buddhists followers and a number of intellectuals would define themselves today as non-Hindus, it is still doubtful that the Dalit masses would follow suit.

Is Indian democracy able to help Dalit emancipation, not just through reservation by law but also through the diffusion of new perceptions among Dalits and non-Dalits alike? The question centers partly on the place given to the individual, and partly on accepted norms. Nagaraj, addressing the problem of violence against Dalits, notes rightly that the village, as Ambedkar saw it, cannot be the basic unit for justice, for traditionally "the structure of justice rests on the consensus of the entire village, which could also mean the unchallenged rule of the upper castes." Here again, the caste ethos has to be rightly assessed: as Nagaraj notes, if an upper caste Hindu misbehaves in the village, this will be considered as an individual act, involving individual responsibility. But if a Dalit break the norms, he will be perceived first as a member of his group, and the entire Dalit community could suffer retaliation. A narrow path is thus open to Dalit militants who seek a way to attack oppression by combining ideology and material domination (hence the importance of the struggles for rights *and* land, which address these two fields), but also by trying to respect the "code of conduct," in the process gaining greater legitimacy in the "traditional" society, which is vital for the success of the Movement. In the meantime, the Dalit activist, "in a paradoxical position," has to recognise that "on him or her is the larger responsibility of creating a new sense of ethics for both the conflicting communities." More to the point, the success of the Dalit movement cannot be delinked from that of other social movements, be they the women's movement, the farmers' movement or the ecological movement. With the latter two, the relationship is not an easy one.

The rule of caste is not so rigid in large cities. But are Indian towns really such an attractive promised land? Urban India might also bring up much more acutely the problem of cultural memory, a memory already challenged either because it is lost in a silent history or because of the contempt it raises not just among non-Dalits but also sometimes among Dalits as well. The fact that some urban Dalit intellectuals who try to theorise Dalitness and emancipation do not always have an intimate knowledge of the psyche and culture of rural Dalits suggest the continued importance of rural movements, rural perceptions and rural memories.

Last but not least stands the Dalits' "rights to cultural space." In Dalit writing in the Kannada language, Nagaraj finds two schools. The "school of social rage" "concentrates basically on the experiences of anger, agony and revolutionary hope." The "school of spiritual quest" transmutes the social rage "into a spiritual vision of equality." Why "spiritual quest?" Not necessarily because of an attachment to a defined religious line, but because this school "tries to understand the world of poverty and untouchability in terms of metaphysical dismay over the nature of human relationship. The ethos of the portrayal of life is not informed by anger and agony, but by a celebration of the joys of life and its possibilities, which also includes the will to change."

Beyond the sphere of literature, these two schools can also suggest a model, a metaphor for the choices offered to the Dalit society at large, or for the types of action open to militants. Those animated by an intimate or spectacular social rage might feel that no middle ground exist between nihilist or desperate intellectual marginality and strident revolutionary advocacy and militancy. But how to build from this anger a moving and intimate connection with the entire Dalit community? Can this rage sustain a durable way, beyond minority extremism, for the political, cultural and social emancipation of the Dalit masses? There is an unavoidable contradiction between activist groupings and larger party politics, the former being generally prone to isolation and/or repression, the latter bringing quickly enough, after the first electoral successes, the need for compromise. On the other hand, the spiritual quest is more prone to being co-opted by the system. The real challenge for the second path is to resist this co-optation while transforming the system. Nagaraj pleads "for a radical reconstruction of villages from a critical-modernist perspective which can also mean a radical revision of existing values along the lines of Indian religious reformers." Some Dalit militants or leftist radicals would call for a complete break with religion, reformed or not. Others would follow Nagaraj in opting for a middle-of-the-road line. A third group might find that this complex goal offers a path of change more acceptable to Indian society, because it is less disconnected from the legacy of a past not entirely encapsulated in upper caste orthodoxy. Whatever paths are chosen, Dalits intellectuals and militants know very well that deconstructing the prevailing Indian social order and constructing a new one will not be an easy process. It will involve Dalits and non-Dalits, the past and the present, the community as a whole and its fragments, and the self. It is a total enterprise, with innumerable implications. But it is clearly a process in which Indian Dalits are engaged today.

At the end of this century, we are on the whole observing a rather confused situation. Indian society is in a state of flux. Castes are very much a part of the political game, but the caste system as such is condemned. The OBCs are asserting themselves everywhere, including in the decisive circles of power. One finds more and more Dalits in positions of responsibility and power, largely through the reservation system, while most of the community is still subject to various sorts of overt or covert discrimination. But there will be no scaling back of expectations now, despite the atrocities still perpetrated against Dalits and the setbacks to protest struggles or revendication campaigns. Promises have neither been fulfilled or forgotten. But the Dalit aspiration for change has become too strong in the minds of millions for backing down. Myriads of daily struggles, spectacular or not, sustain this aspiration, which has now gained access to the media and the political field.

The present state of uncertainty is in itself a victory and suggests that the past cannot perpetuate itself indefinitely. But Dalit emancipation remains a challenge for it raises formidable issues pertaining not just to the fate of the Dalits but also to Hinduism and to the Indian society as a whole. Seven points might call for answers, that only the future will provide:

- The first addresses Dalit identity itself: must the Dalits place themselves behind the blue standard and, faithful to Ambedkar, find a place in the larger society without abandoning their sense of belonging? But how to reconcile the legitimate revendication of a caste (or "macro-caste" if we put all Scheduled Castes together) so oppressed for centuries with the goal of "annihilation of caste?" This goal supposes that members of other castes, both the oppressed and oppressor will let castes be annihilated. Could it be the historical mission of the Dalits to constantly harass the dominant paradigm and shake the old oppressive order?
- The second point is a correlate of the first one: how to preserve Dalit memories? Can the experiences, the history of millions of Dalits simply be abandoned for the sake of joining the mainstream? This could be a temptation for urban intellectuals. But how can the past and the present of more than 150 million people be ignored for long? The urban-rural divide between Dalits becomes an additional challenge. Will the political and the NGOs activists bridge a potential gap between a growing corps of urban Dalit intellectuals and the mass of rural illiterates? The answer varies from place to place, and depends on the types of links preserved by the Dalit intelligentsia with rural Dalits. This relationship will have a decisive impact on the way in which a genuine and practicable emancipation is theorised.
- A third point relates to the nature and the real extent of the "mainstream" Hindu identity. Is there only one Hindu ideality set by the *shastras* of the brahminical tradition? Is there not also a legacy of other traditions on which to build the future, a large and

diverse cultural space which encompasses not just the Dalits but also the Tribals, the reformist movements formulating a new Hinduism where the individual has a place, the secular democratic ideal, not to mention eventually other faiths not based officially on caste? Where do the OBCs stand in this landscape? The fourth varna, the Shudras, were also excluded from knowledge and power by the dominant classical paradigm. Are the survivals of such exclusions strong enough to make possible an alliance between OBCs and Dalits, or is that just wishful thinking? Is Melavalanu an anachronism or a sign that the OBCs, gradually empowered over the past 100 years, are not yet ready to share the cake to which they have just gained access?

— The fourth point takes us to the impact of regional parameters. In the Tamil case, the legacy of the Dravidian movement is decisive. Even if the fragmentation of the Dravidian parties' vote banks opens the field to more autonomous formations, the question of competing identities remains, unavoidably perhaps, a challenge. Dalit or Tamil? It is not by chance that the new Dalit party calls itself "New Tamilnadu." The Dravidian ideology offers a way out of the dilemma of Dalitness/Tamilness, for it offers a seducive interpretation of history: by putting the blame for the scourge of caste and untouchability upon "the Brahmins who came from the North," one may link the future Dalit emancipation to the more egalitarian and secular values attributed to the old Tamil civilization. Beyond the specificality of this case, the question of regional affiliations remains important: will they obstruct a possible pan-Indian union of Dalit movements, or will the circulation of activists and ideas facilitate the incorporation of regional figures from other parts of India, helping to build a new and richly diverse national legacy? As an example, Periyar has now become an icon for the Bahujan Samaj Party in Uttar Pradesh.

— The fifth point queries the possibility of the union of the Red (the Left) and the Blue (the colour of the Dalits).The established Left has always tried to circumscribe the challenge of caste, without really addressing it, and simply denounced caste as a mask for class. With the Dalit issue gaining momentum, it will be more and more difficult for the Left to ignore this challenge for long, partly because Dalit sensibilities on this issue can no longer be ignored and the concept of "oppressed" requires urgent theorising. For the time being, the Communist Parties have not been a part of *bahujan* strategies. There are also substantial differences between the parliamentary Left, which has definitely to answer the challenge of caste parties, and the ultra-Left, for whom the Dalits are the potentially revolutionary subjects par excellence?

— The sixth point is about alliances between the Dalit and other social movements. The alliance between Dalits and OBCs is not simply a matter of political convenience and electoral arithmetic. Politics is not just a matter of power: it is more basically a question of goals, policy and change. What are the forces that are bringing changes to the daily life of millions of Dalits? Will they transform the socioeconomic fundamentals of Dalit life and, indeed, affect the entire social balance?

Dalit emancipation requires the imperative need for fresh thinking amongst non-Dalits about untouchability. On a wider level, how to connect the Dalit movement with the women's movement? Could Dalit women, more and more visible in the present struggles, help transcend caste barriers through gender commonality? And to what extent will an alliance with Muslims and Christians help transcend, through Dalit involvement, the instrumentalised prejudices between the minorities and the Hindu majority, knowing that the "old song" of the irreparable Hindu-Muslim divide is mostly fiction?

— The seventh point brings us back to the difficulty to forge a stronger relationship with OBCs if Dalit emancipation calls for, as many militants contend, a rupture with Hinduism? Or put differently and abstractly: how must Hinduism itself change in relation to Dalit emancipation? If the duality/dichotomy between "the brahmin" and "the untouchable" was a foundation of the caste system, what will happen with the latter rejecting his/her status? Could we imagine that the double process of OBCs' upliftment and Dalit revendication may help a new Hinduism emerge, less preoccupied with orthodox hierarchies, more open to individual or lineage relations to deities in a much more fluid society? The dismantling of the caste system and the politicisation of caste would not hinder such an evolution. In the changing cultural and political context, Hinduism is bound to change, perhaps along the lines proposed by some of 19th and 20th century reformist movements, paying less attention to castes and probably also by inventing new ways of accommodating Dalits. In this context, one cannot underestimate the strategy of Hindutva, which tends, despite the weight of its high caste leadership, to weaken caste differences in order to forge a pan-Indian Hindu identity. Dalits and Hindu tribals are clearly being invited to hitch their wagons to the communal project, and to let them assert an overarching Hindu identity rather than a primordial (caste or tribe) affiliation. Will the saffron hypothesis of the Sangh Parivar offer a major temptation to Dalits to join a new communal mainstream, which would also subvert more radical Dalit leanings?

All these issues, and many more, pose uncertain and difficult questions to which the answers are, as yet, inchoate. But the Dalit movement is definitely here to stay and will probably, as today, continue along diverse paths, tempted sometimes by isolation and at others opening itself to other forces. Blue, red and saffron are the predominant colours of change. In the end a rainbow might emerge from the synthesis of now-divergent paths. At minimum it will have to be a secular, democratic synthesis consistent with the Dalit movement's call for justice, respect and progress. The nature of the Indian polity is at stake as well, and so is the future of India's dominant ideologies and the nature of the social bond. This challenge is not just a matter of intellectual analysis or social theory. In thousands of Indian towns, in hundreds of thousands of Indian villages, the fate of the Dalits will largely fashion India's future, and this is not irrelevant to India's ambition for the next century. Dalits call for equality.

9.5. Dalit Rights Movement

The word dalit means broken or downtrodden in Sanskrit and was "used as far back as 1931 in journalistic writing". Popularized by Dr. B.R. Ambedkar in the 1920s and 30s, and later by the Dalit Panthers movement in the 1970s, the term became a new secular identity for millions of those formerly known as 'untouchables' in India. Today, modern dalit identity is in a discursive competition with various religious identities for control of between one-fourth and one-fifth of India's billion-person population, which is classified as scheduled caste (SC). The life and thought of Dr. B.R. Ambedkar, the father of dalit rights and assertion, as well as the modern Indian constitution, was foundational to this discursive competition, which can be clearly seen in the following quote from Gangadar Pantawane, the founding editor of *Asmitadarsh*, a journal devoted to dalit literature:

> To me Dalit is not a caste. He is a man exploited by the social and economic traditions of this country. He does not believe in God, Rebirth, Soul, Holy Books teaching separatism, Fate and Heaven because they have made him a slave. He does believe in humanism. Dalit is a symbol of change and revolution. Compared to the rhetorical calls by Trailokya Bauddha Mahasangha, Sahayak Gana (TBMSG) activists to work towards a time when "all India will be Buddhist," the above quote provides a stark secular-focused contrast to Indian social activists' penchant for citing religious ideals in order to galvanize the identity of followers. Pantawane's conception privileges dalit as symbolic of a post-modern identity in which caste distinctions have become irrelevant.

Yet, it was the life and legacy of Dr. B.R. Ambedkar that laid the foundation for this competition to win the hearts and minds of dalits. As both a social reformer from within the government, and then later a cultural reformer from the outside, Dr. Ambedkar's life itself represented a balancing between these two, not incompatible, identities. While many people outside the Indian subcontinent are familiar with Mahatma Gandhi, few who live outside of India know much about Dr. Ambedkar, or about the movement he helped spawn. Both his political significance as the foremost representative of the Mahar 'untouchable' community in Maharashtra, and the religious importance he played in changing the social identity and spiritual commitments of that particular community of dalits through a revival of Buddhism, are unrivalled throughout India's long historical development. Ambedkar's prolific legacy culminating in his chairmanship of the drafting of the Indian constitution, as well as his call to all former 'untouchables' to convert to Buddhism has made his continued influence among scheduled castes unrivalled. Though his life narrative is so compelling that Indians of all persuasions have appropriated his image, like other low-caste social reformers, both before and after him, Dr. Ambedkar struggled to create intra-caste bonds; that were lacking even among the lowest of caste groupings who were divided and aggrieved. Dr. Bhimrao Ramji Ambedkar (1891-1956), affectionately known by his followers as Babasaheb, overcame the cultural and economic impasses of being born an 'untouchable' Mahar, one of three lowest-caste segments of Maharashtra society, in late 19th Century Hindu-dominated India. Breaking through countless stereotypes, Ambedkar was taught early of the importance of education, and he used the social cleavages that the British administrative policy provided to transcend his socially prescribed role. Rising to the post of Law Minister in Nehru's first independent Indian cabinet, he was appointed chairman of the drafting committee for the new constitution. From this vantage point, Ambedkar was well-placed to destroy the legal foundations of the caste system, and in 1948 Ambedkar presented his draft of the Indian constitution, which was accepted a year later. In it can be seen Ambedkar's push to get social change codified legalistically. This part of Ambedkar's legacy culminates in Article 17 of the Indian Constitution, which states:

> 'Untouchability' is abolished and its practice in any form is forbidden. The enforcement of any disability arising out of 'untouchability' shall be an offence punishable in accordance with the law.

But despite this important legal success, Dr. Ambedkar slowly began to realize that structural reform was only one means to his larger goal of social change in India. Increasingly frustrated that change was not coming to his people fast enough, he began to believe that social revolution was necessary, which could come only from actively critiquing the cultural structure of Hinduism, as opposed to attempting to change it from within. Similar to later conflict resolution scholars, the trailblazing Ambedkar seemed to ask:

> "Will we contribute to harmony through conflict resolution, but do so at the cost of accepting the continuation of some injustice? Or should we pursue justice for a particular group, knowing that this pursuit may increase conflict rather than resolve it?".

Gradually coming to believe the answer to these questions was a resounding commitment to pursue justice, Dr. Ambedkar began to focus more on societal rather than structural change. By organizing political parties, educating low-caste people, and agitating for change, Dr. Ambedkar pursued broad based change by re-conceiving the meaning of justice in society, not only its structures, but also its social realities.

Ambedkar's identity evolved throughout his life to one of social activist, and the evolution of his growth and thought can be seen clearly in his prolific writings. During

9.5.1. Transnational Advocacy

The latter part of his career, Ambedkar increasingly began to see religion as a valuable means to realize change through sociocultural critique. As an answer to his discontent with the structural violence imposed by the caste system, religion provided a vehicle to restructure social discourse and remake the foundational values of the social system—two important aims of legions of young dalit activists. It was also with a lifelong desire to understand religion that Ambedkar conditioned his analysis of caste. Thus, by 1935, Ambedkar had decided that Hinduism was the root cause of the 'untouchable' problem and had resolved to change his religion as a result. This, he believed, was the best solution for the Mahar 'untouchables' that he now led. Encouraging other 'untouchables' to join this cause, If you want to gain self-respect, change your religion.

1. If you want to create a cooperative society, change your religion.
2. If you want power, change your religion.
3. If you want equality, change your religion.
4. If you want independence, change your religion.
5. If you want to make the world in which you live happy, change your religion.

But Ambedkar saw religion as a social vehicle as much as others saw it for its soteriological commitments to explain life. For Ambedkar choice of religions was a means to social change in the present. By changing religious traditions he, as well as each individual, could change society. Thus, he waged a polemical and rhetorical war against

Hinduism. Declaring Hinduism the root cause of dalit suffering Ambedkar challenged the orthodox beliefs of Indian culture head on, and was either reviled or loved for this audacity. These acts created support, criticism and fierce debate. Gandhi, upon hearing Ambedkar speak, was once said to have remarked,

> "Religion is not like a horse or a cloak, which can be changed at will. It is a more integral part of one's self than one's own body".

Yet, while Gandhi criticized the idea of a choice in religion, Ambedkar studied all the world's faiths in order to find the one, which would best fit his 'untouchable' communities' needs. The act of choosing his religion was, for Ambedkar, the cement of a repositioned identity which was both personal and collective. As the answer to many of the needs of his 'untouchable' community, it was an act of social protest and self-help rolled into one. If his more outwardly social protests brought spite from Brahmins, his repositioned identity as a Buddhist would bring him deification among his own 'untouchable' community—something he himself was said to be uncomfortable with. On October 14th, 1956, on the 2500th anniversary of the Buddha's Nirvana, Ambedkar led a mass conversion of 'untouchable' Hindus to Buddhism. This was the culminating act of his now repositioned identity and in writing his own vows upon taking refuge Ambedkar ensured that he had created what some religious scholars have since called "neo-Buddhism". Through this repositioned identity he legitimated a new social perspective and Buddhism happened to be a means to the end of creating a new world view and social discourse. As the ultimate *upaya* (skillful means), Buddhism itself was to give new hope and confidence to thousands of dalits. However, as Ambedkar died only six months after his controversial conversion, it is not completely clear what form of institutionalization his Buddhism would have taken. He nonetheless ignited a revitalization of Buddhism on the Indian subcontinent, inspiring many a social activist, and living up to his promise to not die a Hindu.

The above leadership narrative provides a common grounding for both secular and religiously inclined dalit rights activists. Yet, depending on the specifics of the story that is emphasized, one can see divergences in social movement organization. Two thousand plus years of caste discrimination has left a void in dalits' collective cultural identity, which Ambedkar attempted to fill. At the same time, future activists will continue to argue as to which void Ambedkar's narrative fills––a clarion call for secular rights or a human need for ultimate meaning?

As Taylor, Bougie, and Caouette have argued, lack of a collective cultural identity is the most socially damaging and difficult to overcome aspect of a group's identity. It seems that Ambedkar's emphasis on the role of religion in society is an implicit acknowledgement of this argument and an attempt to reconstruct a new version of this collective cultural identi. The role of cultural collective identity is not merely for group members to have a shared cultural history. It is a stable reference group against which the individual engages positioning processes on an ongoing basis in order to develop a healthy personal identity.

Ambedkar was a pragmatist, studying under John Dewey at Columbia University, eager to develop a healthy collective cultural identity for those he considered his people—the downtrodden of society. Religious narrative structures were used as a vehicle to attempt to redeploy a self-aware collective cultural identity. But his use of both secular and religious narrative structure as a means is telling. Ambedkar had a modern understanding of religion, which emphasized that belief was not only about ends, but also a means of social interpretation. He saw the wisdom of approaching social conflict from a position, which privileges neither simply religious nor secular explanations.

Unfortunately, Ambedkar's Buddhist followers have failed to openly and fully explore the social and political resources of both the secular and religious narratives they have at their disposal. Despite the fact that Ambedkar dalit activists' discourse seems to strategically use one or the other these narrative structure—religious or secular—to support their cause and build support, an analysis of the social positions that each creates has been lacking. Secular attempts to focus on Ambedkar's injunction to "educate, organize, agitate" have failed to see the added value that creating a new religious identity can bring to oppressed groups' aspirations, not to mention the added value religious institutions bring to attempts at mass mobilization. Similarly, religiously inclined converts to Buddhism have failed to realize that their religious rhetoric can be exclusionary. Though preaching an inclusive and voluntary belief system, converted dalits often fail to realize their emphasis on religious-based explanation sidelines broadbased rights-based opportunities for mobilization. Further, each side of this spectrum of activism has seen the other side as problematic for maintaining their own base of support within the dalit community. In other words, followers of Ambedkar's religious narrative see secular rights talk as problematic since it relies too much on outside notions of liberty, democracy, fraternity, and agency while followers of Ambedkar's secular narrative see religious rhetoric as backward and pre-modern. In order to bridge these two narratives within the dalit rights movement their foundation, structures, and expressions have to be further explored and dissected, as both narratives provide important resources, which have the reach and impact all dalit activists desire.

9.5.2. Activist Narratives

The religious narratives of dalit assertion focus on leaving the Hindu-fold, which is seen as the root cause of the dalit social condition. In doing so, the individual reasserts him/her self and repositions their identity as coming from a religiously converted worldview, as opposed to coming from a certain caste which is seen as a partitioning of society that has been too long sanctified by the hierarchical system now called Hinduism. As such, the religious framework of conversion as a means to social justice fosters a sort of dualistic identity among dalits by empowering dalits not only as newly self-reliant through the experience of conversion, but also as one that has been victimized in an all too recent past.

As Sen reminds us "the adversity of exclusion can be made to go hand in hand with the gifts of inclusion", but this fact should not deter us from seeing that the complexity of identity highlights the difficulty inherent in mobilizing people around "identity justice". In particular, the combination of liberation and victimization is problematic for mobilizing widespread international support. Conversion as the living out of theology's connection to praxis does not have the same universal appeal as a narrative structure which equates dalit rights with human rights. Despite a new identity as Buddhist—or Sikh or Christian—the converted dalit cannot completely divorce him/her self from the psychological legacy and mobilizing power of past experiences of injustice. This dual identity has both advantages and disadvantages for newly converted dalits as they attempt to achieve social justice. Ever cognizant of which identity to engage when, Dalit Buddhist followers of Dr. Ambedkar must navigate an array of dalit aspirations by balancing secular pragmatism with the desire to create a religious community based on Buddhist values.

The secular frame of social justice, by comparison, presents a more unified conception of dalit identity as first and foremost human. While this more materialist perspective on social justice places Dr. B.R. Ambedkar near the end of a long line of important low-caste social thinkers, it also downplays any religious proclivities as subordinate to secular humanism. Simultaneously, this secular frame presents a belief that the problems of dalits can only be cured with the help of the unified action of outside intervention, advocacy, and political agitation, taking the onus for change off the individual and placing it on the collective. From this view, the root causes of a lack of social justice, as contextual and unchangeable by any one individual, are confused by any attempt to focus attention on any sacred ultimate. It is as if religious commitments appear as anathema to those strict adherents of the secular rights frame. It is therefore, assumed from this secular perspective that the root causes of a lack of social justice must be approached from a religiously neutral position of secular re-humanization of the oppressed.

As a consequence the concepts of reconciliation and healing are often overlooked by these secular humanists in a rush to realize the equitable society. In addition, the secular activists adherents' post-enlightenment aversion to religious discourse seems to run counter to the local cultural norms and history. Religion as a constituent part of the South Asian historical and cultural milieu is de-emphasized in favour of a perspective of global interdependence.

9.5.3. Secular Narrative

The secular narrative and social position of dalits as oppressed victim predominates among dalit social actors partly because of the slow, but steady, success of this narrative structure's ability to build transnational support and advocacy networks. Bob argues convincingly that "organizing" and "rhetorical" changes among dalit activists led to increased success of a dalit rights as human rights frame of contention in the late 1990s. But what has this increased reliance on a narrative structure of victimization cost the dalit rights cause? As Polletta explicitly argues:

> while "personal stories chip away at the public indifference" and "elicit sympathy on the part of the powerful," it is also evident that "narrative comes with risks as well as benefits".

While the secular narrative structure has allowed activists to conflate dalit rights with human rights, it has also disempowered many religiously inclined dalits through its aversion to religious language and frames. Further, since transnational advocacy often does not respond effectively to local needs, many disenfranchised dalits are turned off by a secular approach to organizing that sees personal belief systems as irrelevant to mobilization success. In short, there is a cultural divide between Western post-enlightenment rights thinking and traditional thoughts rooted in local contexts that value ritualistic and institutional expressions of culture.

This is not to say that the dialectic between secular versus religious narratives can be explained simply by arguing that a post-colonial clash of civilizations or cultures is either the genesis of the divergence, or the solution to unifying these different worldviews. Rather, noticing this cultural divide does signal the risky footing one stands on if advocating either a strongly secular narrative structure to combat caste or a strongly religious one. As Ganguly concisely puts it:

> "The modernizing desire to first reify caste as a relic of times past, and then to annihilate it, is truly alive and well".

This secular bias away from the traditional is neither the best nor most effective way to create social change. Instead, it often leads to sensational excitement outside of India, while faltering in the local context. The bias among secular dalit rights organizations, which disregard the conversion perspective so prevalent among Indian Ambedkarite Buddhists, serves as a case in point. During the recent, and first ever in the Unites States, Dalit Studies conference, an academic panel on the "Paradox of Religion" failed to raise this issue of religion's relation to traditional manners of thought, much less address the dalit rights movement from a perspective that privileges religious conversion as a crucial factor in the identity of low-caste groups. Beyond the academic community, however, a secular rights-based focus also creates a number of limitations and paradoxes for activists.

DANRIA, the organization portrayed in the second short vignette that began this piece provides a prime example of the dialectical problems that secular activists face in approaching their religiously-grounded counterparts. The DANRIA leaders desire to engage Ambedkar Buddhists, but within a frame of the strictly secular. At a DANRIA planning meeting in May 2007 Ambedkar Buddhist representatives from the TBMSG attempted to develop linkages with the work and resources of DANRIA members, and DANRIA members continually made it clear that their work was to support secular dalit education and empowerment. Partly due to how religion is understood in a postre formation West, such interactions revolve around a judgment that equates support for religious-based organizations as support for the propagation of that religion.

It is the old stigma of religious proselytization; no matter what good work an organization may be doing it must always be scrutinized upon the backdrop of its religious commitments and the assumed privileged priority of those commitments. In this dance of assumptions and commitments, Ambedkar Buddhists try to re-frame their contention to fit the desires of secular activists, while secular activists assume religious organizations' exclusive goals and underestimate their ability and opportunities to mobilize. Secular narrative structures of dalit contention present benefits to go along with the limitations, which they pose. They bring pragmatism to an often-disorganized array of activist decisions and goals. Through an unequivocal support for humanity and secular humanism these narrative structures provide grounding for international mobilization which bridges religious and cultural difference. The International Commission for Dalit Rights' (ICRD's) mission statement demonstrates this tendency to both symbolically and pragmatically bridge these aspects of difference within the dalit movement:

> "Eliminating rights-based human need and fulfilling freedom and democracy is necessary to achieve effective national and global

> development policies and programs, and to alleviate discrimination and extreme poverty."

Sufficiently secular such a statement allows for the possibility of religious responses to lack of freedom, discrimination and poverty. In place of a strong religious commitment, the secular narratives that such organizations profess, are often founded on an enduring faith in ideology. In interviewing Chadra Bhan Prasad, the only dalit writer for a major Indian weekly and a dalit rights activist who tends towards the secular end of the dalit movement's narrative structure, it was immediately evident that he was not even familiar with TBMSG, one of the major purveyors of the religious narrative of Ambedkar and dalit rights in Maharashtra. Though at first surprising, this observation seems more understandable given that Prasad, a native of Uttar Pradesh who is based in Delhi, is a strictly secular Ambedkarite who sees Ambedkar upon the backdrop of a Marxist analytical ideology of change. Now arguing that capitalism is the only thing that will save the dalit, Prasad draws an interesting comparison to the Ambedkar Buddhist activists of the TBMSG who see the solution for dalits as coming through the dharma (Buddhist teaching). This secular narrative structure implies that religious commitment can be sidelined in favour of an underlying, and more basic, commitment to humanism—an assumption, which runs deep in the dalit rights movement. One ICRD dalit activist even stated:

> "Despite the fact that many different dalit groups employ different strategies, our goal is the same."

The idea that dalit activists' deploy diverging strategies despite common goals posits not only that dalit activists have one collective identity, but also that this collective's social justice concerns are all the same. Such broad assumptions, however, limit the effectiveness of dalit organizations by disempowering the potential to reflect on real difference.

Mangesh's sincerity and commitment to social justice through building a peaceful community in which everyone has the ability to reach their potential, is not simply lipservice to a vague altruism—it is lived. His Buddhism is more humanistic than sectarian or scriptural; more philosophical than overtly spiritual. Yet, the inclusiveness of the

TBMSG family of organizations is not simply an expression of pragmatism. The members who carry the mantel of the TBMSG movement are, first and foremost, believers in dharmadatu (all living beings' possess the Buddha-nature), and this belief provides philosophical grounding for an egalitarian social prescription aimed at redefining karma in the Indian society as scientific and not supernatural. As an Indian, but humanist above all else, Mangesh is representative of a young generation of modern Indians who are both newly curious about the world outside of India and armed with the means to explore it. Eager to integrate Western political ideals, such as rights discourse, with Eastern conceptions of the examined life, these modern Ambedkar Buddhist activists see themselves as "the fruit of the movement." In other words, the beneficiaries of their parents' conversion and insistence on following both, their father and mother's example as well as Ambedkar's call to education.

Mangesh believes full-heartedly that focusing on inner change is a priori to attempt at social justice and peace-building. Therefore, teachings of the practice of Buddhism are crucial to the community that he aims to assist. This is a rational, not spiritual belief and the Buddha—from the Ambedkar Buddhist perspective—provided Jeremy Rinker Guiding principles to achieve inner change. Yet, this insistence on rationalism and pragmatism is where a certain bias threatens to stunt the full potential of the TBMSG movement. The symbolic use by movement members of ritual and stories can, and does, get lost when a rational problem-solving approach to the world is privileged. This is not to say that Mangesh's (or TBMSG's) commitment to social change is weak or even unjustified by experience, but rather that a combination of both inner and outer change can be problematic. Exclusively focusing on rational approaches to problems solving can limit TBMSG's ability to affect lasting change of the local level; while a focus on inner-change marginalizes strong believers in other religious and normative systems and simultaneously decelerates the pragmatic realization of TBMSG's wider social justice ideal. That sustainable social change can only come with inner-change may be a truism, but it also places limits on TBMSG appeal and deftness to claim secular support or argue for symbolic senses of meaning. This poses a number of pragmatic problems for the movement, illustrated by the reconstructed narratives above. For one the narrative represents a normative assumption that rationality always explains moral justifications. Mangesh's positioning of Ambedkar Buddhists as consistent believers in scientific processes—while exposing the rational assumptions involved in narrating justice—also acts as an attempt to justify a moral stance via delegitimizing the other. MacIntyre would label such a process as falling within "the When men and women identify what are in fact their partial and particular causes too easily and too completely with the cause of some universal principle, they usually behave worse than they would otherwise do. In reference to this particular narrative, it is not presumed here that it engenders bad behaviour among movement members, but rather that it misses an important realization of the potential for destructive behaviour created by the identity it enforces.

Positioning Ambedkar Buddhists as rational humanists and all Hindus as superstitious anti-rationalists only concerned with pleasing the gods, Mangesh is unconcerned with his own moral denigration of the other and the processes of positioning this type of delegitimization models to others. Mangesh's ascription of unscientific characteristics to others that are associated with under-education, or lack of intelligence, positions Ambedkar Buddhists as freed from the fear of superstition through education and Buddhist practice. This freedom is seen as liberating not only in the sense of being based on methodological reliability, but also in a sense creating an epistemological freedom. Furthermore, Mangesh's own relived experiences of this anti-rationalist thinking provide an emotional energy which legitimizes Mangesh's speech. Paying attention to the uses and processes of social positioning within Mangesh's attack on fundamentalist Hindus as superstitious provides a means to understand the TBMSG social justice narrative upon a spectrum of interconnected meanings.

Coming in the context of Mangesh's description of Ambedkar's sociological analysis of the caste system, this narrative transcription exhibits an opposition between rational and ideal conceptions which is immediately apparent in line one. Positioning Ambedkar as opposed to any ideal (future) system based on scripture, Mangesh develops the image of Ambedkar as an egalitarian freedom fighter. The ideological other becomes the antithesis to actualizing liberty, fraternity, and equality. More than simply pejoratively categorizing mythical or idealistic social constructions, privileging the rational as normatively more valuable and as implicitly congruent with equality has the effect of positioning the superstitious as irrelevant and undemocratic.

Anti-rationalists are thereby equated with anti-democracy's proponents, while simple-minded ideologues are de-legitimized. Mangesh is drawing attention to the unacknowledged role of Ambedkar in the independence movement; yet at the same time branding Gandhi (and his supporters) as advocates of future aspirations ungrounded in reality. Such utterance implies that if these future aspirations are ungrounded in reality, then they are bound to produce unjust social relations and structures. By contrast, the TBMSG ideal is grounded in a scientific methodology, which is attainable from a pragmatic view.

Unaware of the full spectrum of needs in society these Gandhians are utopian thinkers with little by way of concrete analysis and/or proscription for creating their utopia. In citing examples like Rama Raj and test-tube babies Mangesh is essentializing all Hindus as superstitious—equating Gandhi followers with Hindutva nationalists or extreme fundamentalists. Though subtle this positioning process is intentional. Creating a sense of us versus them such crude associations have the effect of reinforcing a TBMSG belief in social uplift through the personal empowerment of education and Buddhist practice. In the context of this speech act, Mangesh is positioning himself and his movement as the original purveyors of Indian democracy and scientific rationalism.

To an audience of foreigners, the Ambedkar Buddhist is positioned as providing a logical method for explaining the world and therefore proscribing change; while the Hindu is the cause of the stereotypical view of India as nonsensical and mystical, thus making them incapable of instituting equitable change. Nuanced and multifaceted, Mangesh's narrative holds multiple levels of meaning, aspects which are often overlooked by both movement members and outsiders. On the deepest level this transcribed narrative is an attempt to position Hindus as falling outside the Western scientific community—as pre-modern and mythical in their world view. But as Cassirer has argued "mythical and verbal thought are interwoven in everyway". Only through metaphor, Cassirer argues, is one able to see the "unity" and "difference" of the verbal and mythical worlds. In line 22, Mangesh uses an evolutionary metaphor, "the big fish ate the small fish," to explain the Hindu justification for caste. This metaphor is then discredited as "a very crude form of social Darwinism".

Since social Darwinism has a negative connotation, the use of this metaphor is aimed at further discrediting the non-rational unmethodological approach of the other. It provides another example of caste Hindus attempts to justify the inequities of the Indian social system as having a rational basis, but by de-legitimizing it as social Darwinism Mangesh reposition the view as unscientific (not founded on the scientific method) and a-historical. In cycling through orienting the listener, developing complicating actions, and evaluating the situation, Mangesh is positioning unscientific culture as detrimental to society and an Ambedkarite restructuring of society as the only prescription able to correct this flaw. This has the dual effect of legitimizing secular humanism and Buddhist practice. Therefore, only through seeing the failure of current social constructs can change become possible and an Ambedkar Buddhist analysis provides the best lens to identify this failure.

In this context, it is also insightful to return to this narrative paying close attention to pauses and other aspects of speech processes in Mangesh's talk. Such analysis not only tells us more about the speaker, but also about the "reflection-in-action" aspects of scripting the talk to his specific audience. Speaking in English is harder than speaking in his native Marathi dialogue and periods of pause are undoubtedly periods of actively choosing specific words and word phrases suitable for the context and the audience.

After debunking the ideal of the Rama Raj, Mangesh—having equated this idea with the father of Indian nationalism—seems to stumble in finding an adequate example to illustrate the superstitious nature of the caste based ideal, which underpins this idea. In setting up the Hindu nationalist ideal—exemplified by the well-known personage of Gandhi—Mangesh then challenges this ideal as scientifically ungrounded and superstitious and casts the work of TBMSG as attempting "to challenge those ideas, the 'so-called' religious ideas". Essentializing the idea as ideal, he struggles to find adequate language to express these ideas. Forced to explain through example and analogy, Mangesh invokes a traditional ideal, a modern discovery (test tube babies), and a scientific theory (Darwinism) as tools to expose the injustice of an irrational social stratification system.

9.5.4. Future of Dalit Activism

Inherent in the promise of these two worldviews is a sort of grounded pragmatism. The mobilization experience, social networks, and common purpose of religious activists, is something that secular dalit right activists can and must tap into. Conversely, the rights based language of secular dalit rights activists can provide social justice ends that are less ambiguous than the rigorous spiritual practice of individual self-attainment. The following reaction to the celebratory Buddhist conversions of October 2, 2006 by a keen observer of the Ambedkar movement underscores the issues at stake when this connection between secular and religious narrative structures goes unattended and unanalysed:

> 'What do they mean: All India will become Buddhist?... These people *need to* live in a world with Muslims and Hindus and all the rest. Dr. Ambedkar wanted to reconstruct the Buddhist tradition so it met the needs of his time. But can the Ambedkarites do the same with Ambedkar's own ideas? Nagaloka [TBMSG's University] should be teaching comparative religion… They need to say what they are for, and leave aside what they are against.'

The seeming incongruence of dalit identities as either victim or as self-aware Buddhist leaves conceptions of social justice, citizenship, and community vague and unbounded. Hence this lack of balance cries for a syncretism between these often competing narrative frames of social justice—an integrated religious/secular focus on individual rights that does not overlook the importance of individuals' spiritual world view in creating social justice. As dalit activists strive for a society open to pluralist ideals they must practice pluralism in the narrative constructions that they deploy. Such a mix of transnational and local strategies for contention redefines the transnational and highlights the need to critically analyse the role of such activists' narratives in the wider global society.

References

Arunkumar: "A case of missed opportunities". *Yojana*, March, vol, 51. 2007

Balley. L.R. *Public services why reservation*? Bheem Ptrika Publications, Jalandar. 1979.

Bharati, Ashok: "Globalization, communalism and Dalits." *Unquiet Worlds, Dalits voices and visions*, Heinrich Boll Foundation, Delhi. 2004.

Choudhari, S N. *Dalit and Tribal leadership in Panchayats*. Concept publishing company, New Delhi. 2004.

Das D, Satapathy M.K. "Education for sustainable development, University News", No 49, December. 2007.

James Massey "India 50 years of independence 1947-97", Dalit issues and concerns, B.R. publishing corporation, Delhi 1998.

10

Educational Development of Dalits

The ancient caste system of India, which has resulted in the social and economic oppression of the Dalits, continues to play a dominant role in India. The Dalits, also known as the scheduled caste or untouchables, have experienced consistent denial to access to education since the 1850s. This decade coincided with Britain's established control over India, which meant many of the improvements to Dalit education were coming from outside influences, rather than from the national government. Because of unchanging social norms and behaviour, incentives to pursue education were minimal for the Dalits who were still physically and emotionally harassed. Increasing efforts to eliminate caste discrimination combined with additional attempts to increase the accessibility and appeal for education have contributed to the slow progression of Dalit education.

The responsibility for social equalization fell fully upon the Indian government when it gained its independence from Britain in 1948. While some benefits of social programs and government policies designed to increase primary education rates can be noticed, the Dalit literate population still remains much lower than that of the rest of India. There remains still, hostility, oppression and flaws in social programs in Indian society that prevent an increase in education growth. Despite efforts to decrease caste discrimination and increase national social programs, the Dalits of India continue to experience low enrolment rates and a lack of access to primary education in comparison to the rest of India.

Deeply entrenched in Indian society is the complex social stratification of individuals known as the caste system. It is a division of society traditionally based on occupation and family lineage. In India, the caste system is divided into five separate classes. The highest class in Indian society is that of the priests and teachers, or Brahmins, followed by the warrior class, the Kshatriyas . Third ranked are those who fall in the farmer and merchant class, the Vaishyas, followed by the fourth ranked labourer class, the Shudras ("The Caste System in Hinduism"). The fifth group, which was seen as being so low as to not deserve being placed in a caste, were the Dalits. Often referred to in Indian culture as the untouchables, these were the people who have the harshest and most unjust restrictions imposed upon them.

The organization of the caste system and its entrenchment within Indian history has resulted in centuries of hostile interaction between classes. In rural areas, Dalits were excluded from temples, village wells and tea shops. In some areas of the country, the Dalits were not permitted to walk in daylight for their shadows were considered pollution. In addition to the cruel and humiliating circumstances the Dalits have been put in, their efforts to improve their situation have often been squashed by assault, rape and murder by upper castes threatened by the Dalits' search for equality. The cruel and unjust treatment imposed upon the Dalits has decreased in frequency as history has progressed, although it still continues in today's society.

After the introduction of the Scheduled Caste and Scheduled tribe Prevention of Atrocities Act of 1989, the practice of the caste system became illegal in India. Despite increased government intervention, the discrimination and mistreatments of individuals of lower castes still occur. Today, the Dalit population represents 16% of the country's population and still struggles to achieve social equality. There remains geographic division within Indian cities and villages which exemplify the role that the caste system plays in today's society. Many Dalits have attempted to avoid the caste system by converting from Hinduism to other religions, although this rarely allows these individuals to escape their social and economic hardships.

The Dalits have experienced a bit of progress in establishing an equal position in Indian society. Under the Poona Pact, a reserved number of seats in the national legislature were reserved for Dalit candidates only who would be elected based solely on the votes of their Dalit constituents. Their movement has also been encouraged by slow societal shifts towards a greater acceptance of Dalit equality and a greater role played by local and international nongovernmental organizations. The Dalit population continues to struggle for equality, though the progress of the past few decades shows hope for an improved level of equality within Indian society.

10.1. Importance of Education

Before beginning to examine methods of improving enrolment in primary education and literacy rates, it is important to know why education is such an important topic in development studies. The past century has been characterized by a global expansion of education. Alongside this growth in education has also been an increase in the gap between different social strata. Education can be a way to increase the incomes of impoverished people. Education helps to ensure that benefits of growth are experienced by all. Economic perspectives see education as a means to make individuals more productive in the workplace and at home. It can also be seen as a means of empowering socially and economically deprived groups into seeking political reform. By using any of these reasons as motivation to pursue educational development, governments are attempting to generate some form of social or economic equality for the population.

Some of those who study development see education as a means of improving social welfare through economic means. When compared to secondary and university level education, rates of return are highest for primary education, which means that the costs associated with providing basic education are much lower than the benefits received from learning to read and write. About 17.2% of economic growth in Africa and 11.1% in Asia between the 1950s & 1960s have been credited to increases in education. In addition to an increase in economic growth, primary education is also said to lead to greater income distribution. Providing primary education to 10% more people would equate to a decrease in the inequality index of 5%. The economic advantages of increasing enrolment rates for primary education emphasize the importance of increasing education accessibility for the dalits of India.

An alternative reason to study education is for its ability to empower the individual to strive for an improved quality of life. A big factor impacted by education is that human beings often base their life goals and everyday actions on what they perceive to be feasible. Education expands the knowledge of possibility to poor individuals, and is often a necessary factor in providing incentive to escape poverty and social oppression.

Development projects focused on increasing access to basic education, rather than ones that increase capital to improve current levels of education, ensure governments are able to know that the benefits of these programs are experienced by all, rather than a select few. As mentioned previously, the rates of return for primary education exceed those of secondary and university levelled education. It is therefore of greater value for governments to focus first on increasing access to primary education before moving onto to increase levels of education. By focusing development on a human-capabilities approach, governments and aid organizations are able to increase the number of people with the fundamental skills of reading writing and arithmetic. These skills allow individuals to communicate, argue, count, and problem solve so that they are able to become more aware and in control of their own lives. This allows them to better deal with problems in their everyday lives including taking a loan out from the bank, defending them in a court of law, escaping unhealthy personal relationships or avoiding jobs which would expose them to unsafe working conditions. Even the value of holding a basic education is in itself a frequently overlooked asset. Education has had an independent effect on life expectancy, increasing the age for educated individuals.

One of the most important Dalit political activists who saw the value of social equity within India was Bhimrao Ramji Ambedkar, who became the chief architect of India's constitution after years of social activism. Throughout the first half of the twentieth century, Ambedkar dedicated a significant portion of his life to improving the quality of life and social status of Dalit Indians. He established the People's Education Society in 1945 which believed that increasing access to education to the Dalits would increase their empowerment. He thought that a higher level of education would cause the Dalits to realize their position so that they would aspire to the highest of Hindu positions, and that they would consequently use political power and influence as the means to an end to their oppression. Ambedkar believed that the value of education was in the empowerment of Dalits to pursue political action for social reform through informed lobbying.

10.2. Educational Development of Dalit Communities

The 1991 census of India reported that Dalit communities were one of the least literate social groups in the country, with only 30% of Dalit children recognized to have basic reading and writing skills (Nambissan 1011). These high levels of illiteracy are a result of insufficient access to primary education. Reasons proposed for this low primary education rate amongst the Dalits have ranged from blaming family values to universal acceptance of social behaviour. In reality, it is a history of constant oppression and missing incentives that have been the reason why India's lowest caste has struggled to take advantage of public education programs.

For centuries, the Dalit population of India were forbidden from gaining access to education. Originally reserved for upper castes only, the denial of conventional education to Dalits was designed to prevent them from increasing their quality of life and to highlight caste divisions. Caught in a colonial struggle between European nations, Indian society had no motivation to determine who should manage social programs until the British established control over India. Then, during the 1850s, the British began the long process of increasing the accessibility of education to all citizens on India.

Signed in April of 1850, the Caste Disabilities Removal Act theoretically abolished all Indian laws which challenge the rights of those who are members of any caste or religion. To most, this was the first step towards social equalization within India. It was also the beginning of a series of attempts to increase accessibility to education for members of the dalit caste. To coincide with the signing of the act, the Indian education system became accessible to every member of society. However, one hundred and sixty years after the Dalits were granted permission to attend schools, the primary education rates of the Dalit population compared to those of upper castes remain as low ever.

There have been a number of suggestions proposed as to why the Dalits have yet to take advantage of open access to education. Some have suggested that Dalits possess an apathetic attitude towards education, and so the thought of attending school seems unappealing and inefficient compared to entering the workforce or doing nothing at all. Another suggestion of the cause for lower access to education to Dalits is that most families are caught in a vicious cycle of illiteracy and poverty. Therefore, not only do parents have no incentive to have their children attend school, but they also frequently lack the financial means to send them to the fee-based schooling system of India. The final and often most realistic reasons for why the Dalits have failed to take advantage of their access to education is a combination of a history of oppression and a lack of access to local, quality education systems.

A historical back-drop of mistreatment and class hierarchies has provided little incentive for the Dalits to pursue education. Throughout the 1800s and into the mid 1940s, conditions for Dalit children within the Indian education system were very poor. Due to discrimination from higher castes, the Dalits did not feel comfortable attending schools. Dalit children were required to sit outside the school, listening on the veranda while those in higher castes would be taught inside. Teachers, who refused to touch the Dalit children even with sticks, would throw bamboo canes as undeserved punishment while children of other castes were permitted to throw mud. The Dalit children, who knew retaliation would result only in increased abuse, would be essentially scared into not attending school. Of the limited number of Dalit children who were attending school, the majority were male; a trait which continues even today.

The 1948 independence of India prompted an increase in responsibility for the government to promote the economic and educational interests of the lower castes and to protect the Dalits from social injustices and exploitations. Over the next few decades, the Dalits would see very little action to support the claims and progress made during the fifties to help improve their access to primary education. The 1950s saw subtle improvements in the number of schools being built in India, as well as the amount of money being allocated towards primary education programs. The efforts being put forward by the government lost momentum over the next few decades however, as the rate of primary schools being constructed slipped from 5.8% in the 1960s, to 2.1% during the 1970s, and eventually down to only 1.3% through the 1980s. This was complemented by a shift in funding from primary school education to middle school education. This transition exemplified the government's shifted focus from increasing primary enrolment rates to increasing the quality of the education provided to those already provided with sufficient access to education.

Between 1983 and 2000, improvements in access to education for all of India have been made, although the difference between education rates for Dalits, especially females, and those in higher castes remained constant. In the seventeen year period, enrolment rates for Dalit boys grew from only 47.7% to a meagre 63.25%. When compared to those males in upper castes, enrolments jumped from an already relatively impressive 73.22% to 82.92%. Even poorer results were observed when looking at the female Dalit enrolment rate, which inched from 15.72% to 32.61%, when compared to their upper-caste counterparts whose enrolment climbed from 43.56% to 59.15%. The education gap can also be understood to translate through the entire schooling system, with the proportion of Dalit to non-Dalit success remaining at a constant low rate through primary, secondary, and post-secondary schooling. Although large improvements have been made to increase enrolment rates in India, statistics show that there has been little progress in decreasing the education gap between castes.

The lack of success in increasing primary enrolment rates for Dalits over the past one hundred and fifty years is evidence that very few projects have had any success in increasing social equality within the Indian Caste system. In the next section, the paper will look at some of the programs which have attempted to provide incentive for India's poorest to seek primary education.

10.3. Education-Based Development Programs

When discussing methods which seek to improve enrolment rates, it is important to analyze which circumstances prevent Dalit children from attending school. A family's financial situation plays a role in whether or not they are able to afford to send a child to school. This is a major contributor to low Dalit enrolment rates since Dalits have considerably lower incomes than those in upper castes, and therefore have a hard time paying for education. Distance also plays a key role in determining a child's ability to attend school. Because Dalit homes are often located outside of a village, it is more dangerous for Dalit children to travel to and from school by themselves without risking assault, sexual abuse or abduction. In addition, teachers at the schools are often members of upper castes who set low expectations for the Dalit children and rarely seek to provide them with a positive learning environment. There are many factors that act as obstacles for Dalits attempting to gain a primary education, and which many development methods have attempted to overcome.

India has attempted many different strategies to help increase the incentive to receive education for Dalit children. Earlier strategies focused on finding ways to give Dalit children an education without exposing them to the harshness of upper castes. As time progressed and the caste system began to weaken in India, there was a greater shift towards equalizing society so as to provide safer and more positive learning environments. Since gaining its independence, the Indian government has continued to make progress on improving the quality of life for India's lowest caste. Modern exposure to international thought has increased access to ideas and methods on how to increase education rates for the Dalits, providing for some of the best results in recent years . The remainder of this section will examine some of the strategies used over the past one hundred and fifty years, attempting to look at how effective they really were.

Following the creation of the Caste Disabilities Removal Act, the British government attempted to increase Dalit school attendance through methods which took into consideration the sensitivity of the caste society. Because the Dalit children were often harassed when they attended schools, the British chose to propose alternative teaching methods, rather than directly addressing the caste issue. One proposed alternative was the use of night schooling for Dalit children. In this manner, children would not need to worry about attending school with members of upper castes, but would still face dangers of travelling without daylight to and from school. Another proposed solution was the use of all-Dalit schools. This solution eliminated the dangers associated with night-time schooling, but also did not help to decrease hostility between the classes. These two methods combined resulted in a 4% primary enrolment rate for Dalit children by 1931, 81 years after education was first opened to all citizens on India. Of these Dalit children, 93% were attending all-Dalit schools. A problem occurred when there were insufficient all-Dalit schools at which children could pursue secondary education. Only 1% of all students at the time ever made it past primary education. It was because of this, that when the British handed over control of the country to India in 1948, the Indian government began thinking of new ways to increase access to education.

Often, governments try to bring in international assistance in dealing with a national crisis like severely low primary enrolment rates. Prescribed to the Indian government by the World Bank, the District Primary Education Program was designed to increase primary enrolment rates within India. The goal of the program is to reduce differences in enrolment between gender and social standing to 5%, and to decrease the dropout rate to 10%. The DPEP receives the majority of its funding from the World Bank. It calls for the formation of local committees that oversee the hiring and management of Para-teachers. These Para-teachers are trained teachers hired by the DPEP program to fill growing vacancies in primary schools. They are hired on a short term basis but are offered extended terms as an incentive to perform well. They are a low-cost alternative to permanent teaching staff and their performance is often higher due to increased incentives. Since the introduction of the DPEP, India has actually managed to see decreasing primary enrolment rates. It is possible that national campaigns to increase enrolment in primary education fail to have a direct intended impact. Instead, the management of such programs are so focused on a top down approach to education development that they are not able to discover and acknowledge specific issues.

A smaller scale, and more capital based approach to development and increasing primary enrolment rates is the allocation of additional textbooks to a community. In developing countries, textbooks are often the only basis for a curriculum in a subject. If a school is not able to purchase its own textbooks, then knowledge resources will be limited. By increasing the amount of textbooks, development projects are attempting to increase the ability of schools to take in more students and they hope that additional resources so that performance in school will increase. The biggest concern which arises out of providing textbooks is that it will not increase enrolment rates. New textbooks provide little incentive for Dalit children to attend classes as they do not alleviate any of the barriers currently blocking them from access education. Increasing access to text books has assisted in increasing the quality of education despite having little or no impact on enrolment rates.

Lastly, this paper will look to an outside approach to increasing school enrolment and attendance by observing how school-based drug treatments to common diseases attempt to provide incentive for enrolment. Many preventable diseases, including hookworm, roundworm and whipworm affect millions of children worldwide every year, preventing them for attending any sort of school or doing any physical labour. In this sense, the free drugs associated with this program not only provide incentive for children to come to school and learn, but they also serve a second purpose in that they keep students healthy, ensuring they are physically capable of returning to school. Children who attended schools which offered this program not only remained healthy, but felt more comfortable attending school on a regular basis. It has been proven that programs which offer medical incentives decreases absence rates by 25%. This method has also. proven to equally increase the amount of girls and boys who are being enticed to attend regular primary schooling.

In a case examined by Miguel and Kremer, female attendance increased by 10% in subject areas, nearly two times that of males. The medication has also proved more cost effective for the organizations administering the medication. This method been proven as a more effective way of increasing education levels compared to food incentives. On average the annual $5 cost of administering deworming medication to a child is six times cheaper than providing the same child with food incentives. School uniforms, which are often so expensive as to prevent young girls from attending school, have had relatively equivalent success in increasing enrolments rates in young females. Deworming, however, remains more effective because costs associated with deworming medication are twenty times less expensive than providing school uniforms. Using medication and deworming medicines as incentives, international organizations including the World Health Organization and The Forum of Young Leaders' campaign, Deworm the World, have developed a successful outside-the-box approach to increasing enrolment and attendance rates.

There have been many attempts over the past one hundred and fifty years to help increase the quality of life for the Dalits of India through development focused on enrolment in primary education. Education provides individuals with the means to increase their income and to engage in economic activities. In addition, it can help empower individuals to lobby for social change through political activism. The lack of incentives to pursue education for the Dalits of India can be traced back to a long history of mistreatment and oppression. Still occurring today, caste harassment makes teaching environments unstable for caste children, it places caste homes on the outskirts of towns so that children have greater distances to walk to school, and it economically suppresses the Dalits so that they are unable to pay for their children's education. Many suggestions, both traditional and modern, have arisen on how to go about resolving issues surrounding Dalit primary enrolment. Night classes and all-Dalit schools provided a safer learning environment for the Dalits, but did not address any issues of caste conflict. Twentieth century policies helped officially decrease some of the animosity and inequality between groups so that the Indian government could have a greater focus on national primary enrolment rates.

Larger operations, including the DPEP cooperative project with The World Bank failed to resolve some of the grass-root issues which deterred Dalits from attending school. Funding increasing supplies of textbooks to Indian schools do not address any of the core reasons as to why dalits are not attending school. Instead of increasing enrolment, additional textbooks only had an effect on increased performance levels. Providing free deworming medication at school has proven successful both in increasing the health of children which prevents absenteeism, and in increasing enrolment levels. Minor increases in incentives for Dalits to pursue primary education have been beneficial, but not sufficient in equalizing the enrolment gap between the Dalits and members of upper castes. In order for significant progress to be made in increasing the primary enrolment rates of Dalit children, development organizations must continue to explore varying levels of incentives and pursue national social equality in India.

10.4. Dalits and Human rights Education

There can be two ways in which the question of human rights can be dealt with in the context of education. One is to state that the education system should facilitate the spreading of an awareness of the importance of human rights and an awareness of the importance of human rights and an understanding of the premises on which they are based as well as the safeguards that are available for the protection of these rights. This can be broadly referred to as Human Rights Education (HRE), and NCERT and UGC documents broadly refer to this. The second is to critically look at the practice of human rights within the education system.

There can be no quarrel with the objective of wanting to strengthen the subject content in relation to human rights wherever it is appropriate in subject areas such as social studies, civics as on. In this context it is probably adequate to integrate the teaching of human rights within the content of what is already being taught rather than introduce an additional subject at the school stage and thereby increase and lad of an already burdened school curriculum. There is considerable potential within existing content areas to do so and it is a matter of how effectively and sensitively this is done.

Of crucial importance to the issue of human rights in relation to education is the practice of human rights within the education system itself. In other words we probably need to first understand the concrete practice of human rights within the education system (and the manner in which the experience of different social groups varies in this context), before we can speak in general of Human Rights Education, the content of this education, whom it should focus upon and so on.

Any one who looks at the schooling statistics in any government document will be struck by the extent to which certain social groups lack even the minimal access to opportunities where they can acquire basic skills of literacy and numeracy, i.e., to the primary stage of education. Today when we are discussing the role of education in human rights literacy it becomes important to see whether children from communities whose human rights continue to be trampled upon are able to receive education with dignity from schools. The school is of particular importance as these are institutions that occupy public space and profess aims of equity ensuring equality of educational opportunity with social justice.

There are two points of importance that need to be remembered in the context of the education of Dalit children. One is that these children come from communities that have been traditionally denied opportunities for education. The lack of exposure of generations to skills of literacy, numeracy, literature and other forms of knowledge considered desirable is likely to put them at a disadvantage where access to school knowledge is concerned. This would imply that such children are likely to require specific pedagogic supp9rt from the school system. This is integral to their right of education. The other point is that Dalit communities have been denied learning in the past specifically because of the caste to which they belong. There is hence need for special vigilance to see that they do no continue to face social discrimination with in the school.

The majority of Dalit Children in both rural and urban areas do not attend schools. Though education documents assure us that schools are available within walking distance to all children in rural areas, this does not even hold if one looks more closely at official statistics. Further, given the spatial segregation of Dalit communities in villages and among them specially those who traditionally remove night soil and the fact that schools are located within the upper caste areas, the question of how socially accessible schools are is also relevant.

Coming to the schools themselves what needs to be seen is the qualit6y of facilities that are available to Dalit children. One knows that the general quality of primary schools in rural areas is poor. What is the condition of schools that cater primarily to Dalit children by virtue of being located in their habitations? Passing references in a few studies and reports give rise to the suspicion that schools where Dalit children predominate may be in poorer conditions than the average rural schools-the minimal facilities may not be available to ensure that education is received in conditions that maintain the dignity of the individual child. Inadequate inputs in schooling, the poor quality of teaching, and as on-likely to be particularly detrimental to the education of children from these communities-are relatively less exposed to the kind of skills required in the classroom.

Equally important particularly for Dalit communities are the social processes within school and classroom that influence the learning environment provided for children. There is not much research evidence on what it means to be a Dalit child within the Indian classroom especially in the rural areas where the majority of Dalit school children are to be found. Scattered references in a number of studies do indicate that the eduation of Scheduled castes may still not be looked upon with favour by upper and dominant castes in many parts of India.

Within the school it appears that Dalit students continue to experience social discrimination and this can be seen both in the official curriculum, i.e., in the approved content of education and the hidden curriculum of schooling. Scheduled caste communities and the experience of untouchability rarely form part of school knowledge. Textbooks are silent about Dalit communities, even in states where these communities form a significant section of the population. Though untouchability and the maintenance of social distance from certain communities still persists in most parts of India such practices are rarely mentioned in school books or discussed in the classroom.

Dalits who look back upon their often painful experiences in school refer not to their invisibility in textbooks but to the distinct message of social inferiority that is conveyed to them by their teachers (the majority of teachers continue to come from middle and upper castes) and peers. Personal experiences of Dalits educated in the post independence period mention instances of Dalit children being asked to sit separately from their classmates, of being refused drinking water and served in broken teacups, made to dine separately and so on. A number of observers have noted the fact that teachers refuse to touch their slates or copies, or even resort to physical punishment for fear of pollution. Discouragement from teachers and indifference on their part to the academic needs to Dalit students is also reported in a few studies. Passing reference is also made to friendship patterns tending to remain within caste boundaries in schools.

The point being made here is that children belonging to communities that belong to the lowest of castes in the social hierarchy continues to be discriminated within the school and classroom. While blatant practices of untouchability may be less common than in the past, discrimination continues to exist in school practices particularly in the attitudes of teachers and school authorities as well as in peer behaviour. The inadequate academic support given to dalit children, the prevailing attitudes regarding these communities and the stereotypes that teachers and other members of the school community hold regarding their educability and their destiny impinges on the right of the child to education with dignity.

Given the scenario that exists regarding social groups that suffer from the backlash of caste in society at large, it is unlikely that human rights education in the abstract will bring about any significant change in the education environment provided for children belonging to these communities. What is required is that school practices in relation to discrimination, or the need for social justice within schools, is directly addressed. How this needs to be done is a matter of democratic debate and discussion but one can point to a few areas of intervention.

One is the official content of school education where a conscious effort should be made to critically analyze the manner in which school text books portray socially vulnerable communities both in terms of their visibility as well as the kind of roles they are seen to play if represented. In the context of what is called the hidden curriculum there is need for a multipronged strategy. One is the need to ensure that all children (specially in the rural areas) are entitled to equal access to facilities within educational institutions and the meting of stringent punishment where there is any form of discrimination.

The other is in the context of programmes to sensitize and create awareness among teacher educators, teachers and school administrators not only of human rights where these children are concerned but also of the deleterious consequences that social discrimination can have for the development of children and the realizing of their full potential. The special role that the schools can play in reinforcing academic inputs for these children need to be stressed. Similarly within the classroom the raising of awareness of human rights requires that such awareness is linked to critical consciousness of school practices including peer group behaviour in as sensitive a manner as possible. For both teachers and students this can be done more effectively through dialogue and discussion rather than in a didactic manner. Group projects can offer opportunities both for the recognition of underlying attitudes and critically looking at them.

Children especially those from Dalit and Minority communities are in an extremely vulnerable position in the classroom. Protection and support to children in order that they can exercise their rights will be important in efforts to create an educational environment conductive to learning with dignity. In this context the links that democratic and civil liberties organisations forge with schools will be critical.

REFERENCES

Bob, Clifford. ""Dalit Rights are Human Rights": Caste Discrimination, International Activism, and the "Changing Educational Inequalities in India in the Context of Affirmative Action." *Demography* 45.2 2008: 245-270.

Crossley, Michael, and Myra Murby. "Textbook Provision and the Quality of the School Curriculum in Developing Countries: Issues and Policy Options." *Comparative Education* 30.2 1994: 99-114.

Freeman, James M. *Untouchable: An Indian Life History*. illustrated edition. Stanford University Press, 1982.

Nambissan, Geetha B. "Equity in Education? Schooling of Dalit Children in India." *Economic and Political Weekly* 31.16/17 (1996): 1011-1024.

Psacharopoulos, George. "Education and Development: A Review." *The World Bank Research Observer* 3.1 (1988): 99-116.

Simon Wigley, and Arzu Akkoyunlu-Wigley. "Human Capabilities versus Human Capital: Guaging the Value of Education in Developing Countries." *Social Indicators Research* 78.2 (2006): 287-304.

11

Emancipation of Dalits in Nepal

In Nepal today, Dalits that constitute almost one fifth of the population have long been suffering from vicious practices of discrimination as if they are second-class citizens. Their living conditions continue to be deteriorated as they lack educational opportunities and thereby consequently don't have access to economic resources. Many of them have been hard hit by the mass poverty at the same time seriously being threatened by the pressure of their survival.Their hopes for their brighter future have been over trodden and several of them are dangerously caught in the prison of frustrations and hopelessness. They are forced to continue their traditional occupations and are poorly paid for their services.

In Nepal, 31% of the total population is living below the poverty line, and 70% of which comprises of Dalit community. Since Nepal has agriculture-based economy and most Dalits are landless, their economic condition is deteriorating. More than 50% of the families in Nepal do not get sufficient food for consumption because of poverty and lack of income source, and 90% of that percentage belongs to families of Dalit community. Even today majority of the families are landless. Looking at their accessibility to land, 80% Dalits are landless and only 1 % of the fertile land is accessible to them. Even though Dalits are Hindus, they can't practice their religion as other so-called upper class Hindus. Likewise, different forms of discrimination badly affect Dalits particularly because they have been marginalized in each and every sphere of their lives based on caste system under Hindu religion. They have lost their self-respect and dignity as a result of centuries of social discrimination, oppression, exploitation and suppression. This caste-based discrimination to Dalits, however, is found not only from high caste Hindus but also it is prevalent within Dalits groups, which has posed challenges for the Dalit upliftment and elimination of caste-based discrimination against them. Dalits also lack proper education, as they don't have proper family and economic environment. As per the 1991 census, the overall literacy of Dalit is 22.8%, while the average national literacy is 39.6%. And, the educational attainment of Dalits is lower. Consequently, there are very few Dalits in public service of Nepal.

11.1. Socioeconomic Status of Nepal

Nepal, one of the countries in South Asia, with the total population of 27 million (HDR-2006 estimate), is bordered by China to the north and India to the east, west and south. It is considered as one of the most diverse countries in the world based on religions, castes, cultures and languages. Nepali People speak more than 73 dialects with Nepali being the official language. The country is divided into 14 zones and 5 development regions. Nepal is of roughly trapezoidal shape, 800 kilometers long and 200 kilometers wide, with an area of 147,181 square kilometers. Nepal is commonly divided into three physiographic areas: the Mountain, Hill, and Tarai regions.

Nepal was under the dictatorial regime of Rana regime for 103 years and was ruled by autocratic Panchyat system for 30 years until the multiparty democracy was re-established in 1990 after people's movement. The multiparty system on its way experienced another revolution led by Communist Party of Nepal Maoist (CPN-M), which is in the mainstream politics after the recent people's movements against the direct ruling of the king. At the time of this research, Nepal has eight party interim government formed on the aspiration of the movement with the mandate of conducting constituent election in the country to draft a new constitution. The king is no more in power by laws, rather the prime minister is representing both as the head of the government and the head of the state.

Communist Party of Nepal-Maoist (CPN-M) is a political party in Nepal. This party started its movement as an underground party Feb.13 with their demand of general public welfare, constituent assembly, establishment of secular and republican state, and the abrogation of all unequal treaties between Nepal and India such as 1990 Peace and Friendship treaty and the 1996 Integrated Mahakali River treaty 1996. Now they are in the mainstream politics of Nepal after the comprehensive agreement with the government in 2006.

Many scholars and Dalits activists state that Dalit in Nepal are the poorest caste in the country that suffers from different kinds of discriminations under the Hindu caste system. Dr. Bhattachan notes that Dalits suffer from 205 different kinds of discrimination based on caste, occupation and descent in Nepal. Likewise, Dalit National Federation (DNF) and some Dalit organization's researches have pointed that there were some 3654 cases of atrocities against Dalits in 2005. The Dalits face caste-based discrimination from High caste Hindus and the indigenous nationalities against Dalits and intra-Dalit caste-based discrimination. This caste based discriminatory practices have driven them to economic, social, cultural and political backwardness that has badly affected in their life.

According to Sharma, 58.6% of Dalits believe that they are discriminated by the elite groups of the society, one forth of them believe that discriminations to them is 'Godmade.' Another 30% of the Dalits believe that both God and religion are responsible for it. While Bhattachan Krishna notes that it is the upper caste that is responsible for the caste-based discriminations in the society. Even if Daits have to undergo various kinds of discrimination, there are very rare cases filed against those discrimination and atrocities. On the one hand, Dalits fear of further discrimination and exclusion from the society, on the other they lack financial resources needed to file the case and go ahead with legal matters. Another reason why they just endure the discrimination against them is that most of them depend on the upper class families for their daily living. Mr. Chakraman Bishwakarma, a Dalit activist of Dalit Welfare Organization (DWO), blaming state being responsible for making Dalits attributes that very poor provision of law and poor provision of punishment against discrimination has been another problem in the elimination of these practices. He therefore insists on formulation of stronger provision of penalty and punishment for those who are guilty of discrimination and untouchability against Dalits.

The Nepalese Legal Code 1854 codified Nepalese society into a hierarchical system with the Bahuns at the top and the Dalits at the bottom. The allocation of rights and the application of law were adapted to give the higher castes privileges and to downgrade the rights of the lower groups. Thus, it makes the clear note that the state itself made this exploitative mechanism, which pushed Dalits behind other castes in the society.

Mr. Padam Singh Bishwakarma, the chairperson of National Dalit Commission claims that religion is the most responsible factor for classifying touchability and untouchability in Nepali society. He further makes the note that without eliminating untouchability, it is almost impossible to make any significant changes in the lives of Dalits in Nepal. Therefore he assumes that religious institutions should play the vital role in abolishing these fatal practices by redefining their religious roles and creating some awareness in the society. Supporting this view, Dr. Mohan Man Sainju insists that since the caste-based discrimination is associated with social structure, the solution of the problem also should be sought there.

Despite the fact that, the Article 11 the Constitution of Nepal 1990, (Sub-articles 1, 2, 3) ensures the fundamental rights of the citizen that all are legally equal, Dalits are still the victims of different forms of discrimination. It also states that no discrimination based on religion, caste, sex, creed, ethnicity or political inclination will be made by the state in the course of law enforcement. Likewise, the sub-article 4 has made the special provision focusing on Dalits that ensures that no one will be discriminated on the basis of caste and creed in public presence, and the use of public properties, and the discriminating behaviour against this provision is punishable by law.

The government of Nepal has recently declared the country in the Pratinidhi Sabha (House of Representative) being a secular country from its formal label 'Nepal: the only Hindu Kingdom'. Many experts assume that this announcement will help more or less in eliminating discriminatory practices under Hindu hierarchical system against Dalits. Except this historical decision to declare the country as a secular country, the government of Nepal has not paid much attention to changing the overall deplorable situation of Dalits in the country, as they suffer from not only social discriminatory practices but also from economic and political underdevelopment.

11.2. Status of Dalits in Nepal

The word 'Dalits' refers to the lowest caste group (the poor and the oppressed persons), the Shudra, in the Hindu caste hierarchy. The politically coined word is generally understood as the untouchables or 'Achoot'. According to the old legal code: 1854, Dalits are called 'pani nachalne choi chito halnu parne jat' (caste from whom water is not accepted and whose touch requires sprinkling of holy water). The term 'Dalits' seems to have been used by Dalit people for their convenience. Yet, defining Dalits remains a problem as different groups and authority have defined them in different ways that have inclusions as well as exclusions in their list. According to the Population Census of 1991, Among four castes (Kshatriya, Brahmin, Vaisya, and Shudra), Shudra is the fourth caste in the traditional four caste division in Nepali society under Hinduism. Most Dalits belong to this category. About 14% of the population belongs to the Dalit community; while some Dalits state that it is almost 20%.

In terms of demographic distributions, Dalits reside in all part of the country though the concentration varies. According to Dalit Vikash Samity (established in 1997), there are various cultural groups as Dalits, while Dalits and Dalit Ayog formed in 2002 identified 28 Dalit cultural groups in Nepal. As there is not clarity in the list of Dalits, so isn't the size of their population. It is estimated that their population ranges from 2 million to 4.5 million.

Due to the lack of sufficient and reliable records, it is a very difficult to trace the origin of caste system in Nepal, Some scholars have attempted to link it with the old legendary sources like Vedas, Mahabharata and Manusmriti. However, the accuracy of origination of caste system is found from the reign of King Jayasthiti Malla (1380-1394). The king is found to have classified the population of Kathmandu valley (present capital city of Nepal) into 64 castes, each with different occupational and functional categories. With the introduction of Old Legal Code of Nepal (Purano Mulki Ain) in 1854, there appeared more precise definition of groups of hierarchy along with the norms and behaviour of different castes in Nepal. According to the code, Nepali castes were broadly categorized into four categories:

1. Tagadhari
2. Matwali
3. Pani nachalne choi chito halnu napaparne, and
4. Pani nachalne choi chito halnu parne.

This last one is considered as the real Dalits or untouchables in Nepal Traditionally, the Dalits have been relegated to doing dirty, menial work, and have been considered unclean and therefore untouchable by the higher-caste groups who have reserved for themselves the right to do business, run the government, and educate themselves. Throughout the history, Dalits have been deprived culturally, politically, economically and socially, by long-standing traditions, and during some periods, by law (Civil Code 1854). In the past, the law New Civil Code 1963 and the Constitution of Nepal 1990 have abolished discriminatory legal provisions, and have enshrined in the constitutional statements ensuring equality for all citizens irrespective of caste, creed, or Vedas, Mahabharata and Manusmriti are the famous religious texts/ books on Hindu religion and its philosophy. It is believed that the texts were written 1500 B.C.

However, discrimination based on caste system is still a reality of life in Nepal. Despite their huge population (nearly 14%), they have no representation in the various aspects of their lives in the society. They were long marginalized, excluded and exploited by the rest of the society. Even today they are expected to earn their living by performing tasks that the rest of society considers to be unclean, and therefore performed only by Dalits.

According to Bhattachan et al, there are many kinds of practices of caste-based discrimination in Nepal. Throughout their history the Dalits have been denied access to education. Even today, their access to education and other resources for escaping poverty is limited, as evidenced by their low literacy rate. Given their limited income-earning opportunities and access to public resources, it is not surprising that approximately two thirds of Dalits currently live below the poverty line. They are living not only being economically deprived, but also being stripped of self-respect and dignity as well. The constitution declares the practicing of untouchability punishable by law, and includes a provision for uplifting Nepal's socially and economically backward communities. In 1997, the government established for the first time the Neglected, Oppressed and Dalit Upliftment Development Committee, the objective of which was to uplift the Dalit community. However, despite these provisions made in constitution and new legal code, discrimination in sociocultural behaviour is still prevalent in Nepalese society.

The ninth and tenth plan commits the government to uplift the social and economic status of Dalits through elimination of all forms of discrimination. But, the elites groups monopolize the programs, while the participation of Dalits remains low in those programs; as a result Dalits remain as they were. The government in recent years has plans for a national committee to be formed for Dalits, including a three-tiered structure (central, district, and village) for the empowerment of Dalits, which the government is doing in partnership with NGOs at the local level. Similarly, in recent years, several NGOs and non-profit organizations (NPOs) have been actively involved in addressing problems relating to Dalits. These include non-political and non-religious organizations such as the Dalit NGO Federation (DNF), the Academy for Public Upliftment (Jana Utthan Pratisthan), the Dalit Welfare Organization (Dalit Sewa Sangh), and the Feminist Dalit Organization (FEDO). However, the success and effectiveness of the programs undertaken by these various agencies have not succeeded to bring remarkable changes in their lives. Although the budget is allocated for the Dalit Upliftment Programs, it ultimately had been diverted to non-Dalits, as Dalits don't know how, what for and where the budget is used. Despites several measures undertaken by the government and CSOs for their capacity building of Dalits, different forms of discrimination, poverty, inequality, injustice and untouchability remain as the synonyms of Dalits in Nepal. They are still the victims of social, political economical and cultural discrimination and backwardness in the Nepali society.

11.2.1. Caste-based Discrimination

Caste based discrimination is one of the most widespread social problem throughout the human history and it is still prevalent even in this 21st century. According to UN Committee on the Elimination of Racial Discrimination (CERD) report 2004, there are 20 different nations where caste based discrimination is still practiced (Algeria,

Bangladesh, Burkina Faso, Ethiopia, Guinea Conakry, India, Japan, Kenya, Libya, Mali, Mauritania, Nepal, Niger, Nigeria, Pakistan, Rwanda, Senegal, Somalia, Sri Lanka, and Yemen). It is estimated that more than 260 million people around the world suffer from caste-based discrimination. The caste-based problem nowadays has been the concern of many scholars, social scientists, UN agencies and CSOs all across the world. It is a common realization that efforts made to fight the discrimination has not been adequate; the problem still remains the rampant in the world, and has proven to be resilient to the normal measures expected to combat it (International Consultation on Caste-based 46 Discrimination: Establishing Dalits Rights in the Contemporary World; the Role of Government, the United Nations and the Private Sector).

In Nepal, caste based discrimination has victimized about 4.5 million Dalits who are considered ritually impure and untouchables. They are placed at the bottom of the society and the state, and are left behind, not only sociopolitical realms, but also in the economic sphere. According to United Nations Development Program (UNDP) Human Development Report-2005 of Nepal, Dalits are far behind the other castes from the same vicinity on wide range of measures. They are marginalized by both caste and nationality from the mainstream development process. In recent years, especially after the establishment of democracy in Nepal in 1990 followed by Maoist movement, discourse on Dalits problem and other minority groups, is underway. The bilateral and multilateral organizations, World Bank, UNDP, United Nations Human Rights Council (UNHRC) and CSOs have also realized the vicious cycle of exclusion and discrimination against Dalits in Nepal; hence they have set their goal to fight it and thereby uplift Dalits at the centre of their development policies. It is noteworthy that the Nepal government has also formulated different policies for uplifting Dalits, but their implementation is lacking. Bhattanhan, a Scholar notes that there are 205 kind of existing practices of caste-based discrimination, which he has categorized in nine broad social categories such as:

1. Dalits are denied with the entry into the home, restaurants/hotels, temple etc.
2. Wearing of scared thread and worship conducted by Dalits are not acceptable

3. Dalits are denied the access to common resources like using water tap, pond, well,
4. They are denied to participate in public activities like government and religious activities,
5. Discriminatory practice of labour some times forced labour such as Bali Ghare, Haliya Partha or bonded labor or to carry the dead animals,
6. They are mistreated and misbehaved (practice of obeisance),
7. There are lots of atrocities against Dalits such as rapes to Dalit women,
8. Dalits are socially boycotted if either of them gets married with high caste Hindu, and
9. There is great tendency of attitudinal discrimination like if one high caste person sees Dalits early morning, it is inauspicious to him/her.

Besides this, Dalits themselves practice the caste-based discriminations among their sub castes. Hindu religion and its caste system is one of the biggest problems of different forms of discrimination against Dalits. The traditional hierarchy of Hinduism places Brahmins (priests and teachers) at the top, followed by Chetris (rulers and soldiers) and Vaisyas (merchants and traders). Dalits or untouchables (labourers, cobblers, and manual scavengers) are the lowest position within the caste hierarchy. One's caste is determined by one's birth into a particular social group. It is therefore not possible to change one's caste or move between caste categories. There is a big impact of these caste divisions in every sphere of human lives. The practices of caste system are also translated in to one's occupation, too. Dalits are typically restricted to tasks and occupations that are deemed too 'filthy' or 'polluting' for upper-caste communities. Unlike discrimination on the basis of ethnicity or race, it is difficult it distinguish one caste from another just looking at the people. Only based on surname, one is distinguished as a particular caste.

11.2.2. Untouchability and Segregation

One of the worst aspects of the caste system and discrimination against Dalits in Nepal is the practice of untouchability. Dalits are often segregated from high castes people only because they are Dalits and are not allowed to even touch high caste people and their belongings. They are often denied entry to high caste people owned shops and restaurants. While being considered as untouchables, they are asked to dine in separate dishes and do dishes after they dine. Likewise, they can't enter into upper-cast temples even though they belong to same Hindu religion. The Nepalese Constitution 1990 in its article has abolished any form of discrimination on the basis of caste, ethnicity and religion; however the discrimination against Dalits are the same. Similarly, there is strict prohibition on inter-caste marriage, particularly between Dalits and non-Dalits, which many Dalits believe, also contributes to preserve caste hierarchies in the Nepali Society. If one member from Dalits gets married with a non-Dalit, the whole society goes against the step and enforces punishments to them particularly the Dalit. Even the so-called educated people and politicians have belief in this system of untouchablility in Nepal.

11.2.3. Education

Throughout their history Dalits have been either denied or have poor access to education. Even today, their access to education and other resources for escaping poverty is very limited. They are generally deprived of acquiring education in schools especially because of their economical backwardness. They therefore have to compromise on achieving education in schools. In rural areas, Dalits are often treated badly by their other upper caste students for being untouchable, and sometimes even by their teachers. Although there are a small number of Dalit teachers in the country, they are also the victims of social segregation that often come from their non-Dalit colleagues.

While the average literacy rate for Nepal's general population is estimated to be approximately 50%, only 24.2% of all Dalits were literate as of 2001. According to a 1997 report, there were only two Dalit medical doctors and fifteen Dalit engineers in Nepal. As of 2002, not a single Dalit held a leadership position in the Royal Nepal Academy of Science and Technology, an independent institution charged with promoting science and technology in the country. Nor do any Dalits hold academic or administrative posts. Consequently, this pathetic situation of Dalit education has contributed to more marginalization of Dalits in the Nepalese society. It needs to be noted that the poor access to education is generally caused by many factors like poor economic power, discrimination and so on.

11.2.4. Political Representation

The common realization of most intellectuals regarding unchanging plight of Dalits in Nepal is their lack of representation in Nepal's political landscape. Despite their one-fifth of the total population, Dalits are extremely underrepresented in government. Since 1958, only fourteen Dalits in Nepal have become members of parliament (upper house) so far, all of them are men. Till the date, only one Dalit has been elected to the House of Representatives. Dalits are also absent from Nepal's administrative and judicial system. A survey revealed that 98% of all civil service posts were held by upper-caste Brahmins and Chhetris. Not much has changed well over a century later. A 1991 survey of Jana Utthan Parishad Nepal notes that 93% of these posts are still held by upper-caste Brahmins and Chhetris. Over a 137-year period, there was only a 5% increase in Nepal's political diversity. According to a 2001 report of NGO Federation Nepal, while Brahmins constitute only 16% of the population, they represent 57% of parliament and 89% of the judiciary.

This pattern of exclusion is repeated at the local government level, where Dalits are severely underrepresented in the administrative system: of the more than 3,000 Village Development Committee chairmen, only a handful is Dalits. The control of local and national leadership posts by upper-caste members has resulted in wholesale disregard for Dalit issues. In the recent months, political parties and intellectuals have been working to make the political system of country more inclusive, which is believed to guarantee the representation of marginalized and disadvantaged groups like Dalits in politics. However, the election of constituent assembly will engineer the framework of the system. It means the concerned actors have come to realize the need of mainstreaming the disadvantaged groups for the development of the country.

11.2.5. Economic Marginalisation

The Dalits have historically engaged in non-farming occupations, with farm income representing only a small portion of their total income. They therefore have had little to fall back on when demand for their services diminish. A survey shows that only 21% of Dalits produce food grains sufficient for 90 days, 19.5% for 4–6 months, and 15.4% sufficient for one year. Only 5.1% of the Dalit population produces food grains in excess of what is required for family consumption. Given their limited income-earning opportunities and access to public resources, it is extremely pathetic that approximately two thirds of Dalits currently live below the poverty line.

Though they comprise over 20% of Nepal's population, Dalits possess only 1% of the nation's wealth, and collectively Dalits represent 80% of the 'ultra poor' in Nepal that forces them to be the victims of bonded labour, slavery, trafficking, and other forms of extreme exploitation. When Dalits are desperate to feed themselves and their children, they have to undergo much other exploitation (JANA Utthan Pratisthan). Collectively, Dalits represent 80% of the 'ultra poor' in Nepal, dramatically increasing their vulnerability to bonded labour, slavery, trafficking, and other forms of extreme exploitation. The practice of untouchability deprives Dalits into work considering them being 'impure' such as manual scavenging or leatherwork. Because of this, they are even excluded from entry into temples, restaurants, hostels, and milk cooperatives because they are considered impure from handling animal remains. Although they are made to do the so-called impure jobs, they are poorly paid for this work, sometimes not paid as well. Because of being Dalits, they have to face lots of discriminatory practices in their economic activities. According to the World Bank-Living Standards Survey 2003/04, more than 50% of the families in Nepal do not get sufficient food for consumption because of poverty and lack of income source. 90% of that percentage belongs to families of Dalit community. Even till today most of the Dalits families are landless. About 15% of hill Dalits and 44% of Terai Dalits (Dalits living in plain area of Nepal) are landless. The landlessness of Dalits also pressurizes them to depend on the wage labour for making bread for their families. Similarly, Only 1% of the fertile land is accessible to them. Statistically, more than 54% of the Dalit population is involved in agricultural activities, another 15.7% in service, an additional 14.2% in non-farm wage earning and the remaining 6.1% in casual farm labour and other low-wage activities.

According to a report of Human Rights Watch, Dalits constitute a great number of Nepal's agricultural labourers, but very few of them posses their land; Dalits own just 1% of Nepal's arable land, while 3% percent of Dalits own more than a hectare of land. As a result, they are compelled to be landless bonded labourers. In the mid-western and far western hills, bonded agricultural labourers, or Haliyas are mainly from untouchable castes. When they need some money for making their lives, they borrow some loans from upper classes wealthy people, but they are charged with higher interest rate. To pay this loan back it takes years for them. And, when failed to pay it, they and their children are supposed to work for those lenders as bonded labours.

The land reform Act of 1964 was introduced to manage the landholdings, but powerful landlords ultimately made Dalits community to work as agricultural labours for claiming their rights on land. Consequently, a large number of Dalits became landless. This pattern of land ownership that expulsed Dalits from land, limited the economic activities of Dalits resulting to excessive poverty. In the beginning the compulsory precondition of citizenship to posses the land is also believed to be one of the main obstacles for less land ownership of Dalits, because this condition restricted Dalits to buy new lands. While on the other hand, non-Dalits bought big size of land in different parts of the country. Similarly, in the domain of employment opportunities in both government and private institutions, Dalits experience discriminations in recruitment, workplace and salary. According to the ILO report in Nepal, approximately 48% of the surveyed Dalits claimed that they would be denied employment due to their caste status even if job openings were available, and 21% of the respondents reported that they had been refused jobs based on their caste status. In addition, approximately 71% of individuals reported that they are paid lower wages and salaries in both the private and informal sectors. At the time of the study, Dalits received an average of NRs. 96 (about US $1.23) for a day's work. The mean wage for a female worker was approximately NRs. 78 (about US $1) while the mean wage for a male worker was approximately NRs. 99.42. By contrast, the mean market wage rate for the same kind of job in the general population was around NRs. 105, with women receiving an average of NRs. 88 and men receiving NRs. 111.43. But, Dalits in rural areas are paid less compared to those of urban areas. These kinds of discrimination force many of the Dalits to go abroad for employment especially in India; some are able to send money to their families back home, but many Dalits return with even more debt, handicapped by the high interest loans obtained from non-Dalit lenders in the community to fund the overhead expenses of foreign employment. Likewise, Dalit women experience aggravated caste discrimination, enslavement and sexual exploitation.

11.2.6. Awareness of Existing Laws

There are many existing national and international human rights laws as well as international laws. But, most of the Dalits have no ideas about the laws and their various rights. The Constitution of the Kingdom of Nepal, New Legal Code of Nepal, the new Legal Code of 1963, the Eight-point Social and Economical Programs declared by the then Prime Minister Sher Bahadur Deuba and many other laws have prohibited discriminations. Similarly, the international laws like Universal Declaration of Human Rights, International Convention on the Elimination of all Forms of Racial Discrimination, Civil and Political Rights, Economic Social and Cultural Rights and many more also defend the Dalits Rights and prohibition of any forms of discrimination based on caste, region, race and ethnicity. Although these laws and rights treat Dalits equal with other communities, the lack of awareness in Dalits regarding these laws is another problem in making them enjoy such rights. Poor access of Dalits to education and their limited time has also deprived them from knowing various rights for them. Sharma et al. makes the note among the total respondents on his research, only 5.6% Dalits were aware of the New Legal Code (1963) and 9.5% Dalits were aware of rights to equality. According to Bhattachan et al, a few Dalits respondents like political leaders, NGO activists. Intellectuals and some educated Dalits were aware a little about national laws; while non-Dalits were rather more aware of it. Due to the lack of proper education, Dalits have failed even to know their rights. This means there is the urgent need of campaign to aware public regarding these laws, which prohibits any forms of discrimination. Besides, since there is a very few research carried about the level of public awareness of these laws and rights, very deep researches are necessary.

11.3. Issues of Dalits

One of the burning problems of Dalit is a lack of access to adequate water supplies and food. It is true that water scarcity affects many parts of the country; but Dalit communities suffer disproportionately because they are denied access to communal water sources for fear that they will pollute the water supply. Dalit women and girls are often forced to fetch water from springs located hours away (Jana Utthan Pratisthan, Nepal). If Dalits attempt to access non-Dalit natural springs, wells, and hand-pumps, they have to undergo many hardships; sometimes even they are beaten to death. In some schools of Nepal there are separate wells for Dalit and non-Dalit children.

Dalit students found drinking from non-Dalit water taps may face disciplinary sanctions, including corporal punishment, by their teachers; particularly in rural areas. Some people believe that even development projects may also reinforce caste hierarchies. Drinking water projects often serve non-Dalit communities before reaching the Dalit community and development plans to increase water access for Dalits are rarely realized. In part, this is due to the lack of Dalit representation in Village Development Committees. In 2005 the Supreme Court of Nepal found that the state was promoting the distribution of separate taps for Dalits and non-Dalits and ordered the defendants not to discriminate in distribution of drinking water and to increase awareness against caste discrimination Ratna Bahadur Bagchand, Important Nondiscrimination Case Won, International Nepal Similarly, in Nepal food deficiency is reported highest in Dalits. Dalits are disproportionately malnourished as compared to the rest of the population. As a consequence of being denied water and land, they are unable to produce sufficient or nutritious food.

Even though some of Dalits have adequate purchasing power, they often undergo discriminatory practices in the markets, shops and cooperatives. In the domain of health, Dalits lack proper access to healthcare. They have very poor health status. In addition to occupational hazards, sexual violence against Dalit women is another painful reality. Consequently, many of them suffer from sexually transmitted diseases. Due to the lack of nutrition and healthcare, Dalits have lower life expectancy of 50.8 years while national life expectancy is 57 years. Similarly, children and infant mortality rate is also respectively 171.2 and 116.5 (per 1000 live births), while the national average of children mortality was 79. They are also the groups with lowest recipients of immunizations. According to Action Aid Nepal, 90% of the Dalit women in its project area had a disease called uterus prolapse. They regularly suffer from various diseases, most commonly from diarrhea and pneumonia. The bitterest reality is that they even don't have access to good health care facilities, as they can't afford for the treatment. As a result, they die of various diseases.

If looked in to the possession of house Dalits, the true picture of their overall reality is well reflected. The interesting thing is that most people in the rural part of Nepal have houses though the quality defers one to another. Most Dalits also possess houses. But the houses of Dalits are of lower quality as compared to that of other groups. Among the low housing status communities, 50% Dalits belong to it. According to the research, 35.7% of Dalits have thatched roof houses, 24.8% of them have brick/stone wall and thatched roof houses, 22.0% of them have brick/stone wall and tin/slate roof houses and only 1.8% of them have concrete houses Children between 5 to 14 years of old working are called child labour.

In Nepal children of this age groups work in various conditions to make their living and to support their family. One research shows that most Dalit children contribute 60% of the adult work to the family's economy. Although the Children's Act 1991 prohibits the employment of any child in any enterprise, around 18% of the Dalit children were involved in their traditional occupations such as sweeping and human waste disposal; leatherwork and midwifery; earthwork and soil-digging; and laundry washing. The very report notes that around 8% of all Dalit children are victims of slavery or slavery-like practices. Children also work to pay back their parents' debts or helped their parents in cultivating the land of 'upper caste' households in return for food or shelter, or both. Dalit children get involved in hazardous and arduous jobs such as picking and collecting rags, metal scraps and glasses; disposing of carcasses; cremating dead bodies; disposing of human waste; pottering; working in coalmines, etc.

This situation clearly tells the story that they are denied with the education and their rights; and rather they have to exploit their labour for their daily living. The poverty causes the child labour pushing them to darker future, ultimately making them poorer in the society. This predicament of Dalit children therefore goes in the cyclic order from one generation to another.

Taking all the above-mentioned situations of Dalits in to serious consideration, it can therefore easily be asserted that they are the victims of all kinds of discrimination in the Nepalese societies. Even though the government and civil society organizations have vividly seen their problems, no any specific and genuine strategy has been undertaken to uplift their existing conditions. On the other hand, deeply rooted discrimination towards Dalits in sociopolitical and economic spectrum of their life, rampant corruption, poor mechanism, and poor performance of CSOs in empowering Dalits lead to the conclusion that; if there are no sound cooperation and commitments from various actors in Nepali society towards empowering Dalits, the life of Dalits will remain almost same for long. Consequently, it will nourish the factors for disestablishing the country in many ways.

11.4. Role of Civil Society Organisations

Civil society in one sense is the complex networks of autonomous institutions sustained by a civil code of conduct that is distinct from; yet maintain effective ties with the State. Civil society organizations known as 'Nagarik Samaj' in Nepal are of different kinds as they have diverse constituencies, sizes, strategies, structure, ideologies, specialization, sources of funding, agenda and power. The organizations are religious, secular or affiliated with political and social groups, and mostly funded by donor agencies, foundations, private citizens and governments and business sector.

There were 131 INGOs and 19200 NGOs and other civil society groups registered with the Social Welfare Council (SWC) and other ministries until February 2006. Besides these, there are many nonregistered civil groups and organizations in the country working for community solidarity. Tracing the line of Nepali civil society to 2000 B.C, historians note that people oriented themselves towards living together and working collectively for peace, public welfare and harmony in the society, and that gave the birth of CSOs. However, the extensive growth of CSOs in Nepal is considered to have sprung after the country turned into democratic country in 1990. As mentioned above, modern civil societies are different in their originations, their aims and goals and their institutional constituencies are also different. The constitution of Nepal 1990 and the interim constitution 2006 providing rights to citizens to set their social, economical as well as political agenda has created more space for the role of CSOs in Nepali society. It is praiseworthy that the CSOs in the country, in many extents, have nourished the potentials for changing the dominant cultural values, political culture and structure, and male domination. Observing the potentials of CSOs, the government of Nepal in 1990 has considered CSOs in Nepal as the partners for development.

Many of the organizations registered with Social Welfare Council (SWC) are working on environment sector, social development, empowerment and upliftment, transparency, economic projects, human trafficking and alike. Given the dynamics of Nepali society and the failures of the government to meet all its needs, the role of CSOs in garnering a healthy society that promotes debate and opposition is a vital and an ongoing dialectic process in the country. In Nepal, after the proven inefficiency of the successive governments to deliver effective services, donors are using I/NGOs as their partner for assistance rather than channelling the whole fund to the government's single funnel. Similarly, the increasing emphasis on human rights, democratization and privatization has led to the growth of the voluntary non-governmental sector. This social phenomenon is being actively promoted by external organizations for economic, social and political transformation.

Human rights politics has remained an integral part of such transitional endeavours. It is a pity that some of the CSOs are politicized because of regular intervention from political parties. It is visible that some of them are all the clutches of either political parties or the donors. The same privileged caste and groups who have long dominated political and administrative spheres of the country run most NGOs and civil society's platforms. Lack of internal democracy, transparency and accountability are common to most NGOs of Nepal. Most of them are attached to private rather than public interest. As they are highly dependent on foreign donors only a few English speaking elites are benefited by NGOs business. Most of the people in Nepal have got very negative attitudes towards most of the civil society organizations because of their dependent and colonized mind that doesn't contribute to the overall development of the country. It is also criticized that civil society organizations have not achieved much success in monitoring and checking anti democratic policies and actions of different social actors. Many experts have noted that most of the organizations lack transparency, accountability and independency in their activities although these attributes are taken as fundamentals of democracy. Although civil society is considered as a value in itself, Nepali civil society organizations have played their complementary role to create a liberal democratic state. It is a fact that making reforms within civil society organizations in terms of transparency, accountability and independency can play another critical role in social transformation. It is an undeniable fact that the organizations have established them as an integral part of Nepali society with their various contributions. However, it needs to be realized that they also need lots of changes in their organizations so as to win over people's trust in the days to follow. Among the civil society organizations in Nepal, there are quite good numbers of civil society organizations which are supporting Dalits through various ways.

11.4.1. Role of Dalit–based NGOs

It is noteworthy that there is the Dalit civil society, which is composed of national and local level Dalit non-governmental organizations (DNGOs). There are Dalit organizations working on the grassroots level as well as national level. It has been estimated that there are about 600 Dalit organizations in Nepal and most of the organizations are found to be working in district level and village level. The society constitute district registered Dalit NGOs, district chapters of national DNGOs, and Dalit community based organizations (CBOs). There are some national level Dalit organizations, which are considered as leading ones: they are Dalit Welfare Organization (DWO), Feminist Dalit Organization (FEDO), Janauthan Pratisthan (JUP), Jagaran Media Centre (JMC), and Nepal National Dalit Social Welfare Organization (NNDSWO). The programs of these organizations have a relatively wide coverage, and most of them have either district chapters or affiliated local DNGOs. These national organizations are mostly involved in advocating the Dalit cause. The DWO mostly focuses on removing the barriers that obstruct Dalit participation, the

FEDO on gender issues; the JUP on Dalit related international instruments, JMC on Dalits and the media, and NNDSWO on Dalits' education. A national federation of Dalit NGOs, the Dalit NGO Federation (DNF) which was formed in 1998 is the only federation representing Nepal's Dalit NGOs, and all of the above five national DNGOs are members. As stated above, there are many NGOs working for Dalits in Nepal involved in education, advocacy, sanitation, health, rights and empowerment, incoming generating and awareness creating activities, have carried out some campaigns against utouchability, programs of sharing food and water with non-Dalits and fighting for their rights to enter into public temples, which have been somehow effective to making people aware. In some points, it can be noticed that their local level programs to support Dalits in their economic activities providing them with some loan without interest has helped Dalits generate more capital. Although their programs are often made limited by insufficient resources, they have also tried to create some social awareness and cultural changing programs through mass media that has generally been effective in attaining their goals. It is noteworthy that within 13 years of time, these organizations have been mobilizing their resources in the benefit of Dalit community. The introduction of reservation system in public services, political representation and establishment of Dalit Bikash Samity, which is headed by the Minister of State, Local Development, can be taken as results of the influence of these organizations, which have made remarkable contribution in Dalits communities.

11.4.2. Contribution of INGOs

Local and national Dalit NGOs have been implementing INGO supported development programs for Dalit communities. These have involved advocacy, income generation, education and awareness raising activities. The INGOs like Save the Children US, Action Aid/ Nepal, Lutheran World Federation (LWF), CARE, Asia Foundation, Helvetas, USC Canada and Save the Children Norway have been supporting these programs. The DANIDA is the only bilateral donor agency to run an integrated Dalit support program and to provide support to Nepal's Dalit organizations. It has supported Dalit Nepal Federation (DNF), Dalit Welfare Organization (DWO) and Feminist

Dalit Organization FEDO to run advocacy, awareness raising, education, and income generating activities. The DWO is running its DANIDA supported program in various places in Nepal. The INGOs have been helping Dalits in several ways: carrying out grassroots activities with the involvement of their own local field offices, helping local NGOs in their operation of the programs and getting involved in their own programs with the cooperation of other local NGOs.

The INGOs and some bilateral agencies like DANIDA, CARE Nepal, Save the Children US, Action Aid Nepal, HUGOU, OXFAM, HELVATES, Lutheran World Service (LWS), Royal Danish Embassy, World Council of Churches Geneva (WCC), The International Center for Integrated Mountain Development (ICIMOD), PACT Nepal and UN agencies have supported Dalits through their various programs in the country. The programs conducted by the INGOs have been effective in the domain of health care and reproductive services. Similarly, their scholarship schemes for Dalit children in the school and counselling on HIV/AIDS have been positive. But, their programs on empowerment, literacy, sanitation and advocacy in total have been catalytic in bringing changes to Dalit communities in Nepal. Dalit NGOs have lacked the institutional capacity and resources to run programs that make a large impact on improving Dalit's standard of living. To strengthen the capacity, INGOs not only provide Dalit organizations with financial assistance, they also give trainings to develop skills.

The organizations have introduced some new strategies to demolish the traditional system in various ways like using separate taps or wells for Dalits and non-Dalits.They have also contributed in ensuring Dalits representation in various committees and organizations in district level. With the support from these INGOs, Dalits have been able to develop their connections with other Dalits, political leaders and civil society actors. As a result, Dalits have secured certain percentage of reservation in local as well as national level in government bodies and public services. Their activeness in claiming their rights in recent years through different forms of movement has also pushed their voice in the center of national policy making level; as a result, the concerned authorities realize the need of some pro-active policies in empowering Dalits. Considering all these achievements, it can be articulated that NGOs have played the tremendous role. Having realized the role played by I/NGOs for uplifting Dalits in Nepal, it is worthy to note that their colonized minds depicts the uncertainty of their future and effectiveness on their programs. Similarly, they are often blamed to have turned corrupted which spreads the bad impression on public. Most organizations that receive funds from donors are concentrated in the cities mainly in the capital where they formulate their projects to attract financial assistances from the donors. This culture has also obstructed to find the real problems of Dalits in the country creating a kind of mismatch of programs and the problems. When the fountain of their resources stops, their programs are often paralysed and ultimately fail. Similarly, many people believe that most of the programs of these organizations are concentrated in more convenient places; while they have to concentrate the programs to some other areas where the situation of Dalits is grave. Making very good relation and coordinating their programs with local level organizations can better address the problems, which is lacking in these NGOs. It is necessary for these organizations to make some independent sources that can ensure the better performance in their activities.

Not making themselves rhetoric by distributing lip services, they should create such environment where Dalits can be motivated to find the meaning of being human beings

11.5. Implication of NGO Activites

Acknowledging the various contexts of Dalits in Nepal, it is a pity that the problem of Dalits seems like a complex problem to be tackled effectively. Taking in account the condition of Dalits in Nepal, it can be safely articulated that Dalit empowerment needs some interventions in the socioeconomics, political aspects of Dalits. And the better access of Dalit people to economic opportunities, education and political participation without any discrimination can be the best way forward to Dalit empowerment. Although Dalits in Nepal lack proper education and therefore don't have enough Dalit people working for Dalits community, good number of educated people are found in the organizations working for Dalit issues. However, it is the undeniable fact that most organizations fall sort of capable, competent, qualified and dedicated staffs. Although they loud their voice claiming themselves being really dedicated to bettering the status of Dalits, some of the organization along with its staff don't have good understanding the problem of Dalits that they are dealing with. It is quite noteworthy that the country itself has been victimized by the evils of poverty and so have been the CSOs working for Dalits, which lack both human and material resources.

Most of the NGOs working for Dalits empowerment in Nepal have same traditional kinds of approaches for empowering. And, since donors and INGOs normally fund them, they don't bother to find some alternative ways to ensure their financial capacity; rather they always extend their hands to donors through their fund attracting projects. This culture, on the one hand makes them dependent, on the other, it limits their achievements, as donations from donors is generally delivered with the interests and conditions of donors, and it doesn't fully accept the local ownership of the funds either. Realizing this fact, the organizations in Nepal need to initiate some fund-raising programs like the PSPD and the WV Korea have done, which proved to be one of the best ways for fund-raising, through which they have been more independent enabling themselves to operate their activities as they plan. Although the organizations might not be able to collect huge amount of money through their strategies as the country itself is in the net of grave poverty, it will still help them to strengthen their institutional capacity in the long run.

Although many people in Nepal suffer from poverty, the lack of clean drinking water, health care and education that play the vital role in the successful implementation of the strategies of South Korean NGOs in Nepal by Nepali NGOs, there has been a significant rise in level of political consciousness among the people over last 15 years. If there is only thing that has significantly advanced during this period is the spread of mass media all across Nepal. The extension of mass media and the twelve years long Maoist insurgency have highlighted the issues of disadvantaged and marginalized groups like Dalits in Nepal. As a result, they are more mobilized and have come up with the various demands for their development. Even people in Nepal also seem to have realized the need of empowering these groups for the overall development of the country. Similarly, the political parties have also emphasized the need of promoting and protecting the rights of Dalits in the country. At present, there is a strong moral support from political parties, civil society organizations and international community for Dalit empowerment. Even the Constitution of Nepal 1990 has established various rights for the people of Nepal such as the rights to equality freedom, press and publication, cultural and educational right, rights to religion, rights against exploitation, freedom of opinion and expression, freedom to assemble peaceably and without arms, freedom to form unions and associations, and freedom to move throughout the country and so on.

From the aforementioned analysis, it is found that not only the government, but civil society organizations working for Dalit empowerment also have not been playing pro-active and influential roles, but they often apply their traditional strategies to meet their goals; consequently their activities turn less effective and sometimes failed. Therefore, they need to adopt some comprehensive and coordinated mechanism that can realize the true empowerment of Dalit in Nepal.

It has been also noticed that even if the organizations realize that they need to create social awareness in the Nepali society so as to eliminate caste-based discrimination and elimination of the various kinds of discrimination against Dalits can be one of the best ways to start with, this research observes that most of them have not paid much attention to this issue. If these organizations want Dalits being treated equally as other people in the society, they need to think over the ideas and means to change the perception of people who discriminate Dalits under the bad culture of Hindu caste system. They also need to pressurize the government and concerned authorities to explore measures to promote implementation of relevant laws, regulations, policies and recommendations to end caste-based discrimination; and need to make the government ensure that all necessary constitutional, legislative and administrative measures are in right place to prevent, prohibit and redress caste-based discrimination.

Optimum use of mass media to creating awareness in the society can help to redefine the religious norms in positive way, which will ultimately contribute in inhaling caste-based discrimination against Dalits. Likewise, civil society organizations need to launch nationwide public awareness campaigns regarding legal prohibitions on caste discrimination. These campaigns should explain in simple terms what actions are legally prohibited and what recourse is available to victims of such discrimination and abuse.

This research has observed that a few N able to make the best uses of modern technologies and introduce innovative strategies that can better address the problems of Dalits. A good organizing capacity of a organization is expected in increasing effectiveness in project management and quality, for example by enhancing communication, mobilizing local resources, and encouraging local cooperation and local organizations are seen as stronger route to civil society by helping local people engage in dialogue or even partnership with the government and NGOs themselves, and more progress in reaching broader consensus and improving cooperation among NGO community. The NGOs need to build long-term alliance with other civil society actors to create a fully dynamic and autonomous federation on the grassroots as well as national level, which can work for Dalit solidarity. And the stronger collaboration among the different social groups is a precondition to realize the aim of capacity building of Dalits.

Likewise, as noticed in the research, the reformation in Nepal's sociocultural environment is needed to change the attitudes and behaviour among both Dalits and non-Dalits so as to eliminate the caste-based discrimination. Unless a change in the social behaviour of the so-called upper caste Hindus and a corresponding attempt on the part of the so-called untouchables to organize them is effected through humanist and right- based education campaigns, it would be impossible to integrate the socially marginalized untouchable castes into the socioeconomics and political processes; Dalit education therefore can play the pivotal role in this regard. Considering this fact, the Nepali CSOs need to influence in the society through educational intervention policies and strategies. To provide education for Dalits, they need to coordinate, cooperate and network with other actors in the society so that it will ensure their better access to education. The reservation system for Dalits along with the creation of economic opportunities to Dalits can play the pivotal role in educating them. Therefore, the CSOs should influence the government, political parties and other actors to make them formulate a good reservation system that ensures good number of quotas for Dalits in public-private sectors, local and government bodies, bureaucracy and all policymaking posts; this will help in Dalit mainstreaming that can improve the quality of Dalit people's life.

To empower Dalits with economic measures, it is necessary to pressurize the government enact land reform legislation that includes land distribution clauses to counter the pervasive landlessness of Dalits, a majority of whom are dependent on agriculture for their livelihood. The CSOs therefore need to influence the concerned authority to amend and enforce existing land reform legislation to prevent land alienation and ensure development of land belonging to Dalits which needs to be backed by the greater access to credit, markets. Besides these, the organizations also need to create economic opportunities, through which they can improve their economic condition making themselves less dependent.

Taking into account the low representation of Dalits in government bodies under the existing political system of Nepal isn't suitable model for ensuring Dalits representation in political bodies, it is necessary to restructure the political paradigm so that it will make possible for Dalits to reach in decision making level. Pluralistic democracy is generally believed to serve minority interest better rather than other political system. The CSOs in Nepal hence need to contribute to institutionalize the inclusive democracy in the country.

Taking in to consideration that several NGOs in Nepal have been working to improve the overall status of Dalits, and given that the massive caste-based discrimination under traditional ideologies and mentalities, lack of education, poverty, lack of awareness among Dalits and non Dalits, under representation in politics all have contributed to Dalit backwardness and marginalization. It therefore insinuates that Dalit people's overall condition can be improved if the above-mentioned deficiencies are overcome or eliminated and Dalits are ensured with their human rights and justice. Results of all of these would guide Dalits to the road of development and empowerment.

Among the principal causes, various forms of caste-based discrimination under Hindu religion and its traditional values, exploitation and negligence of the government, mismanagement of the resources, poor enactment of laws to protect the rights of the Dalits, widespread corruption and state of unaccountability and unfavourable economical as well as political structure of the country that have marginalized and excluded Dalits, have been systematically linked to the overall underdevelopment of Dalits. It further makes notes that underdevelopment manifests in the other areas of Dalit people's life like health, education, land, housing, water, and so on.

The poor access to education caused by poor access to economic activities backed by different forms of discrimination causes the limitations on the access to education; and this cycle goes on in Dalit people's life that hinders in the Dalit development. It implies that unless this cyclic order isn't torn apart and not given priority to Dalits to enhance better access to education and economical activities, the status of Dalits is sure to be more deteriorating, which will ultimately affect in the development of the country.

11.6. Dalit Assertion in Nepal

Nepal is now in the transitional phase towards a democratic change. This transition is the outcome of the 19-Day uprising by people from all walks of life. This time is important to all because we are going to decide several very important issues like the decision for a new setup of the Nepali state, the fate of monarchy, the appropriate electoral system, introducing a new state mechanism to secure the interests of all groups of plural society. Tnerefore, not only the political parties and players but also the people based on caste/ethnicity, region, religion, and gender are now busy in the debates and discussion to influence and intervene in the transition to making it into their favour. Some of the groups organized various protest programs as a means to reach their voices to the authority easily. The ongoing Tarai unrest, ethnic movement and Dalit movement are the examples of such intervening activities of various groups.

In the Nepalese history, an account of the institutionalizing of exploitation of the Dalit communities by the state dates back to the mediaeval period in the 13th century when King Jayasthiti Malla introduced the caste system. Jung Bahadur Rana further formalized the caste system by introducing the Muluki Ain (Civil Code) in 1853.

In the Muluki Ain, the Brahmins, holding highest position in Hindu caste hierarchy, were excluded from capital punishment; while the other castes of people, including the Dalits were subject to such punishment. Accordingly, the atrocities against the Dalit caste people were intensified. Dalits were denied the right to education and they were denied the right to acquire property. They were discouraged from constructing good house and touch persons of higher castes. So much so that certain sections of the Dalits were almost forced to live either in the outskirts of the villages or in the filthy slums.

The hallmark of the caste system and discrimination against Dalits is the practice of "untouchability." Based on the belief that Dalits are "polluted," Dalits are typically restricted to tasks and occupations that are deemed too "filthy" or "polluting" for "upper-caste" communities. Dalits are segregated from members of other castes and are prohibited from touching non-Dalits and their possessions.

In Nepal's rural areas, upper-caste individuals still practice ritual bathing in order to purify themselves following 1 For an overview contact with a Dalit or a Dalits' belongings. The sprinkling of drops of water on impure objects or individuals is also practiced. Dalits are also denied entry into public places, such as hotels, shops, and restaurants. When they are able to enter public restaurants, they are made to drink water from separate glasses, tea from separate tumblers, and eat *daal bhat* (rice and lentils) from separate plates. Still, Dalits have to wash the pots, which they used or touched in the houses of the "upper-caste people", hotels and restaurants.

There is a debate about the number of Dalits in Nepal. Dalit activists and NGOs have claimed that the Dalits comprise between 20 and 25 percent of the population.

The government census of 2001, in contrast, has estimated the Dalit population at 11.66 percent. Whether it is 11.66 percent or 25 percent; it is not a negligible size but constitutes a substantial portion of population of Nepal. However, it is a known fact that the Dalits remain in misery and abject poverty and are socially downtrodden.

While a great number of Nepal's agricultural labourers are Dalits, just one percent of Nepal's Dalits own arable land. Only three percent of Dalits own more than a hectare of land. In addition, approximately 71 percent of individuals reported that they are paid lower wages and salaries in both the private and informal sectors. At the time of the study, Dalits received an average of NRs. 96 (about US

$1.23) for a day's work. The mean wage for a female worker was approximately NRs. 78 (about US $1) while the mean wage for a male worker was approximately NRs. 99. By contrast, the mean market wage rate for the same kind of job in the general population was around NRs. 105, with women receiving an average of NRs. 88 and men receiving NRs. 111.

Going to the educational sector, it is often reported that not only Dalit students but also Dalit teachers are themselves socially segregated from their non-Dalit colleagues. In rural areas, Dalits are often made to sit in the back of the classroom and are treated as "untouchable" even by their teachers that effected in the literacy rate of Dalits (only 24.2 percent of all Dalits were literate as of 2001 where 50 percent of the average literacy rate for Nepalese) as education is basic requirement of the empowerment. According to a 1997 report, there were only two Dalit medical doctors and fifteen Dalit engineers in Nepal.

As of 2002, neither a single Dalit has held a leadership position in the Science and Technology field nor do any Dalits hold an academic or administrative leadership position at Tribhuvan University (one of the country's premier universities)

The situation of Tarai Dalits is worse than that of hill Dalits in terms of caste discrimination, poverty and other human development related indexes. For example, the literacy rate of the Tarai Dalits is only half (21.6 percent) than that of hill Dalits (41.93 percent)

Similarly, since 1958, only 14 Dalits in Nepal have become Members of Parliament (upper house). Only one Dalit from Nepali Congress party has been elected to the House of Representatives during four parliamentary elections after 1959. This pattern of exclusion is repeated at the local government level, where Dalits are severely underrepresented. Among the more than 3,900 Village Development Committee chairmen, only handfuls are Dalits. An ILO study which analyses the 1997 election results from 735 village development committees revealed that Bahun/Chhetri and Janajati represented "54.42% and 39.86% of the VDC Chairpersons respectively. The Dalits constituted only 1.63% of the 735 VDC Chairpersons. The caste/ethnic composition of the VDC Vice-Chairpersons followed similar proportions (Bahun/Chhetri: 52.11%;

Janajati: 37.82%) except that the proportion of the Dalit Vice Chairpersons constitutes 3.95% of the 735 Vice Chairpersons."

Likewise, Nepal Human Development Report 2004 states that Dalits share less than one percent of senior officials, managerial and professional occupation; around a half percent of technical and assistant level profession; and one and half percent of clerk and office assistance kind of profession.

According to a 2001 study, while *Brahmins* constitute only 16 percent of the population, they represent 57 percent of parliament and 89 percent of the judiciary.

In an International Labour Organization (ILO) study on Nepal, approximately 48 percent of the surveyed Dalits claimed that they would be denied employment due to their caste status even if job openings were available; Twenty one percent of the respondents reported that they had been refused jobs based on their caste status.

Discrimination also persists in the Nepal Army. Historically, the Nepal army was built around caste lines. In 1768, Nepal's first monarch, King Prithvi Narayan Shah, built an army whose senior ranks were composed almost entirely of "upper-caste" *Chetris*– the warrior caste. "Lower-caste" community members, including Dalits, were excluded. Only lower service units contain Dalits now a days. According to one estimate, the "upper castes," constituting only thirty five percent of the general population, occupy 98 percent of all army officers.

On the contrary, Dalit women and girls in Nepal endure the double burden of caste and gender discrimination. According to Durga Sob, a feminist Dalit activist of Nepal,"Dalit women's is proportionate and extreme poverty stems from illiteracy, untouchability, physical violence and lack of empowerment"

Among the Dalit women, the literacy rate is merely 3.2 per cent. Life expectancy of the Dalits is as low as 42 percent.

Among the minimal numbers who got opportunities to become Members of Parliament (upper house) or medical doctors or engineers in the name of Dalits in Nepal, all of them men.

After the Janalandolan II there are some substantial changes seen in the situation of Dalit. Credit should be given to the Maoist party which sent a good number of number of Dalit members in the parliament and compelled other political forces to nominate Dalits in the government and parliament as well. For the first time in history of Nepal, two members from the Dalits, with full ministerial portfolio are at the present interim government led by Prime Minister Girija Prasad Koirala.

Earlier in the Seven Party Alliance government, there was also a minister from Dalits having the state ministerial portfolio. Parties have started giving some representation to Dalits by nominating Members of Parliament which is a good initiation. Among the new nominees in the interim parliament, Dalit constitutes 13.74 percent share of total. Dalit in Jana Morcha occupy 66 percent share, which is 14.47 percent in Maoist party, 10 percent in Nepali Congress (NC) and in 20 percent in CPN-UML. Though NC (D), Nepal Sadhbhawana Party (NSP) and Nepal Majdur, Kisan Party (NMKP) did not nominate even one member from Dalits in the interim parliament, all will have compulsion to follow the trend in the future if they want to save their face. It seems that no one will stop Dalits from being in the government mechanism if there is the continuation of the democratic system of government and Dalit assertion. When the eight-party formed the constitution draft commission without including any Dalits or women, pressure from these excluded groups compelled the eight-party alliance to reshuffle the commission and nominate members from those communities. This is a good example about how society can compel political leadership to go with people's aspiration.

11.6.1. History of Dalit Assertion

Dalit movement had also begun alongside Nepal's democratic struggle since 1950s. However, it is interesting that the history of Dalit assertion neither originated in urban areas or from the capital city. It started in a village of Baglung district, the western part of Nepal. Sarbajit Biswakarma, an inhabitant of Thadaswara, Baglung was the person who challenged the caste based discrimination and untouchability at the village level. Later on, in 1947 he formed an organization named *Viswa Sarvajan Sangh* in his village to fight against caste-based discrimination. The Sangh is considered the first Dalit organization to be established.

Successful Pashupatinath Temple Entrance Campaign, 1954 was the first Dalit assertion in Kathmandu valley. It was a forceful temple entrance movement of untouchable community from where they got inspiration and continued attempting such actions in the other parts of the country.

Following the establishment of *Viswa Sarvajan Sangh*, Tailor's Union, 1947, *Nepal Samaj Sudhar Samgh*, 1947 and *Nepal Harijan Sangh*, 1950 were the organizations which were established along with the democratic struggles of 1950s. Organizations such as *Nimna Samaj Sudhar Sangh*, 1951, *Jat* Tor Mandal, 1951, Samaj Sudhar Sangh 1952, Pichadieka-Barga Sangathan, Pariganit Nari Sangh,1955, Achhut Mukti Morcha, 1958 Rastriya Achhut Mukti Parisad, 1958, were established during 1950-60, the first tenure of democracy in the Nepalese history.

Institutionally, for the first time in the history, Interim Government of Nepal Act 1951 recognized the people as 'citizen' with civil and political rights. However, the Dalit movement also got affected after the derailment of democratic system in 1960. Since the Panchayat system was an autocratic political system, not only the Dalits but also all others faced difficulties to form organizations and organize the program during the 30-years (1960-90). Only nine Dalit organizations were established during the Panchayat tenure.

When Democracy was restored in 1990 after *Janaandolan I*, hundreds of NGOs and other organizations came into the fore with the slogan of Dalit emancipation. It is considered that the second tenure of Democracy (1990-2002) has become the productive period for Dalits in terms of their assertion. It is because the then governments were compelled not only to form Dalit Commission in 2002 but also to initiate other affirmative action programs like scholarship for higher education for backward community students, reservation in scholarship and in admission in educational institutes, quota for foreign employment, etc. Though these initiations were not enough to end all sorts of exploitations and marginalization, they helped Dalits to increase their confidence towards further assertion.

Today, we find many more Dalit and pro-Dalit organizations working in Nepal. Every political party has their Dalit wings under which there are also Dalit student wings. Hundreds of NGOs are there to work on Dalit issues. There are at least three umbrella organizations of Dalit NGOs—Dalit NGO Federation, Dalit NGO Federation-Nepal and Nepal Dalit NGO Confederation. There is a Dalit Citizen Movement Central Coordination Committee (DCMCCC) formed after the decision taken by the Dalit Citizens' Assembly, which was held in June-16-17, 2007. The assembly was organized with the support of almost two dozens Dalit organizations to strengthen the Dalit emancipation movement more assertively.

11.6.1.1. Dalit assertion after the Janaandolan II

Dalit participation in the last year uprising was very active though they remain curtailed from participating in social, economic, political, administrative affairs. People amassed in the streets believing that their individual grievances would be addressed with the change in the government. But unfortunately, both the interim constitution and twice-amended Nepali Constitution are unable to address the core agenda and issues of the Dalits.

Dalit frustration came to a head on June 14, 2007 when the Nepalese parliament decided on an allocation of seats for the new Constituent Assembly that will be held in November 2007. The constitution, after its second amendment has proposed that 240 of the 497 Assembly seats go to those with the highest votes ("first past the post"), and there will be the proportional share to Nepal's minorities, including the Dalit, and the country's isolated areas only in the rest 240 seats. The cabinet will appoint the remaining 17 seats.

Calculating the allocation, Dalits reached a consensus that there are only 6 percent seats for Dalits, though the constitution provisioned 13% reservation to Dalit in upcoming assembly.

As mentioned earlier, Dalits were having a belief that their individual grievances would be addressed by the government which has come in the existence after the *Janaandolan* II. In the early days, they used very democratic weapons in raising their issues by bringing their agenda in debate through writing and getting these write-ups published in newspapers, journals and books. In between this, when the Madhesi and ethnic community movement went into a different kind of protest programs like bandh, vehicle strike, sit-in program, protest rallies and so on, and started getting a quick responses from the government, Dalits were also compelled to think otherwise. Most of them started getting an impression that until and unless one announces bandh, vehicle strike, protest rallies and so on which usually invite violent activities though these are also considered facets of nonviolent movement, no one will hear the voice of the organizer. In this point, the direction of the movement in which Dalits was organizing, received a question mark saying that the manner is very passive for launching a movement. Political leaders, media, academicians etc. also started assuming the Dalit weakness or loophole behind the passive movement in comparison to the Madhesi and Janajati assertion. Such assumption made Dalits rethink over the united and effective movement of all Dalits. Great disappointment overcame the Dalits when there were no leaders or political parties raising their voice of concern for Dalit issues and agendas.

11.6.2. Demands of Dalit Alliances

All Dalit organizations state that they are working for Dalit upliftment, proportional participation and for an inclusive society. When the Dalit leadership was criticized by ordinary Dalits, Dalit leaders of different political parties and organizations started organizing for a united Dalit assertion. Till date, there are mainly three alliances which according to them are in the struggle to capitalize the ongoing transition into Dalit favour.

United Republican Dalit Front, Nepal (URDFN) has formed in October 2006 under the leadership of Tilak Pariyar with the participation of Nepal Dalit Mukti Morcha (united) affiliated with the Maoist, Rastriya Dalit Mukti Sangathan, Nepal Utpidit Jatiya Utthan Sangh (united), two groups of Nepal Swatantra Vidhyarthi Sangathan and independent Dalit personalities. URDFN has announced a fresh protest program submitting a 10-points demands by July 25, 2007.

Again, in making an united effort for Dalit assertion, six Dalit wings of major political parties of Nepal—Nepal Dalit Mukti Morcha (United), Nepal Udpidit Jatiya Mukti Samaj, Nepal Dalit Sangh, Nepal Dalit Sangh (Democratic), Nepal Rastriya Dalit Mukti Sangathan, Nepal Dalit Utthan Manch—had organized a joint meeting in February 18, 2007 and come up with a 9-Point Common Minimum Understanding. The [joint] meeting decided to present the 9-points memorandum on the above mentioned demands to the government, eight parties and legislature-parliament, and to make further decisions on the programs of joint struggle based on common understanding as may be necessary. It had formulated a joint committee for struggle and dialogue. However, the alliance could not continue when four organizations quit the alliance.

Those four sister organizations of major parliamentary political parties, after a couple of days of the break up of the alliance of a six-Dalit wings of major political parties, formed another alliance for struggle and dialogue This alliance is holding several discussions about the nature of struggle, common demand of Dalits before launching a united and fresh movement. Since this is a alliance of the sister organizations of ruling political parties, it is having dialogue with the government regarding the Dalit issues, and is trying to lobby within the party and government for Dalit upliftment programs, policies and so on.

When political leadership failed to get united to form a united alliance in launching a united and assertive movement, rights-based Dalit organizations came in the fore to capitalize Dalit sentiment and to compel the government to hear Dalit voice. Some 19-Dalit organizations sat together and decided to organize a Dalit Citizens' Assembly (DCA) to show a united Dalit voice. The objectives of DCA was to initiate discussion on the model of New Nepal, to discuss on Dalit's core agenda, to put pressure on political parties, to fashion the state model into a federal government system, to collect a multitude of perspectives in order to facilitate an inclusive and proportional state model, and to gather ordinary people for creation of vivid discussions on the Dalits' agendas.

The DCA organizers criticized the Dalit movement and its leaders as incompetent to announce a united and effective protest program like those of Madhesi and Janajati. Another reservation towards the leaders of the movement was the continued practice of the culture of sycophancy or loyalty to their mother parties and donors as the Dalits has been doing for a long time. The stated objective of the assembly, according to the organizers was to break the trend of sycophancy, to end the frustrations seen within the Dalit members and to pressurize the parties to do needful in establishing Dalit rights.

In short, this assembly was organized to forge a common agenda through discussion of individual issues, and to strategize for a unified Dalit movement.

The assembly decided to form a new coordinating group, the Dalit Citizen Movement Central Coordination Committee (DCMCCC), to promote the conference agenda and forge unity. The assembly which was able to amass over 2000 Dalits from approximately 61 districts of Nepal held discussions on 17 different topics through parallel sessions which brought out the following 15-points to present to the Eight Political Parties along with the Interim Government. The DCMCCC is given the responsibility for announcing future programs on citizen assemblies and mobilizing the people around the country through publicity, mobilizing support, and pressuring political and governmental bodies through sit-ins, and other actions as needed.

Demands of the alliances As mentioned earlier, six Dalit organizations affiliated with major political parties of Nepal organized through a joint meeting in February 18, 2006 reached into consensus to a 9-Point Common Minimum Understanding as a way forward to move towards fulfilling the basic demands and aspirations of Dalits in the current extraordinary circumstances of Nepalese society.

The 9-points of understanding are:

1. In the context of the declaration of Nepal as an untouchability-free nation made on Jestha 21, 2063 BS by the parliament following the peoples' movement (Jana Andolan 2062/63), untouchability discrimination must be made a social crime of serious nature by the constitution [the main statute] itself, and hard laws must be enacted against untouchability-discrimination and enforced immediately.
2. Implementing the agreement and understanding made among eight political parties, an interim government including Maoists must be formed, and the date of Constituent Assembly (CA) election must be declared immediately.
3. The election of CA must be held based on the system of inclusive proportional representation. A minimum of 20 percent CA representatives must be allocated to Dalit representatives on the ground of proportional representation as well as a means of

additional rights for compensation to Dalits. Similarly, a provision of 20% representation from Dalits at all levels from top to bottom of the state machinery, governmental and private agencies must be made on the ground of proportional representation as well as a means of additional rights for compensation to Dalits.

4. Nepal as a state must be restructured establishing a federal democratic system of state governance based on caste, language and regional autonomy.
5. Rayamajhi Commission Report must be made public, and culprits of suppressing the Jana Andolan must be booked, and stern action must be taken against them.
6. An effective step must be taken to bring the declaration of a secular state and its system into practice.
7. Dalit Rights Commission must be made a constitutional body.
8. Identifying all problems of Dalits, the state must make a [concrete] plan to resolve the problems in all associated sectors.
9. The genuine demands of Madheshi, indigenous nationalities, women must be fulfilled. The 9-points memorandum was the first consensus agenda of different Dalit organizations though it got legitimacy for a short period. When four members of out of total six quit the alliance, the memorandum lacked authenticity. Realizing the vacuum of a united Dalit voice, after the tremendous pressure from civil society and from the grass root level, through a DCA, Dalit NGOs came out with a 15-points decision as demands to present to the eight political parties and the government.

The points are:

1. Issues relating to Nepal's Dalits remain in the corner as the country faces a great change. Recent amendments in the constitution failed to meet the demands of the Dalits giving Dalits only 6% participation in the Constituent Assembly (CA). It is strongly recommended that the constitution is amended once again.
2. There should be proportional representation of Dalits in every sector of the state. It should be guaranteed that 20% of

representatives in the Constitution Assembly (CA) election are Dalits. This is a strong focus and commitment of this assembly.

3. This assembly urges the 8 political parties and Nepali government to provide a date for the CA elections. The monarchy should be abolished along with the declaration of the Federal government system from the parliament.
4. Dalits are currently unable to gain access to social, cultural and political sectors because they don't have access to natural resources. Dalits should be provided with a justifiable mass of land.
5. The major political parties have shown only surface level interest in Dalit empowerment. We aspire for their strong and reliable support for Dalits' liberation and upliftment.
6. The country is heading towards a federal system of government. We hope that Dalits' agendas and issues will be central to the forthcoming government.
7. Because of the globalization and marketization, Dalits are economically sidelined in terms of their professional expertise. Dalits are also curtailed from water resources, electricity and other resources. This assembly strongly demands economic protection for the Dalits. A collective declaration should be presented to economic organizations, multinational companies etc.
8. Due to landlessness, Dalits are forced to migrate and work in dangerous areas. This is affecting their health status and causing social problems. This assembly urges that proper health and livelihood facilities be provided to Dalits.
9. Land related exploitation systems such as the Haliya, Kamaiya, Balighare, Khali, Harawa-Charawa (Bonded Labour systems often associated with the agricultural sector) systems should be abolished as soon as possible.
10. The interim constitution has provided women with 33% representation in government, but there is currently no specified inclusion for Dalit women. The new constitution should include measures which address the social, economic, political, and cultural hindrances that Dalit women suffer. The government

should seek to provide special policies and programs for the rehabilitation of Badi women.

11. There should be special policies to include Dalits in the state and private media. This assembly urges for this representation.
12. Organizational bodies in Nepal currently only provide representation for segments of the Dalits. Dalits in their entirety (including all subcastes) should be provided with opportunities within governmental, private and non-governmental organizations.
13. A new Dalit commission named "The Constitutional Dalit Rights Commission" should be established along with the amendment in the interim constitution.
14. Untouchability and discrimination should be condemned as a serious social crime, and the culprits should be punished severely within the new constitution.
15. Dalit students should be given scholarships with free education till higher education level. Similarly, United Republican Dalit Front, Nepal (URDFN) on July 25, 2007 put a 10-point memorandum, and has submitted it to the government. "We frequently submitted memorandum to the PM and interim drafting committee to provide the chance of proportional representation to the Dalits in the state mechanism but we get no response" Tilak Pariar coordinator of URDFN said after submitting memorandum at the official residence of the Prime Minister

The 10-points demands are:

1. Holding the CA elections in time.
2. Ending all types of conspiracies which obstruct elections.
3. Abolishing monarchy and announcing the country a republic.
4. The provision of 20 per cent reservation in state organs for Dalits, which according the memorandum should also be provisioned in the interim constitution.
5. Provision of stern punishment against those practicing untouchability.
6. Making public the report of Rayamajhi Commission and taking action against those indicted by the report.

7. Provisioning the Dalit Rights Commission as a constitutional organ.
8. Implementing the announcement of secular state in reality.
9. Scholarship and free education up to high-level education for the Dalits and;
10. Fulfilling all the just demands of agitating groups are also included in their demands. Demanding the fulfilment of the mentioned demands, now two different protest programs are being carried out by the DCMCCC and the URDFN. The first had announced a phase-wise protest program to fulfil the demands raised in June at the National Dalit Assembly. In the first phase of strategy, a regional citizen assembly and mass mobilization program is scheduled to pressure the eight political parties, the government, and the diplomatic missions. The second phase of action includes demonstrations in Kathmandu, circling Singha Durbar, Baluwatar, and locations around the country for the first time in Nepal's history.

Since the main demands of the DCMCCC and URDEN are similar, the first has expressed its solidarity to the program organized by the latter Sit-in, hunger strike and arrests/release of Dalit activists by the police have become normal phenomena nowadays. On August 7, 2007, when the Dalit activists had just started their sit-in protest at 10 am, the police intervened and arrested 24 of its activists.

Again in August 9, some four-dozen Dalit activists were arrested from the sit-in program.

Now, the protest program has converted into a relay hunger strike. Earlier, the URDEN organized one-hour long vehicles strike in Kathmandu valley on August 12 followed by a torch rally on August 10, 2007.

Here, one can raise several queries regarding the Dalit initiation to capitalize the transitional phase into their favour. Will the Dalits who comprise about one-fifth of the population, spread all over the country, in a position to mobilize enough resources from the INGOs, be able to make an assertive movement to co-opt the present situation or not? Though Dalits are always placed in the bottom by all other groups, why is it losing its unity time and again? Why did the alliance of six political party Dalit wings break in this crucial period? Why are DCA and

DCMCCC mired in controversy. Leaders of the Dalit movement have to respond to such questions untii they reach a common understanding for the agenda of Dalits.

11.6.3. Assessment of the Dalit Assertion

The Dalit elites who jumped to NGO sector after international community come with the program of social reform are the main actors to divide Dalits which has resulted in a weaker assertion than that of the demand of this time, he adds. He blames them as champion in making the money by selling the naked pictures of Dalit which is captured after offering a peace of candy. He blames that the dual role UML affiliated Dalit wings is responsible for the break-up of the negotiation team which was formed by six major Dalit wings of the political parties in February, this year. A Dalit intellectual and activist who recently got an appointment as a member of Dalit Commission also agreed regarding the division and debate between the Dalit NGOs and political leadership and argued that the agenda "abolishing the monarchy and announcing the country a republic" was only the cause in breaking the six Dalit wings alliance. Here, he sees a high-level party interference to those who quit the alliance and formed another dialogue team. Regarding the assertion of Dalit, he is happy of the way used by the Dalits and argues that whatever the style Janajati and Madhesi have applied was not the only means of assertion. He is satisfied by the achievements whatever has come up by the Dalit assertion.

Another member of Interim legislature from the Maoist party argues that Dalit emancipation is not possible through NGOs which are influenced by the international organizations. He realizes the present influential role of NGOs but argues that they will undermine the Dalit movement if there is the reluctance of political leadership. He credits the Maoist party for bringing the Dalits into the present situation and argues that so long the feudalist and unitary state exists, Dalits have to be assertive to deconstruct the structure.

Though the NGO activists were denounced by politicians, the Dalit NGO activists still have their soft corner towards the political leadership accepting the say, "parties are the ultimate force in democracy to run the country through people's vote." A prominent NGO activist, who is a Dalit woman argue that she is trying to bring all sorts of Dalit leaders into a forum to make a common understanding accepting the fragmentation within the Dalit based organizations that hamper the assertion of Dalit to bring qualititative change of Dalit through the intervention in the ongoing transition.

11.7. Representation of Dalits in the Government

The representation of the Dalits in the government as a whole is also very insignificant as compared to their population size. Despite the promises from successive governments for their inclusion in the government and policy level bodies of the government, their discourse on Dalit empowerment issue as well as the sustainable development of Nepal.

Sociology theorists like Karl Marx, Max Weber and Emile Durkheim understand caste as a form of division of labour connected with the specific Indian form of the Asiatic village, and believed that it would wither away under the impact of industrialization and modern transport and communications. And one of the most important sociologists on caste, Louis Dumont, comes out of the Durkheimian school with its emphasis on the role of Hindu religion and values as binding and defining forces in society that have set the status of Dalits at the bottom of the hierarchical system. Max Weber supplementing Marx's ideologies emphasize on economic class and the mode of production with the role of ideas and ideologies in history. In the similar vein, Dr. Ambedkar, an Indian scholar, clearly pointed out that caste system was responsible for all the evils and different forms of discriminations against Dalits in the existing society. He therefore called for an annihilation of caste. This is possible only when we annihilate the religious notions on which the caste system is founded. Ambedkar suggests the need of reinterpreting the Hindu religious text that carries the philosophical basis of religion, and bring it in consonance with the principles of liberty, equality and fraternity. Similarly, he adds that the old body must die to receive a new body, these implies discarding the authority of the Shashtras.

And, modernization theorists note that the underdevelopment in developing countries was caused by traditional cultures and values. The propagators of this theory like Gabriel Almond, James Coleman, Samuel Huntington, and Lucian Pye argue that only cultural, political and economic modernization can ensure development in developing countries. This school of thought argues that, for the development in the developing countries, the countries should follow the path of political and economic modernization parallel to the one first travelled by the advanced Western nations; and to accomplish this, developing countries should acquire modern cultural values and create modern political and economic institutions.The assumptions of the aforementioned theory also explain the causes of Dalit backwardness, as the traditional cultural ideology of Hindu religion and its norms have been the evil forces to relegate Dalits in various aspects of their life.

Similarly, D B Sharma Bishwakarma, a Dalit rights activist in his conference paper attributes caste-based discrimination as one of the most widespread social maladies of human civilization throughout history and has attributed that it should not be tolerated in the 21st century. He has also stated that there needs the stronger movement against caste based discrimination in Nepal. He further stresses that this movement against outdated caste-based discrimination towards Dalits that has unjustly denied them a dignified life, should not be looked upon only from a national Nepali perspective but from global perspective as well.

According to Bhattachan, the majority of the people of Dalit Community have been suffering every day simply because they have not been carrying on their traditional occupations. They have been socially boycotted or alienated.They even can't enter into public places. Along with child marriage and marriage of unequal status (fake marriage), the number of people engaging in inter-caste marriage is on the rise. In this situation, the Dalits not only have to suffer, but also face banishment from the villages because of the several reasons. The Dalits have been also victims of labour exploitation from the higher castes as considered to be their guardian.Till today they have been compelled to carry on the occupation based on casteism. Action Aid Nepal, an INGO on its research, notes that the Dalit community has been facing social rejection, social exclusion and social boycott because of the inter-caste marriage, rejection of traditional occupations and opposition to traditional degrading forms of discrimination and beliefs. Habitual untouchability as a result of caste-based untouchability is prevalent in the society.

D.B Sagar Bishwakarma presented his conference paper in a special session in Cornell University on 'Social and Religious Fragmentation and Economic Development in South Asia'- 'Urgency of Inclusive Democracy and Reformation of the State to Mainstreaming Dalits in Nepal' AD White House, October 15, 2005.

According to Bhattachan et al. Hindu religion and its cultures are the primary sources of the existing discrimination against Dalit. He articulates that even though this community falls within the Hindu society, it has not been able to practice freely and fairly the Hindu religion and traditions. The discriminatory Hindu values and beliefs against this community are still continuing. The following traditional conservative blind faith is still there. If milk and varieties of food made out of milk are given to the Dalits then, calves, cows and buffalos will die; if the source of water is allowed to be touched, then snake will come out of it; the source of water will dry and the people in the society will be blind; if some one is allowed to enter into a temple, then the person will die in accident; if tea is taken with Dalits, then devastating floods will come; and if the body is touched, then the body must be cleaned with choichito (way to clean up). The Dalits have been deprived from entering the temples and worship there. Dalit community in Nepal is still identified as illiterate, unemployed, landless, poor, foolish, exploited and restrained etc. Customs based on casteism like Balighare, Haliya, Sinophalne, etc. as still prevalent against the Dalit community. Till today the Dalit community is compelled to write the surnames that reflect the traditional occupations.

The different form of discrimination is continuing in the society from time immemorial based on caste like prohibition in entering different places, forced labour exploitation, humiliation, social boycott, exclusion, social alienation and other kinds of caste-based discrimination. It is not only because upper class people and religion are discriminatory, inter-Dalit case-based practices are also equally responsibility for social exclusion of Dalits. Since Dalits themselves practice discriminatory untouchability in their daily lives, the issue of caste-based discrimination remains as a complex texture. According to Dahal et al., social discrimination within Dalits is distinctly observed in eating food and drinking and while performing life cycle rituals. Moreover, marriage between higher caste and Dalits is strictly prohibited. Koirala, another scholar in his research in Bangkot writes that a Damai is Pani Nachalne (water from who can't be shared with) to a Kami and a Sarki, and a Kami and Sarki who claim equal status don't dine together or marry each other. In the same vein, Sharma notes that Damais don't accept cooked rice and water from Hudke (a subgroup within the Damai). The old legal codes, religion as well as inter-Dalit discriminatory practices are responsible for the discriminations against Dalits in Nepal. This clarifies that caste system based on Hindu religion stands as the main enemy of Dalits people in Nepal.

There are, no doubt, multiple causes behind Dalits backwardness in Nepal. Dr. Ambedkar, and Dalit expert clearly have pointed out that caste system was responsible for all the evils in the existing society and different forms of discriminations against Dalits. He therefore called for an annihilation of caste. This is possible only when we annihilate the religious notions on which the caste system is founded. According to him the possible way is through a Kranti (revolution), and not through a simple reformation. For this Kranti, he suggested the following three steps:

1. New doctrinal basis, this means to reinterpret the Hindu religious text of that carries the philosophical basis of religion, and bring it in consonance with the principles of liberty, equality and fraternity;
2. A complete change in the fundamental notions of life, this can be done through the change in notion of purity pollution, encourage inter-caste dining and inter-caste marriages;
3. The old body must die to receive a new body, this implies discarding the authority of the Shashtras.

It can, from the above analysis be perceived that there are some inhuman religious notions in Hindu religion, which has still enlivened the practices of caste-based discrimination against Dalits; these bad and discriminatory beliefs therefore need to be uprooted so as to realize better situation of Dalits in the country. And, to uproot these motions, there should be some pro-active and philosophical interpretation of the Hindu beliefs that can enhance the equality, humanity and fraternity.

Nepal, the poorest countries in South Asia and the 137th poorest country in the world, is basically an agriculture-based country. And 31% of the total population lives below the poverty level. The primary source of economy of Nepali people is land. In Nepal, Dalits are the poorest group in the society. Although they depend on agriculture, they lack the sufficient land to make grains for their living. Dalits have been the victims of different obstacles like ignorance, illiteracy, poverty, social backwardness and exploitation. Consequently, they don't have access to take advantage of common development programs.

Their access to land control and productive resource is extremely low. Consequently, most Dalits are extremely poor. And even those who have land only have a very smallholding of the lowest quality. Their food security is therefore very low. The average per capita income of Dalits is almost half that of the so-called upper caste groups. Even if Dalits own little land, it is either infertile for agriculture production or is occupied by their house. Sharma in his research found that 21% of Dalit households produced food grains for less than three months, 19.5% for four to six months, and 15.4% for one year and 5.1% produced surplus food grains. The World Bank survey further explains that 60-70% of the total population of Dalit community lives below the poverty line while only 31% of the total population is living under the poverty line.

Although Dalits comprise agricultural labourers, very few of them can claim ownership of land. Human Right Watch Nepal on its report observes that in the mid-western and far western hills, bonded agricultural labourers, or Haliyas; hail mainly from untouchable castes. The report also attributes that Dalits are charged much higher interest rates on loans from landlords than are their upper-caste counterparts. This kind of discrimination further keeps Dalits in to the cruel tenterhook of poverty and marginalization. The economic condition of Dalits always remains deteriorating because of labour exploitation as well. Dalits are poorly paid for their work. Those who are involved in their traditional occupations have also not been able to earn their livelihood because of the failure to modernize their traditional occupations. According to Human Development Report 2006, despite the wealth of skills related to their traditional occupations, Dalits almost invariably work at these trades under discriminatory and exploitative conditions. Due to their poor socioeconomic conditions, Dalits are often subjected to exploitative labour practices like the Haliya system. Such duress from poverty also leads to migration of Dalits in search of work. Such relocation for work isolates them from home for long duration thereby increasing their risk to HIV and AIDS due to high-risk behaviours. Vidya Bir Singh Kansakar in his paper, 'Nepal-India Open Border: Prospects, Problems and Challenge' articulates that, While the Land Reform Act of 1964 sought to curb excessive landholding by conferring tenancy right upon landless individuals, in a bid to avoid conferring these rights onto Dalit community members, powerful landlords dislodged Dalit tenants, compelling them to work as agricultural labourers if they wanted to remain on the land. As a result, a large number of Dalits became landless. Jagat Basnet, in his article 'Land First to Fight Poverty' states that the expulsion of Dalits from their land, when combined with Nepal's repressive citizenship laws, placed evicted Dalits in a double bind. As ownership of property was a precondition for Nepali citizenship, Dalits who lost their land were also forced to forfeit their citizenship papers. Furthermore, Bhattachan articulates in one exchange program organized by Friedrich-Ebert-Stiftung (FES) in Nepal that as possession of citizenship papers was a precondition for purchasing land, evicted Dalits were unable to acquire new land.

Dalits are economically backward groups because they are not only limited within their traditional occupations but also experience employment discriminations. Historically Dalits have been involved in their traditional occupation. These days they are engaged in various kinds of occupations for their living. As Chhetri articulated, Dalits do both wage labour and agriculture side by side, because they can't support them well with one. They can never imagine about saving money for their future; rather they have to fight for their everyday living. In Nepal, Dalits have been undergoing rampant employment discrimination that makes it difficult for them to enter into, much less excel in, non-caste based occupations. According to International Labour Organization (ILO), the government is the country's largest employer; discrimination in the workplace directly implicates the government. Even if job opportunities are available, Dalits are simply denied because of their caste status. The ILO study on Dalits notes that approximately 48% of the surveyed Dalits claimed that they would be denied employment due to their caste status even if job openings were available. 21% of the respondents reported that they had been refused jobs based on their caste status. In addition, approximately 71% of individuals reported that they are paid lower wages and salaries in both the private and informal sectors. Despite the overall reduction in poverty in Nepal, the outcomes are not uniform among different social groups, especially Dalits. These kinds of inequalities and discrimination have further widened the disparity among groups contributing to the disintegration in the country. According to Cox Thomas, Dalits are caught in a vicious economic net. They are unable to receive an education that would qualify them for a well paying professional position. They end up working in their traditional caste occupation and/or as unskilled labourers, usually for a limited income. As a result, they are unable to educate their children adequately and the whole cycle repeats itself. Actually, Cox is right to explain the reason behind the cycle of Dalit's backwardness in Nepalese society.

The assertions above make clear that the environment created by people in power and discrimination against Dalits in their economic activities have contributed more in the economic marginalization of Dalits. And, the government has also paid no attention to the issue of economic marginalization of Dalit community. From the above-mentioned literatures, it has been clear that Dalits have been economically poor not because they don't work, but because they are discriminated, underpaid and exploited. The poor access of the community to education, lack of sufficient land and proper help from the government have also contributed in worsening the economic condition of Dalits.

Taking into a serious consideration the economic situation of Dalits and the economic gap between other people in Nepali society, it seems that Marxist theory that sees poverty as consequences of capitalist exploitation is suitable to better explain the reasons behind economical gap and marginalization of Dalits. Dalits in Nepal, who are trapped in the vicious tenterhooks of poverty for long, get fewer prices for their products and are paid lower wages and salaries in their works for land owners, business persons and corporations. With their salaries, it is very hard even to meet their daily needs in their family; they therefore get obliged to get involved even in dangerous works for supporting their family. Yet, they suffer from loans and debt. The Marxists believe that only making change in the economic system of the country that ensures the opportunities by which poor can succeed in their own, can eradicate poverty. If looked into the economical paradigm of Nepal, it doesn't seem to be supportive for poor; Marx's idea of restructuring the economical system therefore is relevant. This claim of Marxist theory is further supported by a new theory called 'Theory of World System'. One of the main propagators of this school Immanuel Wallenstein and Max Webber agreeing with Marxist's viewpoint stress that poverty is the consequence of capitalist machinery believe that capitalistic system pushes the poor in to deeper depth of poverty and make the rich more richer. There was a debate on the need of land reform and distribution in Nepal to solve poverty of disadvantaged groups like Dalits; but unfortunately it has remained as only a political slogan. There is a common belief that the land reform policy will support Dalits to support their families.

Mr. Bharat Shrestha, the executive director of the MODE stresses that land reform is an economic process and, therefore, policy on land should be highly considered on improvement of productivity through appropriate land use and management that will contribute to upgrade the economic status of minorities like Dalits who have no access to land and other economic resources. This idea matches with the idea of Integrated Rural Development paradigm, which many NGOs have pursued with the aim to help peasants develop self-sustaining system of farming. But it is noteworthy that moderate agrarian programs is often undermined or limited by the scarcity of government funds. In addition, delay in bureaucracy and judiciary challenges frequently remain as the other causes that slow down the land reform process. Mr. Shrestha emphasizes that policy need to be 16 deliberately directed towards Dalits; for this process he notes that institutional framework and legislation plays a vital role in land reform policy. However, as Handelman in his book, 'The challenge of Third World Development' articulated, along with land reform Dalits also need some supplemental government assistance together with land distribution so that they can exploit their labour in a right way ensuring more productivity.

In the domain of education, Dalits are far behind compared to upper class people in the country. The educational situation Dalit is very miserable; there is a big gap in the educational achievements between Dalits and other castes in the society. They have long been deprived of acquiring education, as they were not supposed to achieve knowledge through education and thereby do some intellectual work in the tradition. Consequently, they have still remained uneducated and illiterate. Because of the rampant poverty and caste-based discrimination, Dalit children have failed to go to school to acquire education. According to 1991 census the overall literacy rate of Dalits was only 22.8% while whereas average was 39.6%. But some people estimate that the percent is lower than the report of the census. The male literacy was 33.9% compared to only 12.0% of female literacy rate. The rate also differs from the Dalits of one region to another; the literacy rate of Hill Dalit is much higher, 27.0% compared to only 11% of the Tarai Dalits. The male literacy was 42.2% of Hill Dalits. The highest literacy rate was that of Mushar (42%) and the lowest is that of the Guine (31.1%). Likewise, male Dalit literacy rate was 33.9% and female literacy was 12.0%. The education attainment of Dalit was 14.6% compared to 28.6% of national average.

Koirala notes the Dalits in Nepal never had a tradition for writing. In the past, the schooling system was based on the Varnashram model 8, in which Dalits were deliberatively denied with acquiring education. Nepal was governed by Hindu tradition where the Hindu hierarchical caste structure had prominent influence in day-to-day life of the people. Only high caste Hindu people particularly Brahmins were provided the educational opportunities. After the end of Rana autocratic regime in 1950, the door to formal education opened to all groups including Dalits. Although the western system of education was introduced, Dalits always had to undergo number of problems in attaining education because of the Hindu values. They had to undergo various problems not only in getting admission, but also in sitting and eating together with other high cast students in the class.

Likewise the educational attainment of Dalits is lower as much as 14.6%. According to Child Workers in Asia (CWA) there are even many Dalit communities whose children have never attended the schools, therefore have poor potentials in skilled and educated manpower. Hence, it is urgent to uplift their status by giving grave concerns to their situation, so that they can also be in the mainstream educational level, and there by be as competent as other people. The government also seems to have been indifferent to this critical issue of Dalit in Nepal, although it is a prerequisite for Dalit upliftment as education opens the door to further opportunities. Dalits school attendance and education attainment is also poor as compared to that of other caste. Although the primary education is free for everyone in government run educational institutes, Dalit children can't attend schools as they fail even to support for the dresses, Tiffin and other necessary things for their studies. Consequently, they have to rather get involved in some economic activities to make their living easier. The government introduced some policies in its Eighth and Ninth Plan to ensure Dalit people access to education, but they generally turned ineffective. Realizing the deficiencies of the governmental programs aimed at providing education to Dalit people, Mr. Hem Sharma Pokharel of Nepal's Ministry of Local Development admitted that the government's eight and ninth plans were not inspiring. The government of Nepal guided by the objective of 'education for all' aims at improving the access to the quality of primary education. The Plan also has the objective of expanding literacy programs to improve the livelihoods of deprived groups like Dalits.

The government has also announced a new program to provide free education up to tenth grade for oppressed, backward and below poverty line students providing basic facilities in private schools to students from 'oppressed and backward communities' and setting up of a rural Education Development Fund (financed by a levy of 1.5% of the income of private/boarding schools) which would be utilized for funding the education of marginalized communities. Although the government hoped to make some institutional and operational arrangements to provide education to Dalits, mismanagements and misuse of resources in bureaucracy threaten the effective implementation of the governments programs. Likewise, the limited capacity of the government to cope up with the multiple problems in the society and the lack of commitment from the concerned authority leave the formulated programs related to Dalit education unrealized, which makes Dalits illiterate and uneducated in the society. Consequently, they get deprived from various opportunities in the society. Even though the government and bureaucrats very well acknowledge that the development of the country as well as Dalits is possible through providing education to deprived communities, the situation of education in Dalit population is very miserable, which has stood as one of the greatest evils for Dalits in the society.

The cyclic effects of socioeconomics and political backwardness of Dalits characterized by caste based discrimination have been translated into their poor status in Human Development Index (HDI) record as well, which the above mentioned figure vividly describes; the wide gap between the status of Newar (a caste group) and Dalit conveys the pathetic situation of Dalits in Nepal. It is generally considered that there are many dimensions for human development. In the case of Dalit empowerment, education, health, rural drinking water and sanitation are particularly important ones. In addition, basic infrastructure such as access to roads, electricity and telephone communications (particularly in remote areas) can help improve living conditions for the Dalits in rural areas. As noted above, improvements in these areas are mutually reinforcing, and have benefits well beyond their direct impact. Ensuring equitable access to these services and facilities can be especially important for mainstreaming the Dalits. The school of modernization theory notes that transferring of traditional cultures in to modern one opens up the doors for the modernization process.

On the process, the modernization theorists believe that education, urbanization and the spread of mass media play the pivotal role as the central agents of cultural change. Modernization theorists state that in the process of modernization, economical and technological changes will help to the diffusion of culture, which will lead the society to a certain direction of getting westernized. According to Huntington's explanation, as countries modernize, the spread of urbanization, education and mass media consumption produce an increasingly politically aware and mobilized society, whose citizens make far more demands on the government.

Therefore to respond to these demands, developing countries need to create more and specialized and complex political and economic institutions. If the situation of Dalits in Nepal is analysed on the basis of the assumptions of modernization theory, it seems that it doesn't suit while Dalits are already far behind other caste groups. Even though there are some changes like urbanizations, spread of mass media and introduction of neo-liberal economy in the country, the Dalit situation has not improved. The theory also doesn't explain whether the modernization of culture will end up the discriminatory practices in the society. The theorists rather seem to have accepted the persistence and influence of religion in the societies even after the societies get modernized. Ronald Inglehart and Wayne E. Baker of Michigan University USA in their research paper entitled

'Modernization, Cultural Change and the Persistence of Traditional Values' make the point that industrialization promotes a shift from traditional to secular rational values, while economic development continues, the influence of traditional values are unlikely to disappear as the religious values and beliefs are becoming more wide and spread in industrialized societies. This view undermines the statement of Huntington'All Good Things Go Together' and Marx's prediction 'The religion will die out after industrialization and modernization', since the industrialization also isn't sure to guarantee the complete eradication of the caste-based discrimination based on religion. As themodernization theory stresses on the need of following western values and socioeconomic and political values for developing any developing country, it doesn't seem possible in the case of Nepal, as westernizing the values into modern one takes years. Based on the modernization theory, it can be simply assumed that modernization process might bring some meaningful changes in the traditional societies of that of Nepal. But, considering the capability and conditions to modernization and industrialization, the level of literacy in the country, social, political and economic structure of the country, it is not the suitable way to empower Dalits in Nepal.

While on the other hand, contemporary social science theory, which intellectually focuses on the problem of multiculturalism, group rights and representation, nondiscriminatory equal opportunities for all disadvantaged groups on the basis of affirmative action/positive discrimination and policies of reservations in public institutions, advocates that providing special opportunities to disadvantaged groups is the best way to empower them. This agenda of ensuring special rights of caste-based groups is legitimized in the name of making procedural democracy substantive and socially inclusive. The upshot of this approach is that multiple social groups in every democracy have to be identified by the state for purposes of empowering disadvantaged groups by following pubic policies of providing them special rights so that they can achieve a status from where they can eventually compete with other social groups in the free market of opportunities. When Dalits need to be empowered for their better status in the society, the idea of the school of social theory who came out with the argument that, since Dalits were discriminated, excluded and exploited for many years by ruling class or state itself, they should be provided with some special opportunities and rights, which they call positive discrimination or affirmative actions, is the better way to empowering Dalits in Nepal. According to the propagators of this theory, Dalits should be provided with reservations (quota system) in various sectors such as public services, different levels of politics, economic activities, education, lands and health facilities and son on. The theorists believe that, If Dalits are provided such special opportunities; they, by utilizing the opportunities, will reach to the state where other caste people in the society are. This idea is also relevant from the perspectives of human rights as well, as Dalits have been victimized by either ruling class or by higher caste people for hundred of years. In recent years, realizing the positive aspects of this social science theory on marginalized groups, the WB, NGOs and some donor agencies have also been stressing on the reservation system for marginalized groups in Nepal. While there are various ideologies to empower marginalized Dalits, the assumptions of social science theory can be the suitable model to Dalit empowerment in Nepal.

Marxist social theory which firmly situates social relations in the overall structural logic of the production system argues that divided and fragmented groups become 'conscious' through their own struggles, which makes the fragmented exploited groups conscious of the fact that they are an integral part of the majority who are oppressed and exploited in the process of production. Karl Marx argued not only that social production relation are formed within the structural logic of the total productive system, but also that 'liberation' becomes possible only by demolishing the overall exploitive system of production. Further, fragmented labouring classes only can do this when they become socially conscious that they are the majority and not disparate groups who are victims of social deprivation. Dr. Ambedkar who believed that uniting and educating the Dalits to agitate for a new society are important in the liberation struggle also supports this argument. These elements broaden thinking and action process. A dynamic collaboration with all those who work for the empowerment of poor has to be organized as we move ahead in this liberating process. The ideology of Marx and principle of Ambedkar is very important for Dalit empowerment in Nepal, particularly because they emphasize on the organized movement of Dalits against various kinds of exploitation, injustices and discrimination. The aforementioned social theory better explains the overall situation of marginalized groups like Dalits in Nepal, which sees entire historical process of socioeconomics development from the ancient Nepali society to the present day as exploitative mechanism made by ruling class by dividing people in caste groups. As the theory stated, various literatures prove that caste divisions in Nepali society have invariably helped the exploiting classes keeping the exploited classes like Dalits divided amongst them. It is clear that caste-based consciousness exacerbated social divisions and fragmentations and the policy of caste-based reservations has accentuated caste versus caste or sub caste versus sub caste conflicts. The state and the ruling classes have appropriated caste-based multiple identities and instead of addressing the problems of the absolute majority of the marginalized; rather they have found convenient to provide patronage to a caste or a sub caste and thereby manage social conflicts. As the social theory of Marx and Ambedkar's principle stresses on the need of liberation of Dalits for mainstreaming and empowering them, Dalits in Nepal also need liberation from different discriminations and injustices in the society so that Dalits can better access opportunities.

The political system of Nepal has also pushed Dalits back. Though Dalits comprise over one-fifth of the population of the country, they are extremely underrepresented in the government. Although they participate in politics, their representation in village, district and national level very low compared to their population size. Likewise, there are very rare chances to be elected even if they contest in the election, as higher caste people are dominant feature throughout the history. Since 1958, only Dalits have become members of parliament (upper house), ana only one has been elected in House of Representatives (lower house). In the general election of 1994, only 18 (1.2%) Dalits came as candidates, and in 1994 general election 5.5%; which shows the marginal improvement in their participation. But, if we see the number of them who got elected, it is very pathetic. In 1991 general election only one Dalit was elected in the lower house of the parliament; and since then no Dalit has been elected. However, different parties and the king chose some Dalits in the upper house of parliament. They have participated through different parties as well as independently. Parties have created some spaces for Dalits in their organizations. This pattern of exclusion is repeated in local government level, where Dalits are severely underrepresented in administrative system: of the more than 3000 Village Development Committee chairpersons, only handfuls are Dalits. Comparatively, they have more representation in the village level; but in the district level and national level, it is insignificantly low. According to a study in 2001, while Brahmins constitute only 16% of the population, they represent 57% of the parliament, and 89% of the judiciary.

This kind of pervasive control of local and national level leadership posts by upper class people has disregarded Dalit's issues. Their representation in Nepali politics is nominal because of multiple causes. Even today, there is belief that politics and the responsibility of carrying on political administration belongs to the so-called higher castes. There is a lack of participation, representation and leadership of Dalits in politics because of deprivation in the political field continuing from the past. There are different practices of discouraging the Dalit community from representation in the higher level of politics and leadership in the parties. In the same way the practice of preventing the Dalits from contesting the election as well as standing as candidate is continuing. Dalits are also deprived from administrative as well as judiciary system. The 1991 survey states upper class people posses 93% of the posts in the system. The society has been using the weakness of the Dalits like illiteracy, poverty, lack of awareness etc. in a wrong way and has been using the Dalits only as vote banks. This is because of the caste-based discrimination. The Dalit community has been deliberately kept away from the policy formulation and implementation level till today. Another reason why they are not involved in politics is because they have to exploit their daily labour for everyday living; therefore they don't have even time to think about it. Similarly, they lack proper education and financial backup needed for getting involved in politics; that also obstructs them for participating in politics. There was also no presence of Dalits in making of past constitutions that also has got some discriminatory articles. Since they are one of the major beneficiaries but are not included in policy engineering process, the chance to ensure Dalit people's social, political, economical and cultural issues is therefore less. The governments and political parties in the past hoped and promised to established inclusive democracy and reform the state, they failed to fulfil their promises. This is one of the areas that the government has been strongly criticized for. DV Sagar Bishwakarma, a Dalit rights activist in a conference, organized by AD White House, Cornell University entitled 'Social and religious fragmentation and economic development in South Asia' notes that unless Dalits are not represented into socioeconomic and political processes through constituent election, Dalits won't succeed to ensure and realize their rights, equal representation and freedom.

Agreeing with Bishawakarma, while their representation in different level of socioeconomic and politics, it is however not sure whether Dalits will have better life and status even if their representation in various bodies of the government is guaranteed, since the existing practices of caste system and their poor economical status are other big problems. Nonetheless, the constitutional guarantee of their participation in different level will push up their issues in a hot table; which may help them to better their overall status. The government's poverty reduction Strategy Plan (PRSP), which was prepared by National Plan Commission with the support from Department for the International Development (DFID) and World Bank, also have stressed on the inclusion of Dalits in the mainstream Nepalese politics, but the implementation is always lacking. Mr. DB Sagar Bishwakarma reasons out that the poor implementation is because of the lack of insufficient, nonsensitive governance system and lack of proper representation of Dalits in both policy and implementation level. Giving further critical views, he says that so-called high caste groups that control the state, society and the economy have not shown sufficient political will to address this problem of Dalits. This assertion is also supported by the view point of Ian Martin, who articulated that, to address the long standing problem of caste based discrimination effectively, functioning parliament, democratic system with real representation of Dalits is needed. Many experts have almost no differences on the need of Dalits representation in different policy making and implementation bodies. Lena Sudha, the representative of UN High Commission for Human Rights in Nepal also agrees that the lack of Dalit representation in state body is both a system and causes of discrimination, which results in systemic exclusion of Dalit people from the state.

It has been established that the majority model of democracy fails to protect the rights of minorities in many instances where as the consensual or the inclusive model of democracy is believed to effectively protect minority rights. In inclusive democracy, incorporating Ian Martin is the personal representative of UN secretary general in Nepal who has been working for more than a year as the chief of United Nations Mission in Nepal (UNAMIN). He is supposed to contribute in the peace process that is underway for one year.

Minority groups require a more enlightened view of sharing economic and political resources than simple majority democracy. A precondition for building an inclusive democracy is ensuring right to elect representatives and development of a legal framework that protects the right to participation and free expression. After the April movement of 2006 in Nepal, there is very serious debate going on about how to make an inclusive democracy which can ensure the representation of backward and marginalized people in various bodies of government. Political parties have also even working to better address the representation problems the marginalized groups. The reservation system that the government introduced for uplifting Dalits in Nepal has created another very good platform, which is believed to be supportive to make some significance improvements in the lives of Dalits. However, many problems have delayed in the implementation of this system. The interim parliament of Nepal has recently passed a bill amending Civil Service Act 1993, which has guaranteed 45% reservation for deprived people like Dalits, women and Madhesis (people living in the eastern part of Nepal). Out of the total reservation, 9% has been reserved for Dalits. Following the step, the government of Nepal has also decided to provide reservation for the marginalized sections of the society while making recruitment in the police force and the armed police forces. In the 45% reservation, reservation for Dalits is 15 %.

While agreeing on the aforementioned facts, some people blame that the rampant state of irregularities and corruption but with the state of impunity in the country also pose theobstacles in the upliftment of Dalits. According to Transparency International (TA), and INGO dedicated to increasing public accountability and curbing corruption in all walk of life, corruption in Nepal is growing over the past three years, and the country in 2007 ranks the 131st in the world list most corrupted countries among 180 countries with the score of 2.5. The report clarifies that the corruption is rampant in public sector; this fact leads to assume that the April Movement 2006 was the movement against the autocratic monarchy, which had dismissed and dissolved the Nepali elected parliament and the government in 2002, who then had started ruling in the country as both the head of the government and the head of the state. The movement was launched by the seven party alliances along with indirect involvement of the CPN Maoist, which had been revolting against the government for last 13 years. Ultimately, the movement was successful to make the King give up his power and to hand over to the parties.

The underlined poverty and backwardness benefits well beyond their direct impact. Ensuring equitable access to these services and facilities can be especially important for mainstreaming the Dalits. The school of modernization theory notes that transferring of traditional cultures in to modern one opens up the doors for the modernization process. On the process, the modernization theorists believe that education, urbanization and the spread of mass media play the pivotal role as the central agents of cultural change. Modernization theorists state that in the process of modernization, economical and technological changes will help to the diffusion of culture, which will lead the society to a certain direction of getting westernized. According to Huntington's explanation, as countries modernize, the spread of urbanization, education and mass media consumption produce an increasingly politically aware and mobilized society, whose citizens make far more demands on the government. Therefore to respond to these demands, developing countries need to create more and specialized and complex political and economic institutions. If the situation of Dalits in Nepal is analysed on the basis of the assumptions of modernization theory, it seems that it doesn't suit while Dalits are already far behind other caste groups. Even though there are some changes like urbanisation, spread of mass media and introduction of neo-liberal economy in the country, the Dalit situation has not improved. The theory also doesn't explain whether the modernization of culture will end up the discriminatory practices in the society. The theorists rather seem to have accepted the persistence and influence of religion in the societies even after the societies get modernized. Ronald Inglehart and Wayne E. Baker of Michigan University USA in their research paper entitled 'Modernization, Cultural Change and the Persistence of Traditional Values' make the point that industrialization promotes a shift from traditional to secular rational values, while economic development continues, the influence of traditional values are unlikely to disappear as the religious values and beliefs are becoming more wide and spread in industrialized societies. This view undermines the statement of Huntington- 'All Good Things Go Together' and Marx's prediction 'The religion will die out after industrialization and modernization', since the industrialization also isn't sure to guarantee the complete eradication of the caste-based discrimination based on religion. As the modernization theory stresses on the need of following western values and socioeconomics and political values for developing any developing country, it doesn't seem possible in the case of Nepal, as westernizing the values into modern one takes years. Based on the modernization theory, it can be simply assumed that modernization process might bring some meaningful changes in the traditional societies of that of Nepal. But, considering the capability and conditions to modernization and industrialization, the level of literacy in the country, social, political and economic structure of the country, it is not the suitable way to empower Dalits in Nepal.

While on the other hand, contemporary social science theory, which intellectually focuses on the problem of multiculturalism, group rights and representation, nondiscrimination equal opportunities for all disadvantaged groups on the basis of affirmative action/positive discrimination and policies of reservations in public institutions, advocates that providing special opportunities to disadvantaged groups is the best way to empower them. This agenda of ensuring special rights of caste-based groups is legitimized in the name of making procedural democracy substantive and socially inclusive. The upshot of this approach is that multiple social groups in every democracy have to be identified by the state for purposes of empowering disadvantaged groups by following pubic policies of providing them special rights so that they can achieve a status from where they can eventually compete with other social groups in the free market of opportunities. When Dalits need to be empowered for their better status in the society, the idea of the school of social theory who came out with the argument that, since Dalits were discriminated, excluded and exploited for many years by ruling class or state itself, they should be provided with some special opportunities and rights, which they call positive discrimination or affirmative actions, is the better way to empowering Dalits in Nepal. According to the propagators of this theory, Dalits should be provided with reservations (quota system) in various sectors such as public services, different levels of politics, economic activities, education, lands and health facilities and son on. The theorists believe that, If Dalits are provided such special opportunities; they, by utilizing the opportunities, will reach to the state where other caste people in the society are. This idea is also relevant from the perspectives of human rights as well, as Dalits have been victimized by either ruling class or by higher caste people for hundred of years. In recent years, realizing the positive aspects of this social science theory on marginalized groups, the WB, NGOs and some donor agencies have also been stressing on the reservation system for marginalized groups in Nepal. While there are various ideologies to empower marginalized Dalits, the assumptions of social science theory can be the suitable model to Dalit empowerment in Nepal.

Marxist social theory which firmly situates social relations in the overall structural logic of the production system argues that divided and fragmented groups become 'conscious' through their own struggles, which makes the fragmented exploited groups conscious of the fact that they are an integral part of the majority who are oppressed and exploited in the process of production. Karl Marx argued not only that social production relation are formed within the structural logic of the total productive system, but also that 'liberation' becomes possible only by demolishing the overall exploitive system of production. Further, fragmented labouring classes only can do this when they become socially conscious that they are the majority and not disparate groups who are victims of social deprivation. Dr. Ambedkar who believed that uniting and educating the Dalits to agitate for a new society are important in the liberation struggle also supports this argument. These elements broaden thinking and action process. A dynamic collaboration with all those who work for the empowerment of poor has to be organized as we move ahead in this liberating process. The ideology of Marx and principle of Ambedkar is very important for Dalit empowerment in Nepal, particularly because they emphasize on the organized movement of Dalits against various kinds of exploitation, injustices and discrimination. The aforementioned social theory better explains the overall situation of marginalized groups like Dalits in Nepal, which sees entire historical process of socioeconomics development from the ancient Nepali society to the present day as exploitative mechanism made by ruling class by dividing people in caste groups. As the theory stated, various literatures prove that caste divisions in Nepali society have invariably helped the exploiting classes keeping the exploited classes like Dalits divided amongst them. It is clear that caste-based consciousness exacerbated social divisions and fragmentation and the policy of caste-based reservations has accentuated caste versus caste or sub caste versus sub caste conflicts. The state and the ruling classes have appropriated caste-based multiple identities and instead of addressing the problems of the absolute majority of the marginalized; rather they have found convenient to provide patronage to a caste or a sub caste and thereby manage social conflicts. As the social theory of Marx and Ambedkar's principle stresses on the need of liberation of Dalits for mainstreaming and empowering them, Dalits in Nepal also need liberation from different discriminations and injustices in the society so that Dalits can better access opportunities.

The political system of Nepal has also pushed Dalits back. Though Dalits comprise over one-fifth of the population of the country, they are extremely underrepresented in the government. Although they participate in politics, their representation in village, district and national level very low compared to their population size. Likewise, there are very rare chances to be elected even if they contest in the election, as higher caste people are dominant feature throughout the history. Since 1958, only Dalits have become members of parliament (upper house), and only one has been elected in House of Representatives (lower house). In the general election of 1994, only (1.2%) Dalits came as candidates, and in 1994 general election 5.5%; which shows the marginal improvement in their participation. But, if we see the number of them who got elected, it is very pathetic. In 1991 general election only one Dalit was elected in the lower house of the parliament; and since then no Dalit has been elected. However, different parties and the king chose some Dalits in the upper house of parliament. They have participated through different parties as well as independently. Parties have created some spaces for Dalits in their organizations. This pattern of exclusion is repeated in local government level, where Dalits are severely underrepresented in administrative system: of the more than 3000 Village Development Committee chairpersons, only handfuls are Dalits. Comparatively, they have more representation in the village level; but in the district level and national level, it is insignificantly low. According to a study in 2001, while Brahmins constitute only 16% of the population, they represent 57% of the parliament, and 89% of the judiciary.

This kind of pervasive control of local and national level leadership posts by upper class people has disregarded Dalit's issues. Their representation in Nepali politics is nominal because of multiple causes. Even today, there is belief that politics and the responsibility of carrying on political administration belongs to the so-called higher castes. There is a lack of participation, representation and leadership of Dalits in politics because of deprivation in the political field continuing from the past. There are different practices of discouraging the Dalit community from representation in the higher level of politics and leadership in the parties. In the same way the practice of preventing the Dalits from contesting the election as well as standing as candidate is continuing. Dalits are also deprived from administrative as well as judiciary system. The 1991 survey states upper class people posses 93% of the posts in the system. The society has been using the weakness of the Dalits like illiteracy, poverty, lack of awareness etc. in a wrong way and has been using the Dalits only as vote banks. This is because of the caste-based discrimination. The Dalit community has been deliberately kept away from the policy formulation and implementation level till today. Another reason why they are not involved in politics is because they have to exploit their daily labour for everyday living; therefore they don't have even time to think about it. Similarly, they lack proper education and financial backup needed for getting involved in politics; that also obstructs them for participating in politics. There was also no presence of Dalits in making of past constitutions that also has got some discriminatory articles. Since they are one of the major beneficiaries but are not included in policy engineering process, the chance to ensure Dalit people's social, political, economical and cultural issues is therefore less. The governments and political parties in the past hoped and promised to established inclusive democracy and reform the state, they failed to fulfil their promises. This is one of the areas that the government has been strongly criticized for. DV Sagar Bishwakarma, a Dalit rights activist in a conference, organized by AD White House, Cornell University entitled 'Social and religious fragmentation and economic development in South Asia' notes that unless Dalits are not represented into socioeconomic and political processes through constituent election, Dalits won't succeed to ensure and realize their rights, equal representation and freedom.

While their representation in different level of socioeconomic and politics, it is however not sure whether Dalits will have better life and status even if their representation in various bodies of the government is guaranteed, since the existing practices of caste system and their poor economical status are other big problems. Nonetheless, the constitutional guarantee of their participation in different level will push up their issues in a hot table; which may help them to better their overall status. The government's poverty reduction Strategy Plan (PRSP), which was prepared by National Plan Commission with the support from Department for the International Development (DFID) and World Bank, also have stressed on the inclusion of Dalits in the mainstream Nepalese politics, but the implementation is always lacking. Mr. DB Sagar Bishwakarma reasons out that the poor implementation is because of the lack of insufficient, nonsensitive governance system and lack of proper representation of Dalits in both policy and implementation level. Giving further critical views, he says that so-called high caste groups that control the state, society and the economy have not shown sufficient political will to address this problem of Dalits. This assertion is also supported by the view point of Ian Martin, who articulated that, to address the long standing problem of caste based discrimination effectively, functioning parliament, democratic system with real representation of Dalits is needed. Many experts have almost no differences on the need of Dalits representation in different policy making and implementation bodies. Lena Sudha, the representative of UN High Commission for Human Rights in Nepal also agrees that the lack of Dalit representation in state body is both a system and causes of discrimination, which results in systemic exclusion of Dalit people from the state.

It has been established that the majority model of democracy fails to protect the rights of minorities in many instances where as the consensual or the inclusive model of democracy is believed to effectively protect minority rights. In inclusive democracy, incorporating Ian Martin is the personal representative of UN secretary general in Nepal who has been working for more than a year as the chief of United Nations Mission in Nepal (UNAMIN). He is supposed to contribute in the peace process that is underway for one year.

The underlined poverty and backwardness of Dalit people, and the reason behind the ineffectiveness of various programs targeted to Dalit empowerment was also was caused by this phenomenon. According to TI, poor governance characterized by corruption and state of impunity has strong relationship with the poverty of Dalits. Adding on this, former chief of Commission for the Investigation of Abuse of Authority (CIIA) Nepal, Surya Nath Upadhyay points out that the government needs to strengthen its institutions to ensure governance and corruption control ending the state of impunity. Damodar Prasad Gautam, president of TI Nepal in his statement on corruption report Nepal comments that diminishing on the part of government commitment, and efforts from political parties and other agencies to control the corruption has not been enough.

Some writers like Dr. Seira Tamang of Martin Chautari points out the corruption is prevalent even in NGOs, which has created a kind of negative attitudes in people in Nepal towards NGOs. She further notes that NGOs also need to have transparency and accountability in their activities along with the sprit of volunteerism; and they should let the Dalits to represent in policymaking level of NGOs so that they can bring meaningful changes in the Dalit community. Based on the foregone analysis, it's been clear that cruel caste-discrimination against Dalit people, lack of access to educational and economical opportunities, government's insufficient approach, corruption, unaccountability, and exploitative practices have all been responsible to the state of overall Dalit backwardness in Nepal. Although many people, organizations, governments, bilateral and multilateral agencies have come out with several different strategies for the capacity building of Dalits in the past; Dalit people's lives still remain same. It seems that different programs are not going to make any meaningful difference if no measurers are carried out to eliminate the social vices stated above. The growing frustration among Dalit people and widening gap between them and other caste groups also clarify that if the government doesn't introduce some pro-Dalit programs to empower them as soon as possible, there might be some communal conflicts that might not only engulf the government but also might lead to broader disintegration in the country.

Out of the realization that the government of Nepal alone is unable to deal with the multiple problems in the Nepali society, good number of people advocate the need of the activities of I/NGOs as they more or less have been able to be satisfy people with their services; and they, in many cases have made the good impressions proving themselves as reliable agents for social, political and economical development initiatives. The government of Nepal has also considered and promoted NGOs as its partners for development in the country.

The government of Nepal has established Committee for Enhancement of Ignored, Oppressed and Downtrodden Groups (UUDUVS) called as Dalit Vikash Samitty in Nepali in September 1997. The Committee for Enactment of Ignored, Oppressed and Downtrodden group that aims at identifying programs related to economic, educational and social development of marginalized people and implement them, has been undertaken many activities for empowering Dalits. This committee is also supposed to establish a relation with national and international agencies, consult on Dalit issues, conduct Dalit development programs and launch awareness programs. Since it has a very short history it is very difficult to make a concluding remark on its programs. However, its program to provide scholarship to Dalit students is noteworthy.

A part of that, the Dalit Vikash Samitty's various other programs targeted to Dalit empowerment, with the lack of grassroots areas to identify the appropriate projects, budgetary constrains, and egalitarian and equality approach, is believed to have been inappropriate to the development of Dalits. Similarly, the Nepali government has established a National Dalit Commission in March 2002 with the objective of high-level policy making and formulating programs for Dalit enhancement. This generally attempts to protect the rights of Dalits and mitigate the discrimination and social exclusion against Dalits. Some of their programs are believed to be effective; however in general, they have not been able to enhance the better quality of Dalit lives.

In recent years based on the concept of welfare state introduced in the end of 19th century and beginning of the 20th century, there is hot discussion regarding reservation of marginalized groups so as to mainstreaming Dalits in Nepal, too. Many experts like Prof.

Kanak Bikram Thapa, the Dean of Faculty of Law TU articulates that it is undisputed fact that the reservation is the only means for the advancement of the Dalit Community and the elimination of discrimination perpetuated against them. He however notes that there are complications on making of laws, determination of procedure, organizational protection and period for implementation of the reservation policy. He states that if the reservation is implemented in different phases by determining the period of reservation, it can be guaranteed that such system of reservation will not only be more effective but also scientific, reasonable and judicious.

Advocating in the similar way, Mr. Bimal Bishwakarma articulates that reservation is a concept based on justice that means to acquire justice. Unlike him, many experts stress that there is a need of positive discrimination for the eradication of the existing discrimination in the society. Reservation system indicates separate number and quota; it provides security to Dalits and stops the negative effects of open competition on the weaker sections. Since reservation is provided so as to minimize or redress the effects of the discrimination perpetuated by the state and society for the past many years, it is considered as remedial or compensatory justice. It plays an important role in assimilating them with other classes and communities of the society. Reservation according to D.B. Sagar Bishwakarma, is not only to increase the participation of the backward classes in the network of the state, it is also to end to the inequality and discrimination that have been coming down from the past. A part of this, reservation is taken as the tool to establish egalitarian society and completely involve the Dalits in the development process of the Nation.

Many INGOs in Nepal have also come to realize that, to eradicate poverty and for the development in Nepal, the reservation policy needs to be introduced. This means that Dalits need reservation in economic sectors, politics, public and private services, and policy and decision making level. This belief is similar to that of the ideology of sociological theorists. The explanations given for this model are reasonable although the formulation of reservation mechanism and its sound implementation proves its usefulness and effectiveness.

Besides, there are several Dalit-based NGOs in Nepal, which have been working towards Dalit upliftment. The organizations like Bal Vikash Forum, Dalit Jagram Manch, Dalit Walfare Organization, Jagaran Media Center, Jana Utthan Pratisthan, Nepal Uttapidit Dalit Nari Samaj, Feminist Dalit Organization; Dalit Federation etc. have been undertaking various different approaches to reach their goal of helping Dalits. They are involved in cultural change programs through campaign against untouchability, public programs of sharing food and water, and fighting for their rights to enter to public temples; some of them are engaged in women empowerment through education program, advocacy for their rights, education for reproductive and sexual health.

Since 2002, The Jagaran Media center has been a prominent Ngo for Dalit social movement, which, through the creative use of print and electronic journalism, radio broadcasts, and television programming, continues to combat caste based discrimination by generating local and global awareness of Dalit issues. It also has been empowering talented Dalit journalists, writers, artists, and professionals by providing skill-developing training. Realizing the strong influence of the mass media, this NGO has been very successful in awareness creating and placing the pressure on the government for the eradication of caste-based discrimination against Dalits. It has many programs on TV and radios in various parts of Nepal. And, for the bettering their economical status, some of the Dalit based organizations have launching income-generating activities. These organizations in recent years have started to use mass media to extend their awareness programs based on the realization of its great roles in making people aware. It is noticeable that they have also been trying to be working on capacity building programs with their partner organizations through training programs.

It is noticeable that there are three schools of thoughts regarding the empowerment of Dalits in Nepal. First school of thought pronounce that there should be enhancement of Dalit people's traditional skills such as tailoring, shoe-making, black-gold smithing and many other lower level occupations. The second school of thought believes that improvement in quality of lives of Dalit can be achieved by the educational and income generating facilities. And, the third school of thought with an intermediate approach claims that the mix-method of improvement in traditional skills as well as education and employment is better approach to the development of Dalits.

While human development has many dimensions, education, health, rural drinking water and sanitation are particularly important. In addition, basic infrastructure such as access to (even low-quality) roads, electricity and telephone communications (particularly in remote areas) can help improve living conditions for the poor in rural areas. As noted above, improvements in these areas are mutually reinforcing, and have benefits well beyond their direct impact. Ensuring equitable access to these services and facilities is especially important for mainstreaming Dalits. The government of Nepal in its Poverty Reduction Strategy plan makes clear that the government has promoted NGOs in various activities, both to supplement existing publicly managed activities and also to increase the outreach and effectiveness of these programs. In the case of rural drinking water, the implementation of this approach involving NGOs and user groups is believed to have been effective and has shown good results.

However, even after the proliferation of Dalit organizations, NGOs and INGOs, the overall condition of Dalits has remained unchanged over the years because of their weak institutional capacity and insufficient recourse. And their efforts made to combat the severe and systematic forms of discrimination have been inadequate and have failed to even ensure that they are not exacerbating the Dalit problem. Many scholars and experts comment that these organizations have not been very effective in improving the fate of Dalits in Nepal. Hira Bishwakarma, a Dalit activist DNF for example in his article posted in The Kathmandu Post 2005-Jan points out that Dalit NGOs and organizations in Nepal lack institutional capacity and resources to run their programs, which limits the efficiency and effectiveness of their approaches towards Dalit empowerment. Giving his critical views on the role played by Dalit NGOs in Nepal, he blamed these organizations being just the contractors for international agencies rather than calling the government to account for its responsibility to uplift Dalits (International Consultation on Caste–Based Discrimin Dahal Dev Raj of Friedrich Elbert Stiftung (an INGO) in a similar line observes that most NGOs in Nepal lack managerial, program developing, resources mobilization and accounting skills which is required for developing relationship with other agencies and organizations. Likewise, He points out that these organizations have problems in organizing themselves into a solidarity group for collective action sharing their information and regular communication. This lack of solidarity among Dalits and Dalit organizations themselves has also slowed down the process of their development as they have failed to launch their organized projects and movement for Dalit development. As Prof. Robert Putnam, International Affairs and director of the Center for International Affairs in Harvard University, stressed on the need of strong 'social capital' for development, Dalits also need to build social capital that can contribute to their overall development. Having admitting this, it is noteworthy that the Maoist insurgency that paralysed almost all development, economical and political activities in most of the part of the country, also affected in the successful implementation of the programs of the organizations. The above-mentioned analysis clarifies that most policies of national bodies and NGOs have been poorly implemented or not implemented, therefore requires affirmative actions to address the overall problem of Dalits. Making note on the weakness of NGOs working for Dalits, a group of researchers in their research 'Situational Analysis of Dalits in Nepal 2002' found that these organizations not only have insufficient facilitation on social, economical and political empowerment and integration, they but also have not been able to develop strong networking and coordinations with various organizations, political leaders and other actors in the society; they don't have good coordination between local and national level organizations. The research making further critical remark notes that activities of NGOs on empowerment, sanitation and literacy have been catalytic in changing Dalit community.

References

Baniya, Jeevan, "International Forum Civil Society in Asia: Experiences and Perspectives: Civil Society, Its Role in Conflict Resolution and Peace Building in Nepal" *The Korean Association of NGO Studies*, Seoul Korea, 2007.

Bishwakarma, Padma Lal, "Society for the Liberation of Oppressed Dalit Castes, Caste Discrimination and Untouchability Against Dalits in Nepal" *Global Conference on Caste-based Discrimination*, New Delhi India, 2001.

Dalit NGO Federation, "Dalit Empowerment and Integration Project" Kathmandu Nepal, 2003.

ILO Nepal, "Dalits and Labor in Nepal: Discriminations and Forced Labor" ILO Office Kathmandu Nepal, 2005.

Pradhan, Rajendra & Shrestha, Ava, "Ethnic and Caste Diversity Implications for Development" Asian Development Bank, Kathmandu Nepal, 2005.

UNDP, "Human Development Nepal Report 2006" United Nations Development Program, Kathmandu Nepal, 2006.

Bibliography

Aditya Nigam, "In Search of a Bourgeoisie: Dalit Politics Enters a New Phase," *Economic and Political Weekly* (Bombay), Vol. XXXVII (13), March 30, 2002

Aiyar, Mani Shankar, "Recognising the Rights of Forest Dependents", *Yojana*, Vol. 52, September, pp. 59. 2008.

Arunkumar: "A case of missed opportunities". *Yojana*, March, vol, 51. 2007

Balley. L.R. *Public services why reservation*? Bheem Ptrika Publications, Jalandar. 1979.

Bandhu, P. Dalit Women's cry for Liberation: My Rights Are Rising like the Sun, will you deny this sunrise"? Edited in Rao. *Caste and Gender. Kali For Women*, New Delhi.2003.

Baniya, Jeevan, "International Forum Civil Society in Asia: Experiences and Perspectives: Civil Society, Its Role in Conflict Resolution and Peace Building in Nepal" *The Korean Association of NGO Studies*, Seoul Korea, 2007.

Bano, Zenab, "Tribal Women : The Gender Issues", *SAJOSPS*, Vol. 3, No. 1, July-December, pp. 24-28. 2002.

Bharati, Ashok: "Globalization, communalism and Dalits." *Unquiet Worlds. Dalits voices and visions*, Heinrich Boll Foundation, Delhi. 2004.

Bishwakarma, Padma Lal, "Society for the Liberation of Oppressed Dalit Castes, Caste Discrimination and Untouchability Against Dalits in Nepal" *Global Conference on Caste-based Discrimination*, New Delhi India, 2001.

Bob, C. "'Dalit Rights are Human Rights': Caste Discrimination, International Activism, and the Construction of a New Human Rights Issue." *Human Rights Quarterly* 29 (2007) 167-193.

Bob, Clifford. ""Dalit Rights are Human Rights": Caste Discrimination, International Activism, and the "Changing Educational Inequalities in India in the Context of Affirmative Action." *Demography* 45.2 2008: 245-270.

Chakravati, V *Reconceptualising Gender; Phule, Brahmanisam and Brahminial Patriarchy,* edited in Rao. *Caste and Gender*, Kali for women, New Delhi. 2003.

Chitnis, V *Human Rights of the vulnerable groups*, Futuristic Digital, Pune. 2005.

Choudhari, S N. *Dalit and Tribal leadership in Panchayats*. Concept publishing company, New Delhi. 2004.

"Cong takes up quota issue with pvt sector," *Hindustan Times* (New Delhi), September 3, 2003

Crossley, Michael, and Myra Murby. "Textbook Provision and the Quality of the School Curriculum in Developing Countries: Issues and Policy Options." *Comparative Education* 30.2 1994: 99-114.

Dalit NGO Federation, "Dalit Empowerment and Integration Project" Kathmandu Nepal, 2003.

"Dalits must get their full rights: Digvijay", *The Hindu* (New Delhi), January 6, 2002

Das D, Satapathy M.K. "Education for sustainable development, University News", No 49, December. 2007.

Das, Gurcharan. *India Unbound*. New York: Alfred A. Knopf, 2001.

Department of Social Welfare, Government of India. *Report of the Committee on Untouchability, Economic and Educationl Development of the Scheduled Castes and Connected Documents* (Delhi,1969).

Dietrich, G . *Dalit Movement and Women's Movement*, Edited in Rao 2003 *Caste and Gender*, Kali for women, New Delhi. 2003

Freeman, James M. *Untouchable: An Indian Life History*. illustrated edition. Stanford University Press, 1982.

Fuller, C.J., ed. *Caste Today*. New Delhi: Oxford University Press, 1996.

Galanter, Marc. *Competing Equalities: Law and the Backward Classes in India.* New Delhi: Oxford Univeristy Press, 1984.

Gaur, K.D. and Rani, Poonam, "Women Empowerment in India : Socio and Economic" in *Women Empowerment*, (ed.) Agarwal, Meenu, Mahamaya Publishing House, New Delhi, pp. 33-46.2007.

Gautam, D.N., ed. *Fifty Years of Indian Constitution*. New Delhi: Manak Publications, 2001.

Gupta, S.K. *The Scheduled Castes in Modern Indian Politics: Their Emergence as a Political Power*. New Delhi: Munshiram Manoharlal Publishers Pvt. Ltd., 1985.

ILO Nepal, "Dalits and Labor in Nepal: Discriminations and Forced Labor" ILO Office Kathmandu Nepal, 2005.

James Massey "India 50 years of independence 1947-97", Dalit issues and concerns, B.R. publishing corporation, Delhi 1998.

Javed Anand, "Dalit Drishti: Dateline Bhopal", *Communalism Combat* (Mumbai), N0. 75-76, January-February 2002

Jogdand, P *Dalit Women, Issues and Perspectives*, Gyan Publication, New Delhi. 1995.

Joseph, Vinod, "Tribal Development during the Five Year Plans", *Kurukshetra*, Vol. 51, NO. 8, pp. 23-28. 2003.

Mary, G. *The Struggle of Dalit Women, Resource Sheet* Paper Presented In Dalit Theology Seminar, Barmingham. 2004.

Michael, S.M., ed. South Asia Edition. *Dalits in Modern India: Vision and Values*. New Delhi: Vistaar Publications. 1999.

Nambissan, Geetha B. "Equity in Education? Schooling of Dalit Children in India." *Economic and Political Weekly* 31.16/17 (1996): 1011-1024.

Panandiker, V.A., ed. *The Politics of Backwardness: Reservation Policy in India.* New Delhi: Konark Publishers Pvt Ltd, 1997.

Pandey, G.S. "Environment and Development" in *Tribal Development: Options* (ed.), Samal, P.K. Gyanodaya Prakashan, Nainital.1998.

Parikh, Sunita. *The Politics of Preference: Democratic Institutions and Affirmative Action in the United States and India.* Ann Arbor: University of Michigan Press, 1997.

Pradhan, Rajendra & Shrestha, Ava, "Ethnic and Caste Diversity Implications for Development" Asian Development Bank, Kathmandu Nepal, 2005.

Pratap Bhanu Mehta, " New agenda for Dalits — I", *The Hindu* (New Delhi), February 14, 2002

Psacharopoulos, George. "Education and Development: A Review." *The World Bank Research Observer* 3.1 (1988): 99-116.

Punalekar, S. *On Dalitism and Gender,* edited in Jogadand, *Dalit Women's Issues and Perspectives*, Gyan Prakashan, New Delhi. 1995.

Rajesh Ramachandran, "Private sector for Dalit cause: Party", *The Times of India* (New Delhi), July 10, 2003

"Reserved Signs: Politicians can only offer job quotas but no actual jobs," *The Times of India* (New Delhi), June 2, 2003

Sharma, Kusum. *Ambedkar and Indian Constitution.* New Delhi: Ashish Publishing House, 1992.

Simon Wigley, and Arzu Akkoyunlu-Wigley. "Human Capabilities versus Human Capital: Guaging the Value of Education in Developing Countries." *Social Indicators Research* 78.2 (2006): 287-304.

Sinha, Archana, "Economic Empowerment and Amelioration of Tribals in India", *Kurukshetra*, Vol. 54, No. 9, July, pp. 3-13. 2006.

Srinivas, M.N. *Caste: Its Twentieth Century Avatar.* New Delhi: Penguin Books India Ltd., 1996.

Steven Ian Wilkinson, "India, Consociational Theory, and Ethnic Violence," *Asian Survey.* Vol. XL, No.5, September/October 2000, 767-791.

Susan Bayly, *Caste, Society and Politics in India.* Cambridge: Cambridge University Press, 1999.

Swaminathan S Anklesaria Aiyar, "Diversity doesn't mean reservations", *The Economic Times* (New Delhi), July 23, 2003.

UNDP, "Human Development Nepal Report 2006" United Nations Development Program, Kathmandu Nepal, 2006.

United States Office of Strategic Services, Research and Analysis Branch. *The Depressed Classes of India.* Washington, D.C., 1943.

Venkatesan, V. "The Dalit Cause." *Frontline*, Vol.19:3, February 2-15, 2002.

Wadhwa, Kamlesh Kumar. *Minority Safeguards in India: Constitutional Provisions and Their Implementation.* New Delhi: Thomson Press (India) Limited, 1975.

Wax, E. "In an Indian Village, Signs of Loosening Grip of Caste." *The Washington Post.*August 31, 2008.

Zelliot, E. *Dr*. Ambedkar and the Empowerment of Women, edited in Rao *Caste and Gender*, Kali for women, New Delhi. 2003.

Index